LANDSCAPE CONSTRUCTION

Landscape Construction

M. F. DOWNING

Reader in Landscape Design at the
Department of Town and Country Planning,
University of Newcastle-upon-Tyne

LONDON
E. & F. N. SPON

First published 1977
by E. & F.N. Spon
11 New Fetter Lane, London EC4P 4EE
© *1977 M.F. Downing*
Typeset by Hope Services, Wantage, Oxon.
and printed in Great Britain by
T. & A. Constable Ltd, Edinburgh

ISBN 0 419 10890 4

Distributed in the U.S.A. by Halsted Press,
a Division of John Wiley & Sons, Inc., New York

Contents

Acknowledgements   page   x
Introduction   xi

1. Site investigation   1

Introduction   1
Planning context   3
Stages of information gathering   7
Base plan   7
Value of air survey methods   9
   Black and white photographs   9
   True colour air photographs   9
   False colour air photographs   10
   Extensive black and white air survey   10
Geology   14
Topography   14
Climate   15
Soils   18
Vegetation   24
   Species   24
   Height   24
   Stem girth   26
   Age   26
   Condition   27
Artefacts   27
Services   31
Legal restraints   32
   Restrictive covenant   32
   Tenancies   32
   Wayleaves or easements   32
   Rights of way   33
Conclusion   33
References   33

2. Earthworks   36
Introduction   36
Methods of survey   37
  Field survey   38
  Air survey   39
Landform design   41
  Criteria for landform design   41
The calculation of earthwork volumes   42
  Spot levels   43
    Grid of levels, 44   Individual spot levels, 47
    Computer application, 48
  Cross-sections   49
  Contour lines   57
    The use of the planimeter, 57
  Variation in volume in transported materials   59
Angles of slope of material   60
  Establishment of steep banks   63
Drainage ditches   65
Structural solutions   65
The use of earthmoving machinery   69
  Face shovel   69
  Draglines   70
  Grabbing crane or clam shell   70
  Universal excavators   71
  Pushing machines   71
  Dozers   71
  Graders   71
  Scrapers   73
Influence of machines on the design of landform   75
Summary   76
  Instructions to contractors   76
References   80

3. Drainage   81
Introduction   81
  Rainfall   81
  Nature of ground   83
  Concentration of drainage water   83
    Formulae for the calculation of run off, 85
Removal of surface water   85
  Flow in pipes   87
  Flow in channels   89
Drainage of fields and open spaces   94
  Material for underdrainage   96

Procedure for drainage 96
Mole drains, 99   Drainage in special situations, 100   Forestry
drainage, 102
Drainage problems of reclaimed land 104
Drainage of playing fields 105
Drainage of paved areas 107
Quick removal of surface water 107
Maintenance of drainage systems 111
Chambers on sewer lines, 112   Junctions between closed and
water courses, 113   Man-holes, 114   *Back drop man-holes*, 115
Interceptors, 116   Silt traps, 117   Inspection chambers, 117
Soakaways, 117
Summary 117
British Standards 118
References 119

4. Surfacing 120
Introduction 120
Hard surfacing of banks 120
Purpose of hard surfacing 122
Ground conditions 122
Flexible and rigid road construction 123
Sub-grade and formation level, 126   Pavement, 126   Sub-
base, 126   Base (or road base), 127   Surfacing, 127   Bound
surfaces, 127   *Asphalt*, 127   *Coated macadam*, 128   Wearing
qualities of bound surfaces, 133   *Unbound and water bound
surfaces*, 133   *Dry bound macadam*, 133   *Hoggin*, 133
Water bound macadam, 135   Gravel, 135   *Sealed gravel*, 136
Soil cement stabilization, 136   Gravel, 137   *Proprietary
surface mixes for games etc.*, 137   Dolomite, 137   Rigid
roads, 138   *Reinforced concrete*, 138   *In situ concrete (unreinforced)*, 140   *Other paving*, 141   *Interlocking paving
blocks*, 141   *Granite setts*, 144   *Brick paving*, 148   *Cobbles*, 152
Tiles, 153   *Slab paving*, 153   *Natural stone*, 158   *Other
surfaces*, 159   *Grouting*, 159   Edging and trims, 163   *Timber
edging*, 165   *Metal edging*, 165   *Concrete edging strips*, 167
Kerbs, 167   *Other edgings*, 167
Drainage of paved surfaces 168
Summary 168
References 169

5. Construction of simple structures 170
Free standing walls 171
Drystone walls 171

Random rubble uncoursed, 172   Random rubble coursed, 172
Squared rubble, 174
Other forms of walling 174
Ashlar, 175
Brick walls 177
1. Foundations, 179   2. Damp proofing, 180   3. Copings, 182
4. Mortar, 182   5. Stability, 182   Expansion and movement
joints, 184   Concrete block walls, 184
Retaining walls 185
Facing of retaining walls, 188   Steps, 188
Fences 191
Timber fences 195
Sizes of timber, 198   Cleft chestnut pale fencing, 198
Close board fencing, 199   Wooden palisade fencing, 201
Post and rail fences, 203   Woven wood fences, 203
Metal fencing 204
Continuous bar fencing, 204   Mild steel or wrought iron un-
climable fences, 205   Woven wire fences, 206   Strained wire
fencing, 206   Chain link fences, 207   Anti-intruder chain
link fencing, 208   Other fences: specialist manufactured type, 208
Selection of standard manufactured items and standard details, 208
Other fences: low fences, knee rails etc., 209
Maintenance of fencing 209
Other means of demarkation: bollards and posts 210
Gates 212
Street furniture 212
Timber structures 212
Summary 215
References 215

6. **Water features** 216
Naturally based lakes 218
Treatment of banks 220
Constructed lakes with a natural appearance 222
Clay puddling 223
Flexible linings 224
Concrete construction 226
Formal water bodies 229
Control of water level 232
Means of cleaning pools 236
Recirculation of water 237
Irrigation 240
References 242

Index 243

For Sonia,
Tim and Jane

Acknowledgements

Any volume by a single author must owe a great deal either directly or indirectly to others. This is the case with this book in which the contents derive from much more than one person's limited experience. Many people have provided advice or information, either specifically in relation to the writing of this book or in connection with landscape design problems, and they are too numerous to mention individually.

I must however acknowledge the debt I owe to my colleagues Brian Hackett and Kenneth Hale, as sources of encouragement, advice, information and wisdom. This volume has to a great extent been shaped by generations of students whose questioning and often sceptical approach may well account for any value it may be found to have. Certainly their, often unwitting, contribution should not go unacknowledged. Many other, authors, designers and others' work has been consulted and quoted in the text. Where this has been done, it has, I hope in every case, been acknowledged in the text.

Introduction

This simple volume is an attempt to gather in one place information on a number of aspects of construction required by landscape architects. It is not exhaustive but if it answers a present need, it may, should further editions be called for, provide a framework for a fuller exposition. Many topics dealt with here in a simple manner are discussed in other volumes in more precise and scientific detail. In many cases, however, landscape architects and others dealing with small earthworks, drainage, or construction problems, for example, do not need to be involved in very exact engineering calculations. Where complex problems are encountered these simple 'rule of thumb' methods must give way to move something more accurate. In this case either more advanced texts must be studied or alternatively it may be an indication of the need to obtain the advice of a specialist in the relevant field.

One of the aims of this volume is to provide an introduction to techniques and methods upon which a student can build as his knowledge increases. While a good deal of factual information is included to assist in the solution of construction problems there are very few worked examples or standard details. There are quite enough of these, if not too many, available from other sources. Architects have been known to complain that their profession is becoming work and more one of assembling and arranging standard units designed by someone else, and manufactured in bulk. The same danger seems to exist for landscape design in detail through the proliferation of standard details which can be selected, as if from a catalogue. Apart from the boredom of uniformity from site to site, town to town and country to country, there is the equally serious likelihood that a design detail prepared for the individual conditions of one site in a specific locality will not precisely meet the conditions of another site in another place. Indeed the use of standard details could be compared to the traditionally quoted dilemma of round holes and square pegs, or vice versa. A standard design solution might be the use of an octagonal post, which would go into both shapes of hole, but would not fit either exactly, and would almost certainly be less satisfactory than the correct shape for the hole concerned.

In the modern context of designers being rushed and often not feeling able to devote time to thinking out design solutions at length, the use of standard details may seem to be desirable solution, but this should not be accepted without consideration of the long-term consequences of a less than perfect design detail for the situation. If this volume can help to provide the background information that the designer, and particularly the student, needs to undertake the wide range of landscape construction work, and enables him to develop his own vocabulary of design in detail, the author will be more than happy.

1 Site investigation

Introduction

Modern landscape design essentially rests on a knowledge and understanding of
the working and balance of natural forces. It employs that understanding to
ensure the creation of new designs which utilize the special qualities inherent in
a site or an area. A successful design may rely upon the natural relationships
between plants and animals which has developed in a particular place, as a result
of conditions of climate, soil and topography. Alternatively it may attempt to
create new relationships not found in nature, but capable of providing a
balanced arrangement, although this approach is not always acceptable to
classical ecologists. As early as 1949 Hackett was advocating an approach to
bring human development much closer to the pattern of nature in which a community of plants and animals reaches a climax or a more or less permanent
state of equilibrium under particular conditions of land and climate. He concluded that by studying and following the principles underlying the evolution
of 'natural' landscapes, it seems likely that a way can be found to absorb man's
artificialities into the rural landscape. This approach could be applied at the
broad scale as well as for detailed design. In the case of the former, Hackett
again (1964) referred to the 'physiological understanding of landscape (being)
allied to the manner in which an ecologist considers the inter-relationships in the
communities of plants and animals. It is, in fact, the broadening of ecology to
extend to the concept of the landscape of a region having large scale inter-
relationships between environmental factors and between rather than within
plant communities'. The same relationships are of interest in the present context
as they affect both design and construction, for, of course, the two are inextric-
ably bound up one with another.

   In the 18th century, the exhortation to 'consult the genius of the place',
the *genius loci* of Vergil, was the guiding principle of all designers, and those
improving their country house parks. Nature 'imitated in any measure . . . gives
us a nobler and more exalted kind of pleasure than what we receive from the
nicer and more accurate Productions of Art' (Addison, 1712). Sir John Vanbrugh
must have made one of the earliest acknowledgements of the value of natural site
attributes in his reference to the grounds at Castle Howard which he had laid
out, and of which he said 'I may commend them because Nature made them:

I pretend to no more merit in them than a Midwife, who helps bring a fine child into the world out of the bushes, Boggs and Bryars'. With less poetry and more pragmatism we now insist on the approach to landscape design depending on a thorough survey or inventory of the attributes of the site to be developed and its surroundings. A valuable contribution to the understanding of the need to undertake proper inventories of the landscape was that of Barnard (1965). In the broadest planning terms selection of uses for sites, and of sites for special uses, will depend on political and economic factors; population, accessibility, transport, labour and commodity markets: in short the factors resulting from human, social and commercial structures. It is important that in the face of this, often strident, array of arguments for particular forms of development in specific areas the inherent qualities of land and its variability are not ignored.

These qualities result from specific physical attibutes, or a combination of natural factors such as geology, soils, climate or flora. In this case the effect of the factor or factors may be to influence the functional use of an area; as topography or geological conditions may affect the suitability of land for building purposes. In other cases historical items or currently perceived aesthetic qualities might influence the use of a site or area for some recreational or amenity purpose. The former case is a good illustration of the way in which a design decision must be dependent on an understanding of the actual process and limitations of construction processes. It may well be that the success of structure plans, now being prepared in the British Isles, will depend in a very considerable measure upon the way in which the input of information is balanced to take account of the landscape qualities, scales, and intricacies of the areas in question. If the resulting development fails to fit the landscape and does not respect its inherent qualities, man's environment in these Islands will suffer further deterioration in the name of planning and progress.

Much of the information needed for the actual carrying out of landscape design works on the ground will have been gathered at an early stage in the design process. Planning and design decisions are, or should be, influenced by site conditions; the nature of the soil or rocks; the presence or absence of vegetation; the drainage pattern and the topography; as well as the influence of artefacts, all play a part in arriving at a design solution. This depends not only on an understanding of the need to preserve the best features of landscape in the commission of an efficient and attractive design. Social and economic factors may outweigh those which are intrinsic to a particular landscape, and result in decisions which do not take the best advantage of actual landscape qualities. From the first land use decisions of a strategic plan, all stages of decision-making bear directly, to a greater or lesser extent, on the final details of construction. It is important, therefore, that all the relevant information is available at the various decision-making stages, the different factors are given the correct relative values, and the implications of any decision are fully understood. A simple illustration in terms of land use may help to clarify this point.

If a small town which is a considerable tourist attraction requires additional car parking facilities when large numbers of visitors arrive in the high season, a number of factors enter into the discussion of how these are to be provided. The intrinsic qualities of the land would lead the choice of flat ground, on gravel soil, which would require no regrading or special surfacing to provide a suitable site for this sort of occasional use. It might well be that there was no land of this sort available, or that it was not within reasonable distance from other facilities, or alternatively that it was not available at a suitable price level, being more valuable for some more productive use. In that sort of event some intrinsically less suitable land would need to be sought, which could be made suitable either by surfacing or regrading, or both.

Whether a commercial operation or a public service is to be undertaken, the cost relative to the value being provided is most critical and must take account of the advantages, or their lack, of any site. The cost of operations required to bring the land into use for a specified purpose must be included in such calculations. Among many cautionary tales which can be brought to mind to illustrate this, is the story that a certain university site was chosen because the land would be obtained cheaply, being well on the outskirts of an old town. It was only when the land was purchased that it was learned that the cost of the provision of services, including main drainage, would make the development more expensive than on prime building land which was more central.

It is necessary to divide various aspects of landscape work for teaching and communication purposes, but the wider implications of approaches to construction cannot be overstressed. An approach to design, or even planning on a wider scale, will encompass the broadest structural considerations and more detailed investigation of these aspects will accompany every stage in the process. According to the stage of detail associated with detailed plans and drawing for construction purposes only minor elements of the landscape may remain to be taken into account. Even this, however, may involve quite detailed and exhaustive surveys, to ensure that nothing, which might affect the methods of construction or the cost, is overlooked.

Planning context

The 1968 Planning Act provided for a framework of development plans within which all future proposals would be evaluated, and the form and content of these was clarified in an explanatory volume (Ministry of Housing and Local Government, 1970). For local authorities these range from structure plans, to local plans for districts, and to action area plans. Structure plans are essentially written documents with only diagrams as illustrations, no specific scale is recommended but they are likely to be not greater than 1 inch to 1 mile in rural areas or 6 inch to 1 mile in urban.

In order to emphasize the diagramatic nature of the structure plan, the key diagrams as they are called are recommended to be drawn without the inclusion of any OS Base. In the case of the structure plans, local planning authorities are required to undertake surveys which, *inter alia*, will examine the principal physical characteristics of the area of the plan, and hence of the authority. The survey is 'a factual study of an area and the changes occurring within it, directed towards understanding the present and future problems and potential', and the report of the survey 'the description and analysis of survey data'. Beyond this, the collection of survey data is not subject to any detailed recommendations. It is clear that the structure plan should be derived from the survey and survey report, which will include economic, land use, population and communication factors, besides those of the physical landscape. What is not clear is the specific input that might be expected. There is no suggestion of systematic assessment of physical features as proposed, for example, in *Terrain Analysis* (Way, 1973). Where the influence of geology and its consequent topography is considered in relation to a number of standard issues of site development, those concerned with the physical elements of landscape have grounds, perhaps, for feeling that these are not given the value they merit. It can be argued that the physical elements are the most permanent and unchanging and as such should be the fundamentals upon which the plan is built, rather than being only incidental considerations. In practice the physical content of the structure plan will be limited to major physical elements of topography, and landscape policy will be shown on the key diagram, this information being supplemented on an additional diagram devoted to landscape and recreation. Country parks, recreation centres, green belts and areas of landscape protection, national parks, and areas of natural beauty, are all included, together with nature reserves, and areas of especial scientific interest. The development plan manual also recommends the inclusion in the landscape and recreation plan of information about urban expansion proposals and new and existing transportation patterns. The curious omission from either the Act or the Development Plan Manual of specific instructions on the nature of survey work to be undertaken has already been commented upon and is not really explained by reference to the increasing complexity of survey techniques. The decisions implicit in both written statement and diagrams are obviously dependent on quite detailed knowledge of physical aspects of landscape if they are to have any validity and not be merely paper plans. Reasonably detailed information of geology, topography, soils, climate, vegetation and cultural factors would all need to be recorded (see also Countryside Commission for Scotland, 1971).

In a country such as Britain, where the landscape can be described as fine grained, the scale at which information has to be gathered must almost inevitably be at a much larger scale than that of the structure plan diagrams, unless a very generalized level of data only is required. It is this limitation which makes the adaptation of some systems of landscape evaluation success-

fully used in the United States, where, for example, the variations in landscape
character are larger in scale and less sudden, relatively difficult for British
conditions. This is true for methods involving the interpretation of landscape
by use of limited number of grid points as is the case with computer programmes. At Harvard, Steinitz *et al.* (1969) concluded that for computer
operation of resource analysis material, a cell size of 1 km² was generally suitable and this scale with each cell representing 250 acres was consequently
adopted as the basic spatial unit for the Harvard comparative study of resource
analysis methods. Some previous American studies had adopted a larger grid,
up to 10.4 km² , while at the other extreme the lowest scale used was 1/250th
km grid (1 acre) in an urban situation. Simple exercises with students in the
North East of England have shown that the use of this grid size with a 6 inch/
1 mile map resulted in considerable loss of definition of features which would
materially affect land use decisions. The scale of the map itself is adequate to
reflect the influence of quite minor variations. Although for some specialist
purposes a smaller division is perhaps necessary, the traditional division of the
landscape into fields gives a reasonable breakdown of homogeneous units. This,
however, does not coincide with an even grid. Other than in exceptional cases,
one must conclude that any grid method of resource analysis in this country
can only give the most generalized results and will not be suitable for any
detailed planning activities. Some sort of inventory must, nevertheless, be taken
and must be based on physical units within the landscape. In fact, a considerable
collection of information on a national scale is already available as outlined
in the paragraph below, under the heading Base Plan.

As it is important to base major siting decisions on knowledge of qualities
of landscape, either functional or aesthetic, so it is important at a lower scale
to carry out detailed planning on a similar basis. The selection of parts of a
site for particular uses will be upon the basis of a compromise between factors
of access, proximity of users, ease of providing services etc. and natural factors
such as geology, topography, bearing capacity of ground, climate, ground water
movements etc. Again the technicalities of construction enter the decision
making process, as knowledge of the way in which things are constructed enables
decisions to be made on the best situation for any particular feature according to
the criteria of the landscape. Furthermore, it is not only the natural landscape
which can be considered in this light, a range of artefacts can give rise to
development potentials of different sorts. The appreciation of these potentials
may depend only on simple or obvious facts, or may be more subtle and require
considerable expertise.

From the planning and design point of view the presentation of detailed
survey information about an area or site in a systematic way, so that it is readily
available when required, and can be interpreted in the light of physical requirements for construction and development, is an important aspect of landscape
work. At the later stage, when all the planning and design decisions have been

Table 1.1 Survey information topics for landscape work

Base plan	Published maps (Ordnance Survey etc.). Air photographs and maps derived from them. Field survey.
Geology	Published maps and written memoirs. Field investigation.
Topography	Published maps. Air photograph interpretation.
Climate	Regional and local climatic data. Meso-climate data inferred from observation or obtained from local records.
Soils	Engineering qualities Site investigation. Cultural soils (some generalized conclusions may be obtained from published material).
Land	Site observation.
Vegetation	Species. Heights. Girth (trees). Age. Condition. Plant communities and habitats of interest should be recorded.
Artefacts (and buildings)	Site investigation. Records of estates, mines etc. Air photographs. List of buildings of special architectural or historic importance — local authority.
Services	Site investigation. Records of public utilities: Electricity — CEGB overhead — high voltage. Local board — underground — low voltage. Gas — trunk or distributor local board. Water — trunk or distributor Sewers — Surface water Foul local authority Combined Telephones — overhead/underground — Post Office Cable television and radio — overhead/underground private company
Legal restraints	Legal searches. Restrictive covenants. Tenancy rights. Rights of way. Easements. Other restrictions.

made, the detailed inventory of a site must include not only those positive assets which are to be retained and enhanced but all those items, the removal of which will involve time and trouble. Thus it will be reasonable and, it is hoped, useful to enumerate within this chapter the information it is necessary to amass before undertaking any design. In doing this, particular emphasis will be placed on the constructional implications of this information.

Stages of information gathering

Because of the importance of the implications of construction on planning and design and the interconnected relationship of these processes, much of the information required for the detailed construction of a site may well have been obtained at the earliest stages of planning and design preparation. Where, as in the case of large developments, the level of detail has to be supplemented at a later date this can be done for the construction work. Thus the collection of survey becomes a two-stage process with major elements, primarily useful for planning and overall design, included in the first stage and further details in the second stage.

It is, of course, possible to classify the constraints on planning, design, and construction in a number of ways. Thus, it may be felt to be desirable to classify these according to the way in which they can be surveyed or the way in which they exert their influence. These can result in quite similar divisions. Survey information can be gained either from direct physical observation of the site or from investigation of documents, plans and records, one method supplementing the other. Alternatively, one might take constraints in the two categories as those that are intrinsic in the site itself, and those which are imposed as a result of external facts. In this category might be limitations resulting from planning legislation or from rights of way, or easements, or other legal hindrances. The clarity of both methods of classification is a little clouded by the problem of such things as concealed artefacts which are certainly ascertainable by direct physical observation of the site, but may well be more easily and clearly defined by a document search elsewhere. The limitations of the site itself must then be sought in broader searches than within the site, whereas the limitations of outside pressure, although less likely to be clearly seen as a result of site survey may nevertheless be evident at this level of investigation. For the purposes of this volume it is perhaps reasonable to adopt the division between the actual limitations resulting from physical conditions of the site itself and those arising as a result of the restraints which may be imposed through external causes.

Base plan

The first necessity for the development of a site is the acquisition of a plan

on which the outline of the site is displayed. For this purpose the enlargement
of the ordnance survey plan is the most frequent base employed in Great
Britain. For construction purposes the plan scale is likely to be 1:100 (equivalent to the imperial 1/8 scale) or 1:200 (1/16). A scale of 1:500 is the
smallest that is likely to be employed for this work (see Harley, 1975).

The ordnance survey base has been used for a range of maps giving specialized
information as follows:—

(1) OS maps (1 inch to 1 mile: now replaced by 1:50 000) physical features,
     contours at 50 ft, woodlands and artefacts. Also at 2½ inch to 1 mile
     (1:250 000 scale, with more detail).
(2) Geological maps (solid or drift) 1 inch to 1 mile (to be replaced by
     1:50 000). Series incomplete, also ¼ inch to 1 mile.
(3) Land Utilization Survey of Great Britain. Survey maps of the second Land
     Utilization Survey prepared by Alice Coleman, M.A. (scale 1:25 000).
     2½ inch to 1 mile recording actual use of land at a given point in time.
(4) Agricultural Land Classification Maps of England and Wales 1 inch to
     1 mile (1:63 360). Classification into 5 agricultural and 22 other categories
     of land by A.D.A.S The whole of England and Wales is covered by 113
     maps of which, by June 1974, 99 had been published.

In areas where maps of a suitable scale and accuracy are not readily available
the use of air photography from which accurate maps can be prepared is an
alternative. Developments in this area in recent years have been very dramatic
both in the techniques of map making, and in the advance of interpretative skills.
According to the scale of photograph, determined principally by the height
above ground, a degree of accuracy of a certain level can be achieved. This is
usually within perfectly acceptable limits and indeed because the costs of
achieving a high degree of accuracy in this work are likely to rise in a geometric
rather than arithmetical progression it is often desirable on economic grounds
to establish clearly what level of accuracy is required. To work to very high
accuracy is very costly and when this is greater than necessary it will result in
a great deal of unnecessary expenditure. From air photographs all surface
features recorded in the photograph can be plotted on the map, although some
ground control will almost certainly be necessary to provide detailed information. With the use of a 'stereo plotter', contours can be delineated on a base
map from the information contained on a pair of air photographs. The most
accurate form of maps produced by air survey means is the orthophoto map in
which the highest degree of accuracy of map making is combined with an air
photograph. The point should perhaps be made here that air survey methods
have the disadvantage (at its most intractable in orthophoto maps) that upper
layers can obscure what takes place beneath them; thus the presence of trees
covered with foliage may completely conceal the details of the ground surface
beneath. These can be added as a result of ground survey work to maps drawn
from air photograph data but it may be more difficult to incorporate such

additions on an orthophoto map, although contours and reference grid data can be shown.

Values of air survey methods

Although it is important to bear in mind the limitations in this respect that affect the air survey, the advantages must conversely be outlined. So much information over and above the simple facts of the spatial arrangement and dimension of the elements of the site can be gained from the use of air survey techniques. There are three principal methods of taking vertical air survey photographs for the purpose of preparing accurate plans. These are black and white, the cheapest and most common; true colour; and false colour.

BLACK AND WHITE PHOTOGRAPHS

One of the most dramatic applications of the black and white air photograph has been the way in which it has brought to light archeological features as a result of the effect known as crop marks, where the presence of underground objects result in differential growth of crop plants and outlines of foundations stand out at certain times of year, and in particular climatic conditions. This, of course, is not limited to vertical shots accurately taken such as are needed for map production, but may be shown up also by more casually produced photography. In addition to this, which requires some expertise in interpretation, other areas of survey information can be deduced by experienced interpreters from aerial survey alone. Such matters as the nature of rocks, bedding and mineral veins; the condition of soil, which could be freshly ploughed or subject to compaction and disturbance on a building site; the presence of water in pools or marshes; the types, ages and even species of vegetation, trees, or crops, or the condition of grassland; the nature of roads, hard surfaces and tracks are only some examples of the information that can be interpreted from air photographs. In addition to the plan shape of items found on air photographs, something of the elevations of buildings, height of trees etc., can often be inferred from shadow lines. It is, however, the plan details which are the basic items of information obtained as a basis for more detailed survey, with any further detail that can be gained from interpretation of air photographs as a means of short-circuiting more protracted and laborious ground survey work.

TRUE COLOUR AIR PHOTOGRAPHS

The use of true colour provides greater ease than with black and white photographs. Vegetation and changes in land use and cropping from field to field are also shown with greater clarity than in black and white.

FALSE COLOUR AIR PHOTOGRAPHS

These appear to offer the most complete information being particularly useful in determining the condition and use patterns of open space and vegetated areas. Different tree species, disease in crops, wear on grass and new or freshly mown grass can all be distinguished with limited practice on these types of photographs. Water and moist areas show up and pollution of water may be easily detected using false colour although this may also be revealed with true colour. False colour also is the best indicator of the presence of springs and issues. It should be mentioned that it has been suggested that an experienced interpreter may well be able to obtain almost all the same information from black and white coverage. On the other hand, where finances permit, any approach which simplifies interpretation and leaves less margin for error is clearly to be preferred.

EXTENSIVE BLACK AND WHITE AIR SURVEY

Cover exists of parts of the country, principally from high level flights, from which photogrammetric maps at scales of 1:2500 and 1:1250 can be prepared. From these contour plans can also be prepared to a scale even of 1:500 with a high degree of accuracy. Errors can be corrected by control and checking at ground level but the effect of variations in topography will result in distortion increasing towards the edges of the photograph, in proportion to the topographic variation, and this will be reflected in the accuracy of the map that can be produced. For really high accuracy, maps may be produced using orthophoto mapping techniques. Since 100% accuracy in mapping is unattainable, and the orthophoto method is relatively expensive, it is important to determine the accuracy of map reproduction necessary and relate it to cost. Low level flights of small areas may be used to provide maps at scales as large as 1:60 for specific projects.

The most extensive coverage of air survey photographs suitable for map making is in black and white. Information concerning the coverage available is held by the Department of the Environment, The Scottish Development Department and the Welsh Office. The National Coal Board has commissioned coverage of extensive areas within the country's coalfields and these are held for the Board at the Air Photo Library of Fairey Air Surveys Ltd. This firm has coverage of Berkshire, Derbyshire, Glamorgan, Northamptonshire, Nottinghamshire from recent flights and other flights are constantly being run. Hunting Surveys Ltd, and Meridian Air Maps Ltd are two other firms which have further coverage and some local authorities also have commissioned their own.

In addition to material on a national basis readily available in map form, other information can be obtained from a variety of agencies and will be assembled at the planning stage. It may be that much of this will be too generalized to be of great service at the detailed design and construction stage but will require specific investigation of particular topics. Some will not be in plan form and will require to be related precisely to the ground. In other cases

Fig. 1.1. Vertical black and white air photographs may be used as an information base in a number of ways. Specialist equipment or expertise enable a very large range of information to be interpreted. Information can be gained also on vegetation, including its health, on wear on grassland, on animal populations and in some conditions on buried artefacts.

Fig. 1.2. Orthophotographs provide a very accurate record with all the features of the landscape in their correct position. This is a rectified version of the photograph in Fig. 1.1, corrected to allow for distortion resulting from topography.

no source of information will be available other than the landscape itself, and a
field survey will be necessary. It should here be emphasized that a thorough
and detailed knowledge of sites is considered to be an essential prerequisite
of any design process, and it is not intended to suggest that the investigation
of the site should be the last resort in the sequence of information gathering.
It is important when initiating original survey work to ensure that it is related
to the forseeable requirements. In many cases this can be achieved by making
use of a method of classification already prepared for a topic, to known criteria.
Such a classification, similar to the agricultural land classification of A.D.A.S.
as above is the land use cabability classification prepared for the Soil Survey by
Bibby and Mackney (1969). In this system seven classes of agricultural land
are identified in relation to agricultural use, particular limitations being noted
within the classification code. The system is intended to give a more precise
delineation of agricultural land use than the more generalized 1:50 000 scale of
the A.D.A.S. and enables parcels of land or part parcels to be identified for their
agricultural potential. There are five sub-classes relating to problems namely
wetness, soil limitations, gradient and soil pattern, liability to erosion and
climate. The classification of any piece of land thus becomes, in this system, a
synthesis of a number of individual factors which define the optimum agricultural use of the land. In the same way that the inherent qualities of the land
determine its potential for use in the present climate of technology, so the use of
land for a wider range of purposes must be limited. The value of soil survey to
planning of land use is further discussed by Bartelli *et al.* (1966).

Where a wider range of uses is to be considered or where an even more
open situation, with no preferred end uses, exists, it is most likely that the
individual factors will need to be recorded separately. A requirement of land
for a particular use can then be considered against the individual factors in turn
and a composite plan be produced to give a number of choices on landscape
grounds. It may, or may not, be possible to rank such choices, and of course
external factors will influence the final choice of land for particular uses. A
greater degree of complexity is introduced when more than one land use
competes for the same land area and when the 'return' from different uses needs
to be computed against the capital expenditure necessary to establish the use in
each case.

The factors commonly considered in the inventory of information are listed
below with some explanation. Their classification depends on understanding of
structural or constructional limitations of sites and where broad observations
may be adequate for overall planning exercises a finer degree of detail must be
achieved for detailed site arrangement. It is important however, not to rely too
heavily upon generalized survey information as this can lead to a need to revise
plans as a result of structural limitations discovered only at the stage of
construction drawing.

Geology

Having provided a base plan, information relevant to the design and construction of the site can be plotted upon it. Of this, the most fundamental category might be taken to be the geology. The presence of economically valuable minerals may be the reason for the development of a landscape plan following extraction of a site. Alternatively it may be a reason for limiting development to certain zones, or to activities that can be provided on a temporary basis. The geology of a site may affect the decision as to where to place buildings or water bodies, for example, based on the knowledge of the strength of different rocks and their impermeability. The selection of sites or parts of sites based on natural conditions, and the understanding of the physical requirements of particular functions so that advantage can be taken of the natural qualities is an important contribution to ease and economy of construction. While for major works of civil engineering it is probable that the most detailed investigations of the geology will be necessary at a preliminary stage, there are many other cases where it is necessary only to obtain generalized information at this stage. Subsequent detail affecting the design of features within finer limits will be ascertained at the later detailed design stage. The sources of geological information are, for large scale work in the British Isles, the British Regional Geology series volumes as well as the solid and drift geology maps listed above.

This information is supplemented for many places by the publication of geological memoirs dealing with the complete spectrum of geology or with different geological periods, and by unpublished survey material collected by the Institution of Geological Sciences in London, or at the regional offices of the Geological Survey of Great Britain, which is a constituent body of the Institute. For more detailed and precise information borehole samples obtained by specialized investigation will be required.

Despite depletions due principally to enemy action in the Second World War, it is not immodest to suggest that information on the geology of the British Isles is possibly fuller than for any other part of the world. This is in some measure the result of the excellence of the OS maps available. The Institute of Geological Sciences has available information relating to overseas work, overseas geological surveys being incorporated within it. Survey information is available nationally in many other countries but is often at a much smaller scale. Extensive coverage exists of the United States, for example (Way, 1973) at scales ranging generally from 1:250 000 to 1:2 900 000. The area of New England is generally surveyed at the larger scale range and some parts of this area have been surveyed at 1:125 000 scale. Some parts have been depicted at a larger scale, notably the District of Columbia and Hawaii at 1:62 500.

Topography

This is a factor of some importance when considering matters of construction, coupled in many cases with knowledge of geology and soil types. A number of authorities have from time to time set down generalized limits to certain activities in terms of topography. These are often applied in the planning process, although they are frequently derived from constructional difficulties. Limitations may result from the difficulties of access or construction of housing on slopes above a certain angle, from the need for flat or comparatively flat land for some activities, notably formal recreation and industry, or conversely the positive advantage, for some forms of casual recreation, camping, or picnicking, of broken ground. All this assumes development without alteration of existing topography. Even when this is possible the actual slopes to be found will provide a measure of control over development because the proportion of land that can be graded as a result of cut and fill from a slope will vary according to the angle of the slope.

Whereas with a slope of 10% it is possible to regrade to make use of 80% of the land, the proportion in the case of a steeper slope will be much smaller; for a slope of 20% being 60%, or for 30% being only 40% usable, all with 1 in 2 slopes. The law of diminishing returns operates in this case as the volume of earth moving necessary to achieve satisfactory new grading increases in proportion to the slope. At the steepest end of the range of slopes, limitations are dictated by the angle of repose of the materials, which will vary from solid rock down to wet clay and silt. At the lowest end the ability to drain land so that surface water is not left standing, or the surface becomes ill-drained, is a further limitation. The use of machinery, combined harvesters or ploughs or grass mowing equipment may be a very important limiting factor on cultivable land.

Generalized topography is included in OS maps up to 1:10 000 scale. More accurate information can usually only be obtained by plotting from air photos or by actual field surveying. On economic grounds, it is usually only very small areas, of a few acres only, that will be levelled by field methods. Trained labour being an expensive commodity limits quite severely the extent of areas which can be more cheaply undertaken by field methods, particularly where air photo coverage exists. This is most limited when a site involves complex topography such as frequently is the case with derelict land.

In matters of detailed construction the stability of slopes according to the nature of the ground material will be a critical factor. Surface movement on steep slopes may prevent the regeneration of vegetative cover and the development of a soil profile in some soils, engineering or structural works in the vicinity of embankments may be particularly liable to result in weakness and collapse.

Climate

The controls exercised by climate on the approach to construction is something

Table 1.2 Slopes of land in relation to use (gradient, angle and % slope)
(With slope classification used by Bibby and Mackney, 1969)

Gradient	%	Angle	Bibby and Mackney slope classification	
1 in 1	100	45°	Very steeply sloping	Angle of repose of rocks in embankment 38° – 42° (B.S.1:1959)
1 in 1½		26° 37'		Angle of repose of dry clay (Hackett, 1967)
1 in 2	50	25° 00'		Angle of repose of wet clay and silt (Hackett, 1967)
				Maximum pasture angle of slope to avoid soil creep and formation of paths by animals across slopes (Bibby and Mackney, 1968)
1 in 3		18° 26'	Steeply sloping	Maximum slope for Grade IV agricultural land (M.A.F.F. 1968). Angle of repose of very wet clay and silt (Hackett, 1967)
		18° 00'		Mean recommended incline for artificial ski slopes (Nat. Ski. Fed. 1967)
1 in 3½		15° 00'		Maximum slope for traditional grass mowing machinery; Maximum slope for normal crop rotations (Bibby and Mackney, 1968)
		11° 00'	Moderately steeply sloping	Maximum slope for 2 way ploughing (Bibby and Mackney, 1968)
1 in 5	20	11° 19'	Strongly sloping	Durham County Council permitted maximum slope for regrading on reclaimed land; Maximum slope for operation of combine harvester (Bibby and Mackney, 1968) 10° – 12°; Maximum slope for Grade III agricultural land (M.A.F.F. 1968)
1 in 6		10° 00'		Maximum slope for general house building (Holmes, 1968)
		7° 00'		Maximum gradient for forest roads (Huggard, 1958)
1 in 10	10	5° 43'	Moderately sloping	Maximum slope for design of pedestrian ramps, for prams, etc. (B.S. 1:1960); Ruling gradient for forest roads (Huggard, 1958)
		3° 00'		Maximum slope for trouble free use of agricultural machinery (Bibby and Mackney, 1968)

Slope		Description	Angle
1 in 20	5	Maximum slope for house building without special provisions (Holmes, 1968)	2° 52'
1 in 30		Recommended cross fall for gravelled open space areas (Beasley, 1960)	
		Maximum slope for commercial and small industrial buildings (Holmes, 1968)	
		Optimum cross fall for waterbound macadam road surfaces (B.S.1:1960)	
1 in 40	2½	Maximum lateral slope for playing fields (Gooch, 1963). Minimum slope for overland run off on pastures	1° 25'
1 in 48		Optimum crossfall for concrete and hot rolled asphalt road surfaces (B.S.1:1960)	
1 in 50		Maximum slope for large industrial buildings (Holmes, 1968)	
1 in 60	1⅔	Recommended cross fall for concreted paved areas (Beasley, 1960)	0° 43'
		Recommended gradient for winter games areas 1 in 60 – 1 in 80 (Gooch, 1963)	
1 in 72		Recommended cross fall for slab paved open spaces (Beasley, 1960)	
1 in 80		Minimum desirable cross fall for cricket squares (Gooch, 1963)	0° 34'
1 in 90		Maximum desirable slope for piped land drains (DES, 1966)	
1 in 150		Maximum recommended slope for hard porous recreation surfaces (NPFA, 1968)	0° 23'
1 in 200		Minimum recommended slope for hard porous recreation surfaces (NPFA, 1968)	
1 in 250		Minimum practical fall for piped land drainage (DES, 1966)	
		Minimum gradient for gutters and drainage channels (M.O.T. 1966)	

Gently sloping

which perhaps requires some emphasis, because the overall effect of the climate of an area may be taken for granted by those who work within that particular regime. The vernacular design of an area will develop in response to its particular conditions of climate, and this provides the design context within which details of new proposals are worked out. It is important, however, for the designer who, more and more, may be involved with designing in widely spaced and differing areas of the globe to be aware of the limits and variations in climate which affect the design requirements not only in general terms. He, or she, needs to see beyond this and appreciate the influences of local conditions which give rise to a particular selection of materials for special purposes, and to the particular way in which they are used. Designs for mediterranean conditions might be principally preoccupied with the need to create shade and to provide the access and circulation of cool air between buildings and into areas of recreation. A similar development for the extreme north of England would almost certainly have the opposite objectives of making the best use of the limited available sunshine, and creating the best shelter from draughts. In the former case the selection of materials would be on the basis of the effect of heat not merely on the material itself, including its stability, but also its influence on the area, and the user. For example, materials which retained heat or reflected it would not be selected, preference being given to those materials which would remain cool and would not bounce the heat back on to the user.

In northern climates the general approach to design might well be based on a general premise, derived from predominant conditions, that areas for open air use should be constructed with materials that raise and, in the context of a generally cold climate, enhance the ambient conditions of temperature. Materials in colder climates must withstand extremes of cold and those in climates where great variations occur between day and night must likewise be proof against such extremes in the situations in which they are used. Within the climate which generally predominates an area or zone there are quite a range of local climates resulting from topographic variations; aspect and shelter, and these give rise to particular problems or advantages from the point of view of design and construction. It may be necessary in such circumstances to make some special provision as a result of the prevailing conditions. This may amount to measures which are intended either to ameliorate local climate effects by construction, or by details of materials, to ensure that the structure will withstand local conditions. The former might involve the design of screens or features to deflect cold air or frost damage while the latter might consist of the selection of materials to be proof against extremes of temperature or frequently alternating wet and dry conditions.

Soils

The nature of soils found on a site are likely to be taken into account at the planning stage of development proposals rather than at a later time. This applies both to the civil engineers' definition of soil, and to the soil as defined by those concerned with crops and plant growth. The nature of vegetable soil in fact has very little bearing on the approach to construction. Engineering considerations on the other hand will enter into the detailed design of walls, structures and areas of hard surface. Investigation of the nature of an engineering soil will need to be undertaken in some detail to enable decision making about the exact nature of foundations or the depth of sub-base material for roadways. In certain very simple and clear cut cases it may be possible to make decisions on the basis of very generalized information. Where anything more complex or critical is involved further tests of individual conditions are necessary. For overall classification engineers divide soils into seven categories according to particle sizes ranging from boulders with an average diameter of 75 mm (3 inch) through sands and gravels to the finest clay (Table 1.3). This range accounts for

Table 1.3 Engineering soils classed according to the Cassagrande scale

Major divisions		Approximate California bearing ratios (%)
Coarse grained soils	1. Boulders and cobbles	80
	2. Gravels and gravelly soil	50
	3. Sands and sandy soils	20
Fine grained soils	4. Soils with low compressibility (silts and fine sands)	10
	5. Soils with medium comprssibility (Clays with medium plasticity)	10
	6. Soils with high compressibility (Fine silts and clays of high plasticity)	5
	7. Fibrous organic soils (peats etc.)	2

Note: The figures for C.B.R. give only a broad indication, proper tests must be made prior to any construction work.

six categories, the seventh being that of peat, which has unique properties. This classification gives a preliminary indication of the structural performance of individual soils. More detail is provided by the use of a series of standard tests which may be necessary to establish the strength of a soil. These include the determination of the California bearing ratio. This results from measurement of the penetration of a plunger into the soil, and is expressed as a percentage of a standard pattern of results achieved with different weights on a soil of high strength. The strongest soils thus have the highest percentage figure, or bearing ratio. Limitations of the California bearing ratio are that the tests cannot be operated at the extremes of the particle size ranges of soil types. The equipment cannot be used with particle sizes over 19 mm (3/4 inch equivalent) and at the other extreme, wet cohesive clay soils do not yield accurate results. These soils occupy a very large proportion of the area of the British Isles. None the less the Department of the Environment have produced a table, illustrated in Chapter 4, of road base and sub-base depths necessary with varying conditions of soil and this provides a generalized indication of the relationship of California bearing ratio to different types of engineering soil.

Further information about the strength and stability of soils (as this may affect the approach to construction) is gained from tests designed to determine the dry density, the liquid limit and the plastic limit of the soil. A picture of the strength of the soil in particular conditions, not limited to the condition at the time of testing, can be built up. The stability of a soil depends on the shear strength characteristic, which in turn is determined by its density, moisture content and condition and by its bulk density and conditions on the site. Shear strength itself can be ascertained by a direct test involving an apparatus which exerts a measurable force on a prepared sample of standard volume in such a way as to push the upper half of the sample laterally across a flat plan line of fracture overcoming the resistance of the friction of particles and cohesion, where present in cohesive soils. It is necessary for these tests to be undertaken by civil engineers when any critical structural work is involved, but in many of the situations in which a landscape architect is involved it may be only the knowledge of the general behaviour of soils and the judgement of what situations require this additional detailed investigation that is necessary. In many circumstances fairly simple 'rule of thumb' methods can be adopted for designs and structures undertaken by landscape designers.

From the foregoing it will be seen that the decision to develop on a site for a particular purpose may well turn on initial investigations into the bearing capacity of the soil, if not on technical or economic grounds. On the other hand, once the major decision has been made on whatever basis, the detailed handling of paved areas, retaining walls and structures will vary according to the conditions and the details of construction will only be determined at a comparatively late stage in the proceedings. Some of the constraints affecting the design of cuttings and embankments and the placing of structures or excavation in relation to them are discussed in a later chapter.

Information about the nature of vegetable soil may contribute to decisions at an early planning stage. The use of the Agricultural Development and Advisory Service agricultural land classification of England and Wales mentioned above, for example, may be used for preliminary guidance in the selection of areas for development. While other factors may ultimately be decided as the most important the fact that an area consists of first class agricultural land may be taken as a powerful argument against its use for other purposes. The A.D.A.S. Classification (Table 1.4) consists of five grades of agricultural land and two categories of non-agricultural use. The conclusions of these maps are generalized, being on a countrywide scale, and may be able to obscure quite significant

Table 1.4 Cultural classification of soils and land use capability

A.D.A.S. (1974)	Bibby and Mackney (1969)	Klingebiel and Montgomery (1961)
Grade 1 Land with very minor or no physical limitations to agricultural use.	*Class I* Land with very minor or no physical limitations to use.	*Classes I to IV* Suitable to varying degrees for cultivation of crops.
Grade 2 Land with some minor limitation which exclude it from grade 1.	*Class II* Land with minor limitations reducing choice of crops and interferring with cultivations.	
Grade 3 Land with moderate limitations comparatively due to soil relief or climate.	*Class III* Land with moderate limitations that restrict choice of crops and/or demand careful management.	
Grade 4 Land with severe limitations due to adverse soil relief or climate.	*Class IV* Land with moderately severe limitations that restrict the choice of crops and/or require very careful management practices.	
Grade 5 Land with very severe limitations due to adverse soil relief or climate.	*Class V* Land with severe limitations that restrict its use to pasture forestry and recreation.	*Classes V to VIII* Unsuitable for anything but limited recreation and casual use.
	Class VI Land with very severe limitations that restrict use to rough grazing forestry and recreation	
Other categories Land predominantly in urban use.	*Class VII* Land with extremely severe limitations that cannot be rectified.	
Other land primarily in non-agricultural use.	*Note:* Sub-class may be obtained by defining the kinds of limitations namely: W. Wetness S. Soil limitations G. Gradients and soil pattern limitations L. Liability to erosion C. Climatic limitations These would be defined by number and letter.	

minor variations, while presenting divisions between soil types which are in reality comparatively indistinct as though they were sharply defined. They will almost certainly need to be supplemented for any detailed study of an area. It is a matter of interest that the majority of agricultural land (48.9%) is in class 3 with classes 4 and 5 comprising a further 33 — 7%. The value of class 1 is appreciated when it is realized that only 28% of agricultural land in England and Wales is in this class (Ministry of Agriculture, Fisheries and Food, 1974). In Britain a system which can be adopted in the field is that from the joint work of the Macaulay Institute of Scotland and the Soil Survey of England and Wales. As this divides land according to land use capability into seven categories, this provides the opportunity for more detailed breakdown of areas. The method which derives from an American original is described in the succinct paper-back volume entitled *Land Use Capability Classification* (Bibby and Macknay, 1969) previously mentioned. In fact it is the intention of the Soil Survey to produce a series of maps covering the country at 1:50 000 and 1:25 000 based on this classification but very little of this work has so far gone ahead. At present only two sheets have been prepared at 1 inch scale, for Melton Mowbray and Church Stretton. So far only seven maps have also been prepared at 1:25 000 matching the outline edition of the soils maps.

In the United States the method used by the United States Department of Agriculture, Soil Conservation Service divides land into eight categories: 1 — 4 being suitable for cultivation and 5 — 8 having only limited value. A wide range of maps is available for different areas varying in accuracy, chiefly according to age, the oldest having been prepared in 1899. The American method from which the British system of Bibby and Mackney is derived is that of Klingebiel and Montgomery (1961). The Canada Land Inventory has published a series of maps at the scale of 1:250 000 on which the suitability of land for agriculture according to seven classes is shown. These adopt similar values to the other methods. The Canada Land Inventory also included assessment of recreation potential and suitability for forestry and wild life and has produced a series of land capability analysis plans combining these aspects. The methods introduced here can all be described as reconnaissance in type, and more detailed and individual assessments may need to be obtained for areas under consideration. In Britain such information is sometimes available from the local offices of the Ministry of Agriculture, Fisheries and Food Soil Service whose officers have carried out extensive and detailed soil surveys over areas of the country.

Mention should be made here of the small coverage of maps prepared by the Soil Survey of England and Wales and available from the Ordnance Survey, Romsey Road, Maybush, Southampton. At present 26 sheets based on third edition OS maps at 1:63 360 and 3 composite sheets at the same scale or further 29 outline edition soil maps have been issued, again covering widely dispersed areas of the country. The information obtained from these sources is mostly too generalized to be helpful at the small scale stage of making detailed plans but the structural implications of both geological maps and soils maps, which may be either positive or negative, should enter into the land use decision process at an early stage.

For sites that are to be developed a knowledge of the depth and nature of topsoil is important, because a number of decisions have to be made at an early stage of contract operation on the site. It is assumed that a primary objective must be the conservation and reuse of all topsoil of any reasonable quality. This being the case, decisions about the quantity and methods of soil storage must be made. In many cases it is only necessary to lift and store prior to construction the topsoil in the immediate area of building. In that case the topsoil saved can be used elsewhere as the existing soil in the surrounding area will not be disturbed. Some provision should be made in these circumstances for making good levels and filling up depleted areas, but use can be made of the majority of the soil removed on other sites. In other cases where the building contractor is liable to run over the site extensively with heavy equipment and particularly when the existing soil is likely to be churned up by operations carried out throughout the season or even extending over several seasons the solution may be to lift and store all the topsoil. Only areas which can be guaranteed protection from damage should be left *in situ*.

It is important for these purposes to know the depth of the soil and its nature, to determine the volume to be stacked and the sort of limitations which should be set upon this operation. Two of the most important attributes of topsoil are the soil structure which can be developed as a result of cultivation and plant growth, which is associated with a healthy soil and the aerobic bacteria which are to be found in such healthy soils. Careless handling of topsoil, handling when wet stacking in heaps which are too deep and too wide will result in deterioration of the quality of the soil. This also results from the soil remaining in stacks for too long a period. While there is probably a considerable variation in the susceptibility, or conversely the storage capacity, of different soils a general recommendation is sometimes given that topsoil should be stacked in heaps not exceeding 1½ m in height and 3 m in width and should not be allowed to remain in the heaps for a period longer than six months. If any of these limitations is exceeded it is likely to result in rapid deterioration of the soil to a point where its value as a material does not warrant its retention. It appears likely that clay soils are most liable to very rapid and serious deterioration. It may well be that it is necessary to take special precautions to encourage the return of the topsoil to a good condition after storage and replacement. Doubleday (1970) has indicated problems associated with the use of stored topsoil and emphasized that material which has been subject to this treatment could not be expected to behave as it would had it remained undisturbed. A study of the effect of storage of topsoil on its condition and quality was made by Hunter and Currie (1956) and described in the Journal of Soil Science.

Clearly any programme for development of a site which is to be intensively built upon must include detailed consideration of the retention and storage of topsoil. Space has to be allocated for stacking and the programme should allow for the minimum volume to be stacked at any one time, and the stacking period to be kept as short as possible. It is sometimes, although not always convenient to organize the stripping and removal of topsoil in step with phases of a building contract to reduce the need for the storage of large volumes over a lengthy period. Alternatively the solution of removing topsoil from one area about to be developed and placing it immediately, without any storage, on a developed area is an even better one, which often justifies the administrative headaches it causes. It is, of course, important that any stripping avoids the danger of excavating subsoil with topsoil because this seriously reduces the value of the material.

Vegetation

The retention of existing vegetation in the development of new proposals is something which must be carefully considered. A detailed survey of vegetation must be made for this purpose and for the organization of the removal of trees and shrubs or hedges or even to enable that decision to be made. For trees, the following information, in addition to the precise location and ground elevation, will be necessary to enable the making of decisions and the specification and estimation of subsequent action leading either to the protection or removal of the trees in question. It may be convenient to number trees marked on a plan and use a form to record information of the initial survey. This information may then either be shown direct on a plan subsequently prepared in the drawing office or separately presented as a supplementary schedule to a plan on which the tree numbers only are shown. The accompanying Table (1.5) (see page 25) illustrates ways in which this may be undertaken. Information should be grouped under the following headings.

SPECIES
No explanation is required of this. It is not always possible to give a specific attribution and in this case the recognition of genera may be adequate.

HEIGHT
The height of trees at the time of survey will be a valuable and important piece of information, indicating for future reference the sort of contribution the existing vegetation makes to an area at the time, as well as its potential. Very accurate measurement is not usually necessary, although the method used by foresters of viewing along the hypotenuse of a set square, where the other two sides are respectively vertical and horizontal may be adopted. In this method the distance from the viewing position to the tree pole plus the height of the observer is the same as the height of the tree, provided the ground is flat, that

Table 1.5 Tree survey information schedule

No. on plan	Species	Height	Girth (tick) (mm)					Approximate age	Condition (tick)			Notes
			Below 150	150 – 300	300 – 450	450 – 600	Above 600		A. Essential to retain	B. Retain if possible	C. To be removed	
Total												

the line projected from the hypotenuse is to the top of the trees, and that the
vertical side is truly vertical which can be checked by the use of a plumb bob.
It is not a difficult job to construct a simple measuring instrument on this
basis. Alternatively the height of a man standing at the foot of a tree trunk
can be used as an approximate gauge of the overall height of the tree, which
might be eight or ten times the height of the man.

STEM GIRTH

It is important to record the girth of trees approximately, particularly when
their removal may be required. Although not as accurate as the measurements
required for the calculation of timber content by foresters this may give some
indication of potential timber value but also show the extent of the felling
and removal of timber which may be required of a contractor. This will enable
him to make an accurate estimate of the costs involved in the work. Foresters
traditionally measure timber by the quarter girth of a trunk measured at chest
height. It may be desirable to adopt a similar height although the use of the
specialist measurement may not be justified. Where a different measurement
height is adopted, it may be necessary to indicate this on the record form. For
purposes of site clearance it is common practice to group trees into trunk sizes
and these might be expressed as diameters, the following categories being identified: below 150 mm; between 150 − 300 mm; between 300 − 450 mm; and
between 450 − 600 mm (Imperial equivalents would be below 6 − 12 inch;
12 − 18 inch; and 18 − 24 inch). Any individual trees of larger diameter would,
in other than exceptional circumstances, be specified separately. This method
of classification within ranges, rather than specifying the individual dimension
of trees may be adopted where a number of trees are to be measured and can
be used as a measure of height as well as for the recording of girth.

AGE

The age of trees may be inferred from the other observable features of a tree:
thus the height and girth may give a good indication. It is sometimes the case,
however, that particular species in certain conditions show misleading growth
symptoms and may develop much less well than would be expected. Failure
to appreciate this might result in assumptions being made that certain trees
would develop further with age, when in fact they have reached the age of
greatest development already without achieving full growth. This could have
serious consequences. It is not easy to detect trees of this kind which have failed
to achieve the growth which would be commensurate with their age. The extent
of growth attained by annual increments may provide some clue, otherwise it
is necessary either to undertake borings to extract a plug of timber and from it
the annual rings in the trunk or to attempt some archive search to discover
the date of a particular planting.

CONDITION

Trees retained for amenity purposes are often of considerable age and may
be described as 'post mature'. This is to say that they are past the age at which
their timber value is at its greatest. With careful attention trees in this category
may be maintained for many years as healthy features of the landscape, and
proper tree surgery and fertilizer treatment can add 20 − 30 years to a life
of even a post mature tree. It is important that some note of the condition of
individual trees and tree groups is included in the survey, because although
the final decision may rest on much more detailed investigations of the extreme
and cost of necessary tree surgery some indication of the likely problems of an
area of existing plantry should be made initially. This also extends to groups of
younger trees which are affected by being too close together for example, or
may have been damaged in different ways. It may also include species that are
growing with varying degrees of health and success. Within this category it is
again possible to make classifications within ranges. The sort of plan that may be
adopted is the following simple scheme of:

(a) Trees making a great contribution, healthy and important to be retained.
(b) Trees which should be retained but which are less important and may be
     lost if the development proposals make it necessary.
(c) Trees which are either so old or so unhealthy as not to be worth retaining,
     or so insignificant not to matter, which are all to be removed. In this case
     an assessment of the extent of removal of roots should be made.

Shrubs and hedges may likewise be recorded according to species, height,
age, and condition, as should also any significant groups of herbaceous plants.

The value of existing vegetation varies considerably according to the conditions of different areas. In some parts of the world where growth is rampant
existing vegetation may rate comparatively little esteem. In others the meanest
stunted tree or clump of wind carved bushes may be infinitely precious. This
is true for example, in the North East of England where the establishment of
new vegetation is made arduous by conditions of exposure and industry. In such
conditions the establishment of new vegetation may require an approach based
on an ecological succession from pioneer plants to the final required species mix.
Even then the ultimate desired mature plant development may be difficult to
achieve. The value of existing vegetation will be not only in its visual contribution but also for the shelter it may provide for new planting. This is a point
frequently overlooked by even quite experienced practitioners, unfamiliar
with the climatic conditions of a particular area and perhaps better used to more
temperate zones.

Artefacts

A great number of sites are affected by the presence of artefacts in one form
or another. These may either be visible on the ground or may be concealed.

They include historic objects and derelict structures of no value and may comprise items in each class dating from the recent past, to those of considerable antiquity. It is important to establish the presence and extent of such objects in some detail both to indicate the nature of any items which might be of historic interest, or the extent of the problem as far as demolition and removal of obstacles is concerned. The simplest objects may be adequately recorded in a survey by brief notes of site observations. All but very small items are likely to be plotted on survey maps prepared either from air survey or from field survey. For purposes of demolition or removal it will be necessary to confirm the dimensions of the object, the thickness of walls or the area of concrete bases for example. It is also worth looking for clues about the method of construction; whether reinforcing materials are likely to have been used, which could give rise to demolition problems, or other similar complications. At the same time some assessment should be attempted of the likely extent of the object below ground, depth of foundations or extent of any structure which might be covered by tipped material, or have been built with an embankment.

Some thought should always be given to the possibility of historical interest in objects found on sites. With the rise of interest in industrial archaeology and the increasing appreciation of the value of such objects as contributing to popular understanding of social history, care is needed in this quarter. It may be necessary, as it would be in the case of more obviously historic and interesting relics to call in an expert who can identify the remains and give some assessment of their significance. With remains of sufficient importance overall proposals can be amended or the design so arranged that they can be incorporated in any layout. Alternatively arrangements may be made for dismantling under supervision for reconstruction elsewhere. At worst, for the archaeologist, the opportunity to make records of the object prior to its destruction should be provided. Not all features, however, will be readily visible on the surface and the question arises as to whether a site which has no visible signs of any hidden objects can be accepted on its face value. The startling disclosures of objects beneath the surface resulting from air photography are by now widely familiar. The study of air photographs for this purpose must take account of the fact that the outlines of the structures only show up at certain times of the year and in particular conditions. Crop marks depend on variations of growth in plants being affected by the moisture conditions of the soil. In this way the outlines of walls and foundations beneath the surface can be shown up in certain circumstances although they may equally well remain completely unsuspected for considerable periods throughout the year.

It is important that contractors should be made aware of the need to proceed carefully where items of interest might be expected, and that there should be some consultative procedure laid down to cover those occasions when an unexpected 'find' is unearthed. Such a situation is covered as far as legal responsibility is concerned in the Institution of Civil Engineers, general conditions of contract (1955 fourth edition, amended January 1969) paragraph 27 under the heading 'Fossils'. The contractor may consider this responsibility as one of minor significance it is not always easy to obtain full compliance with this requirement. More of interest is discovered only after disturbance or damage and it seems likely that more is destroyed without ever being noticed. One cannot legislate to ensure that a contractor will recognize an item of antiquarian interest. It may be necessary where material of interest can be anticipated, to lay a special contractual liability on the contractor to take precautions. The Institute of Landscape Architecture conditions of contract (I.L.A., 1973) curiously are less satisfactory and fail to require consultation with the engineer before removal of any objects of interest, nor does it make any specific reference, as does the I.C.E., to structures or other remains, or things of archaeological interest. The same applies to the R.I.B.A. general conditions.

Areas which are known to have any history of industrial use must be approached with a good deal of caution. The presence of excavations, not strictly artefacts themselves, may be one of the dangers to future development. Bell mines of the seventeenth and eighteenth century are a hazard in this category well known in the North East of England. These were shafts sunk to shallow seams of coal perhaps 25 — 50 m in depth with excavation at the base of the shaft into the coal seam as far as could be achieved without the roof collapsing. Where coal was good, the shafts would be close together and numerous. Not only was the operation of extracting coal a hazardous one, the method of backfilling was often very haphazard. More recent mining operations prior to the establishment of the National Coal Board left a great number of sites where only scanty information of the disposition of shafts and other features is available. National Coal Board sites are usually well documented, and the Board attempts to maintain complete records of all the sites it has inherited but frequently is unable to obtain adequate data. Even when the positions of pit shafts are known it is not always possible to establish with any certainty the method by which they have been made safe. Some early methods were extremely primitive, in contrast to the standard method adopted by the N.C.B. of constructing a concrete cap over the mine shaft top, sometimes at a depth of several metres to avoid disruption of surface activities. Some sites may conceal other features; buried surface water conduits for example, or other features which have become submerged beneath deposited materials with the passage of time. Although there are frequently tell-tale signs of previous use, this is not always the case and searches in local records should be instigated to ensure that the best possible information is available before any design or construction decisions are taken.

The same is true of sites which may have some historic or archaeological interest, in which local archives offices may supply valuable information.

Table 1.6 (a) Depth of underground services

	Mimimum mm (ft)	Maximum (m)
Electricity		
Over 22 kV	750 (2½)	2
	(protected with tiles)	
Under 22 kV	600 (2)	2
Gas	600 (2)	2
Water (main)	900 (3)	2
Telephone cable	350 (1½)	
Television	350 (1½)	
Main sewers	1.2 (hard surface)	
	(4)	
	900 (under grass)	
	(3)	

Table 1.6 (b) Clearance for overhead services

Electricity high voltage overhead services require clearance from both permanent objects in proximity to the cable, allowing for its swing, and also from the possible movement of vehicles etc. in proximity to the cable.

The following minimum clearance requirements are set out by the CEGB.

| | kV of line | | | | |
| | Up to 33 | 33 –66 | 132 | 275 | 400 |
	m (ft)	m (ft)	m (ft)	m (ft)	m (ft)
Ground	5.2 (17)	6.5 (21)	6.7 (22)	7.0 (23)	7.6 (25)
Roads	6.6 (20)	6.5 (21)	6.7 (22)	7.0 (23)	7.6 (25)
Artefacts	3.65 (12)	3.65 (12)	3.65 (12)	4.6 (15)	5.5 (18)
Orchards	3.63 (12)	3.65 (12)	3.65 (12)	4.6 (15)	4.6 (15)
Hop gardens	6.1 (20)	6.1 (20)	6.1 (20)	7.6 (25)	7.6 (25)

Services

Another important area of enquiry will be into the presence and nature of any services which cross or affect the site of proposed works. These may be services above or below ground level. The latter which include electricity, telephone, and 'piped' radio and television are easily seen from site investigation. The former comprising gas, water, sewers, oil, electricity, 'piped' radio and television and telephone lines will need to be established by reference to the local offices of the utility concerned. In both cases searches should be carried out to establish the nature and if possible the projected life of any service to assess its influence on a design proposal. Services consist of mains or 'trunk' services, as they are often called, and local supply lines. The cost of diversion of mains can be very high and this cost must be weighed up in the decision making process. Overhead power lines require a minimum clearance distance between ground and structures and cables, and this may extend also to the use of the site on all but the most irregular basis. For example, a small lake at Seaton Burn, north of Newcastle-upon-Tyne, could not be used for sailing because it was crossed by high voltage overhead power lines. It was not possible to use the lake for sailing without traversing the line of the cables and there was not sufficient height between the cable and water level to allow an adequate clearance between the masthead and cable even using the smallest sailing dinghy. Similar limitations will be placed on landform alterations where immovable underground cables and services are to be found. Utility companies will usually insist on a minimum depth of cover over their supply lines to reduce the danger of casual exposure and damage. In the case of major pipelines for such services as water or gas, a maximum depth may also be stipulated, as too great a depth could lead to damage resulting from ground pressure. A special problem of diversion relates to sewage systems which rely on gravity for the movement of their contents. They will have been designed to critical falls and directions and this will limit very severely the possibilities of any realignment.

It is important to establish whether information supplied by utility companies represents the services as 'laid' or the design drawings prepared before construction. Site conditions often result in departures from the designed layout of service lines which, although often quite minor, nevertheless result in an underground service not being in the position on site where it is expected, with dire and even fatal consequences.

Minor services, for example, those supplying small groups or individual houses will often be abandoned when the properties are abolished and in any case the costs of replacement will be very small in comparison with that for mains.

The information about services is important not only for the somewhat negative reasons already described. In the majority of cases some connection, usually to surface water or foul sewerage systems will be needed for site development proposals and for these it will be necessary to establish the position and level of any suitable point of access to the sewage system. Connections can only be made with the agreement of local authorities in the case of sewers, when work will be done under the supervision of the local authority or by its own staff. Statutory undertakers will also undertake connections and the supply of services required as part of design proposals.

Legal restraints

Sites may be restricted in many ways which are not visible from a physical inspection. The limitations of concealed objects have been discussed in the preceding sections but sometimes the restrictions are of a less tangible or concrete nature. They may be of several sorts as follows.

RESTRICTIVE COVENANT

The sale of land may be subject to restrictions upon the way in which it is used and developed. This often applies to land which has been sold for development purposes when covenants are applied for the mutual protection of owners of individual parcels of what had perhaps been a single estate. Other covenants may represent no more than the views and foibles of a previous owner. While many covenants have a very reasonable basis, others may not, or may no longer have their original validity or relevance and in many circumstances they may be set aside in law. The possibility of such restrictions should, however, be investigated for any area of development.

TENANCIES

Planning legislation requires that land affected by agricultural tenancies is subject to procedures designed to ensure that tenants are adequately informed of any proposals which may be the subject of a planning application. It is important that any proposals for development include in any schedule of programming a sufficient period for any notice which needs to be given, and any rights which accrue to the holder of a tenancy are properly extinguished either as a result of lapsing with time or by agreement.

WAYLEAVES OR EASEMENTS

Sites may be affected by wayleaves granted to undertakers which could in some circumstances make the rerouting of services etc. a difficult legal problem, although this rarely occurs in practice. In the same way easements may have been agreed on some land by owners with owners or tenants of adjoining property. This might include the right of passage over the land for certain purposes. The same rights might have resulted from established custom and this could create problems in the development of new landscape designs.

RIGHTS OF WAY

Many sites are affected by the presence of public footpaths or rights of way. These may be diverted temporarily or permanently within the terms of existing planning legislation. Exceptionally they may be extinguished, or they may be temporarily closed during the course of operations. Where a permanent diversion is not to be sought and the operations on site are not so radical as to demand temporary closure of the right of way it is usually difficult to justify closure without providing some temporary route. In these cases it will be part of the duty of the developer to maintain and to protect the right of way for the benefit of the public during the progress of works and restore it completely on their completion.

Conclusion

It should now be clear that the planning and design of the landscape and the positioning of uses and features within it rests upon a clear understanding of the detailed processes of design and construction involved in different operations, for the best advantage to be made of the landscape. Landscape design should be a logical process in which the requirements of use are related to the site by means of a survey of the site, an analysis of its qualities in relation to the proposals, and ultimately a design plan which derives from the survey and analysis. In order to undertake a survey it is necessary to understand something of the requirements of the plan, and thus its analysis. To draw plans requires understanding of construction methods and limitations. The survey information is one half of the base upon which the operation of design and construction rests. The other half consists of the requirements of the uses and activities that are to occupy the area. Ideally all the necessary information in the form of the survey should be put together in a single plan so that it relates together to other aspects and to the site and its surroundings. This is not possible in every case but the task of analysing the qualities of a site and subsequently that of drawing up a plan based on both survey and the analysis is made much easier if this can be done. This involves the development of techniques of draftsmanship to show different information so that each item is clear and legible and the relative importance of different matters within the survey is reflected in the presentation of the information as far as this is previously ascertainable.

References

Addison, J. (1712). *The Spectator* **414.**
Barnard, E. (1965). Symposium on *'Developing the rural landscape to balance the increasing urbanisation of countries'*. IUCN Landscape Planning Committee, Newcastle-upon-Tyne, pp. 6 − 9.

Bartelli, L. J., Klingebiel, A. A., Baird, J. V. and Heddleson, M. R. (1966). Soil Surveys and Land Use Planning. *Soil Sci. Soc. America and Am. Soc. Agromony*, Madison: Wisconsin.

Bibby, J. S. and Mackney, D. (1969). *Land Use Capability Classification*, Technical Monograph 1. The Soil Survey of England and Wales.

Countryside Commission for Scotland. A *Planning Classification of Scottish Landscape Resources*. CCS Occasional Paper No. 1.

Department of Education and Science (1966). *Playing Fields and Hard Surfaces*, Building Bulletin 28, H.M.S.O.: London.

Dickinson, G. C. (1969). *Maps and Air Photographs*. Edward Arnold: London.

Doubleday, G. P. (1970). *Landscape Reclamation* (University of Newcastle-upon-Tyne) I.P.C.: London and Guildford.

Gooch, R. B. (1963). *Selection and Layout of Land for Playing Fields and Playgrounds*. N.P.F.A.: London.

Hackett, B. (1949). Design in Rural Landscape. *Planning Outlook* 3.

Hackett, B. (1959). Design in Rural Landscape *Planning Outlook* Vol. 1, 3 Newcastle-upon-Tyne.

Hackett, B. (1964). 'The Landscape Content of the Plan' *Planning Outlook* Vol. VI, 2, Newcastle-upon-Tyne.

Hackett, B. (1967). Earth works and ground modelling. In: *Techniques of Landscape Architecture* (Ed. Weddle, A.E.) Heinemann: London.

Harley, J. B. (1975). *Ordnance Survey Maps*. A descriptive Manual. OS: Southampton.

Huggard, E. R. (1958). *Foresters Engineering Handbook*. W. Heffer: Cambridge.

Hunter, F. and Currie, J. A. (1965). *J. Soil Sci.* **7.1** 75 − 80.

Holmes, J. (Planning Group) (1968). *The Moray Firth.* A plan for growth in a sub-region of the Scottish Highlands. Highlands and Islands Development Board.

Institute of Landscape Architects (1973). *General Conditions of Contract (with quantities)*. I.L.A.: London.

Institution of Civil Engineers (1969). *General Conditions of Contract* (4th edition 1953, amended January 1969). I.C.E.: London.

Klingebiel, A. A. and Montgomery, P. H. (1961). *Land Capability Classification* Soil Conservation Service, U.S. Dept., Agric. Handbook no. 210, Washington, U.S.A.

Ministry of Agriculture, Fisheries and Food (1968). *Agricultural Land Classification map of England and Wales: explanatory note*. M.A.F.F.: London.

Ministry of Agriculture, Fisheries and Food (1974). (ADAS) *Agricultural Land Classification of England and Wales*. M.A.F.F.: London.

Ministry of Housing and Local Government (Welsh Office). *Development Plans: A manual on form and content*. H.M.S.O.: London.

N.P.F.A. (1968). *Notes on Hard Porous and all Weather Surfaces for out door Recreation.* National Playing Fields Association: London.

Steinitz, A. *et al.* (1969). *A Comparative Study of Resource, Analysis Methods.* Harvard, U.S.A.

Way, D. S. (1973). *Terrain Analysis.* A guide to site selection using aerial photographic interpretation. Dowden Hutchinson, Ross.

2 Earthworks

Introduction

The introduction in recent years of large scale, efficient machinery capable of moving large quantities of material with comparative ease has opened up the possibilities for major civil engineering works and construction programmes. A positive approach to the design of landform can thus be adopted, making use of these modern facilities. The number of opportunities likely to arise when ground modelling on a large scale is adopted as a feature of landscape design independent of the needs of civil engineering or reclamation works is likely to be limited. On the other hand the positive benefits that can be achieved by careful planning of the disposal of waste materials extend from financial savings to enhanced possibilities for land use, climatic improvement, and the creation of a more attractive and interesting landscape. At Basildon new town the creation in the early 1960s of an artificial hill on the town park site provided a feature of interest in an area of otherwise unremarkable topography and at the same time resulted in the saving of considerable sums of money in the disposal of material excavated from roads, housing areas and factory sites. This would otherwise have had to be hauled a greater distance, with increased costs, and would probably have involved the payment of tip charges. The same positive approach was adopted to the disposal of spoil from the excavation of motorway material in Newcastle-upon-Tyne where it was deposited to make a new hill on the town's central open space, the Town Moor. On a smaller scale the positive use that can be made of what would otherwise be regarded as waste material in ground shaping on housing estates and industrial areas has been demonstrated in inumerable examples. It also provides one further argument for the involvement of the landscape architect at the very earliest stages of planning and design, when his expertise and different viewpoint add a new perspective to the solution of design problems (Hackett, 1964a, b, 1967).

The satisfactory completion of earthworks on a site depends on a sequence of planning, design, and execution which begins with an adequate survey of the site, with particular reference to topography. The method of general survey was discussed in the previous chapter. With this information the designer is in a position to commence the design stage which involves a round of design

sketch proposals and calculations which may be repeated any number of times
until an optimum solution compromising between minimum earthmoving and
perfect land form is achieved. Initially the design process is undertaken as a
sketch with no accurate measurement of quantities involved, but for the
purposes of estimating and finally carrying out the work, more accurate information must be provided. In the same way that knowledge of the operation
of the earthmoving plant is essential to the design process, and experience of
that process gives the designer an ability to arrive at a design solution more
rapidly, so knowledge of the two enables the survey to concentrate only on
those facts which are relevant and ignore all others. This is a relationship which
is, of course, not limited to this topic, and has been discussed in the previous
chapter.

Methods of survey

The traditional method of topographical survey has been that of taking measurements on the ground. This has been true for vertical measurement as for other
aspects of preparing maps, involving plotting the disposition of objects in a
horizontal plane. Details of survey methods are outlined in a number of volumes
on surveying and it is not necessary here to repeat this information (see Clark,
1949; Middleton and Chadwick, 1955; Whyte, 1969). Two points should however be made about field methods of taking levels. The first is that accurate
information is only obtained for a series of points or spots which are actually
measured and which can be defined on the map. These may be sited in a comparatively random manner, to ascertain only the relative levels of specific
objects, or spaced in a close grid to give a regular series of recordings, or in a
variety of intermediate ways. The important corollary to this is that the information about the height of points between spot levels is obtained only by
inference or educated guess work, although often quite accurately. A contour
plan based on field measurements, then, is quite likely, by the laws of chance,
not to be based directly on a single measurement, in the sense that no contour
goes through a spot level, but only on a series of interpretations, interpolations
and inferences. It is also possible for different operators to interpret the same
spot level information to give different contour patterns, although variations
are usually minor in nature. As in so many cases where information is used
interpretively it is important to understand the nature of the information,
the way in which it has been obtained, and its accuracy, in order to be able to
evaluate it. It is, in fact, possible to gain a reasonable representation because, by
the law of averages, errors tend to cancel each other out. Being equally likely
that an error will be made on either side of the correct 'line', it is a very unfortunate and unusual situation where the balance of errors tips the map representation a long way from overall accuracy.

Surveyors trained to the exacting standards of precision required for engineering operations such as the layout of roads, drainage and sewers, or mining operations are often surprised at the apparently lackadaisical approach to earth-works' surveys. They themselves, however are measuring points with great accuracy with even grades, in straight lines, or with flat or angled planes between measured points. They are also, in their most accurate measurements, concerned with finished levels in solid and fixed materials. A discussion of the nature of the process and the properties of material gives a clear indication of the level of accuracy of measurement that is necessary for earthworks where no such limitations exist.

FIELD SURVEY

Surveys on the ground may be undertaken by teams of surveyors using a level, which may be one of a number of closely related patterns, and a staff. The principle of this process is that the level is sited in one place and the staff placed on the 'spots', the heights of which it is intended to measure. It is only when variations in topography make it essential, that the instrument itself is moved, and then the sequence of levels is kept constant by repeatedly moving the instrument in relation to a spot level previously measured, which is remeasured with it in its new position. Ideally in any survey the cycle of measurements is 'closed' at the end by measuring back to the first spot height taken, to see that the survey is accurate. Certain earthworks problems may require only a straight line survey of levels; a survey across a valley for example, or a series of random spot measurements. The most usual thing is for measurements to be taken on a regular grid from which a contour plan can be prepared as discussed above, based on interpolation. The critical factor is the selection of an appropriate scale for the grid, which should be the largest, small enough to pick up the significant topographical variations of a site. Both when taking the survey measurements and for any subsequent calculations which are necessary, the smallest number of measurements that can be used to provide an acceptable data base should be taken to save labour. As it is usual for the topography of an earthworks programme to be more complex after completion than before, for most normal purposes the existing ground shape can be taken as the guide for grid size. Appropriate grid sizes have been worked out by Roberts and Stothard (1968) depending on three factors:

(1) plan scale;
(2) topographic variation;
(3) average slopes.

Table 2.1 (see page 39) gives grid point spacings which will provide an acceptable level of information under the relevant circumstances for earthworks operations. Survey on the ground in the most complex topography calls for a grid with measurements taken at intervals of 25 ft and it will be seen that this involves a very large number of readings (81) in an acre compared with 4 for an area where the ground shape was regular and the contour shape even. When,

Table 2.1 Grid point spacings related to ground and contour shape. Measurements in feet, metres in parenthesis

Contour shape	General ground shape (average slopes)			
	1:100	*1:50*	*1:25*	*1:10*
Regular	150 (50)	100 (35)	75 (25)	50 (20)
Uneven	100 (35)	75 (25)	50 (20)	25 (10)
Very irregular	75 (25)	50 (20)	25 (10)	25 (10)

	Interval ft (m)	*No. per acre*	*No. per hectare*
Average number of	150 (50)	4	9
readings required	100 (35)	9	9
per acre	75 (25)	9	25
	50 (20)	25	36
	25 (10)	81	121

(After Roberts and Stothard, 1968)

as in the case of derelict sites, this great number of readings is coupled with a need for frequent repositioning of the instrument, the whole exercise becomes extremely laborious. For earthworks where the surface variation is small in relation to the depth of material to be moved, a low level of accuracy can be accepted and this may be the case, for example, for the open cast coal operations. It is not likely, however, to serve much contour work with relatively shallow grading. For most purposes, and on all but the most limited sites advantage is now taken of the opportunities presented by air survey for obtaining accurate level information.

AIR SURVEY

Making use of matched pairs of vertical photographs it is possible to plot contour lines using stereoscopic plotting machinery. The photographs are viewed through binocular eyepieces and are seen as an apparently three dimensional model. A small black dot which can be manipulated to move about the surface of the model is linked to a plotting arm by which the movement of the dot can be reproduced on an adjoining table. The dot, in addition to horizontal movements can be set at different apparent heights and the machine incorporates scales upon which the height can be read off. When the height of the dot coincides with that of the ground on the photographic model, the dot appears to rest on the ground, if too low it appears to be below the surface, whereas if too high it creates the impression of floating above. It is possible by trial and error to guide the dot about the surface of the model and reproduce the lines of contours on the adjoining plotting table. Experience in this work enables an operator to become sufficiently familiar with interpretations of air

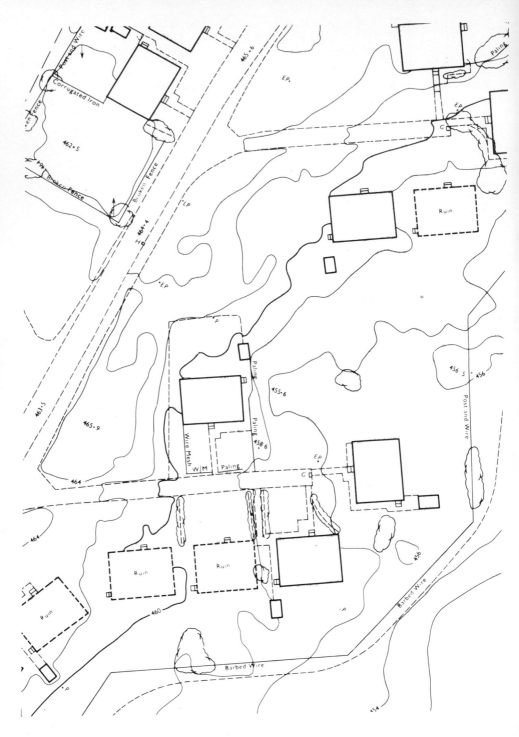

Fig. 2.1. Part of a contour plan obtained by aerial survey methods. This shows buildings, roads, and vegetation as well as fences. The information on the actual fence types is obtained by ground checking.

photographs to be able to make contour plans reasonably quickly.

Landform design

The design of new landform is most commonly achieved with contour plans, superimposing a new pattern of contours on the existing. The design process may involve several draft exercises in landform design, starting perhaps with an idealized concept of the landform desired and amending it in stages to conform to acceptable practical criteria. A number of these govern the design of landform and can be expressed as follows.

CRITERIA FOR LANDFORM DESIGN
(1) Regrading proposals must conform to levels of adjoining land and to common law requirements.
(2) Designs must take account of the natural drainage pattern of the site and surroundings and allow for free drainage.
(3) Designs must ensure that existing vegetation to be retained is not disturbed by raising or lowering ground level.
(4) Designs must ensure that major services, the movement of which cannot be justified on cost grounds, are not disturbed. Information should be sought on critical tolerances from the appropriate service organizations including:
    (a) Clearance of high voltage overhead cables.
    (b) Prevention of operations with heavy machinery over gas and water mains and main pipelines.
    (c) Maintenance of adequate cover over sewers, gas, water, and other pipelines, underground electricity, telephone and other cables.
    (d) Prevention of excessive depth of cover over trunk water or gas mains, or high voltage (e.g. 132 kV) underground electricity cables.
(5) Designs should bear some visual and functional relationship to the surrounding landscape.
(6) Functional requirements include the attempt to create an improved landform in terms of aspect, shelter and microclimate in general terms, or in relation to particular uses.
(7) Designs should take account of minimum and maximum slope criteria which may be determined by the dominant natural topography but which are also subject to the requirements of free drainage and the prevention of erosion. The prevention of storm water build-up is important and particularly so where adjoining land could be affected by the proximity of steep banks.
(8) Except where particular circumstances dictate to the contrary, designs should be prepared with the aim of balancing the movement of material within the site. Cut and fill volumes should be equal and the importation of additional material or the exportation of excess should be avoided.

Fig. 2.2. The use of cardboard models, using sheets of cardboard of the approximate scale height of vertical intervals, cut out along the contour lines provides a good visual representation of the finished earthworks proposals. This can be valuable to the designer and help also the client to visualize what is going to happen.

(9) Designs should aim to optimize the existing ground conditions as far as possible. This will involve attempting to achieve the maximum effect for the minimum movement of material both in terms of volume and distance.

(10) Designs should take account of the practical operating and economic limitations of machinery available for regrading. The design of shapes should, unless some special effect is to be sought, take account of the movement pattern and method of operation of the most economic machinery. The use of scrapers should be thought of in relation to gentle vertical and horizontal curves.

The calculation of earthwork volumes

Methods for obtaining information on the existing topography of a site have been described in previous sections of this chapter devoted to field and air survey. Given this basic information and the nature of the problem to be solved, which might range from a site where regrading is to accompany the removal of a known volume of material, or one where no change in overall volume is intended, to one where the proposals involve the incorporation of additional fill material, a variety of methods of volume calculation is available. Even before discussing these it is perhaps important to make the point that the nature and condition of materials to be handled may vary very considerably and give rise to the need for adjustments to be made to the calculations, for the effects of bulking of very dense material, or compaction of loose deposits. This will be discussed in greater detail later.

Classical measurement of earthmoving volumes naturally has been related to the methods of determining and displaying the topography, already described. There are thus three methods which can be described as measurement from:
(1) Spot levels
(2) Cross-sections
(3) Contour lines.
Of these, the first two have been developed to include sophisticated computer applications of the method. The third, by contrast is suitable only for limited special situations and has not been similarly developed.

Although the methods are dealt with fully in standard works on surveying it may be appropriate to give an outline description sufficient to provide a working knowledge of each suitable for solving simple problems.

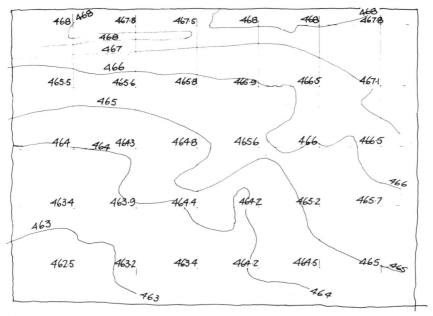

Fig. 2.3. A section of a contour plan with grid of levels superimposed.

SPOT LEVELS
Some authorities suggest that this method is appropriate for large scale excavations with vertical sides only, although this limitation need not apply if sufficient care is taken in relating the vertical measurements correctly to the horizontal area of either cut or fill. The most common application of this is by use of a grid of levels, although alternative methods dividing up the site into a

series of rectangles, squares or triangles may be adopted in some circumstances.

Grid of levels

A grid of levels may be used to calculate changes in volume at the design stage, initially quite roughly but with increasing precision as the design proceeds. For most common purposes it is reasonable to assume that the finished grading will not be designed to give very broken topography, whereas land to be regraded is often very uneven; thus the grid of levels chosen to reflect the criteria set out in Table 2.1 (see page 39) for the existing ground will usually be satisfactory for the new landform. Where this is not the case, the design intention will usually be clear at the outset and the grid dimension can be selected to fit in with shapes and gradients of the design. The grid may be used with a sketch design to determine roughly the balance of material before and after regrading without any attempt to assess movement within the site. For this purpose it is necessary to find the average level of the site before regrading by the simple process of adding up all the grid levels and dividing the total by their number. This is then repeated for the proposed levels. The difference in the average level, which may be higher or lower, multiplied by the area of disturbance will give a volume of either cut or fill material, to be removed from or brought on to the site. Excessive volumes can be eliminated by amendment of the design, until an acceptable balance is achieved, within the broad limits of tolerance allowed.

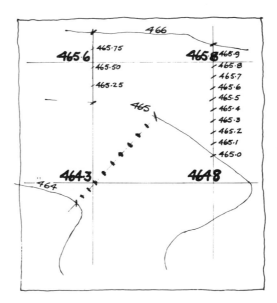

Fig. 2.4. Interpolation of spot levels from contours or vice versa assumes a straight fall between measurements. The distance between can then be divided into equal parts and spot levels interpolated from contours from spot levels.

A more detailed indication of what is occurring on a site can be obtained by defining separately the areas where either cutting or filling is going to take place. When this is done the resultant volumes of material in each area can be used to show the total volume of material to be moved about within the site as well as any excess or shortfall of material generally. It is possible to use the grid to determine quite accurately a series of points between adjoining spot levels where areas of cut abut areas of fill. These points can be interpolated in the same way as are whole number levels for demarcation of contours.

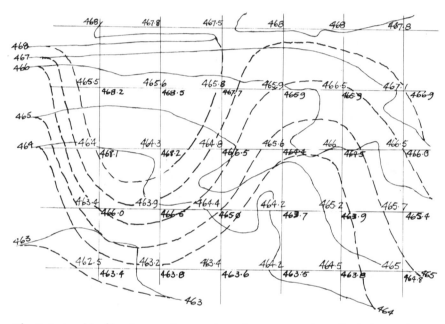

Fig. 2.5. A grid of levels superimposed on the contour plan of existing and proposed contours and showing the existing and new grid levels from which a reasonable approximation of the volumes of material can be calculated.

As contour plans can be produced by joining contiguous points at the same level, so lines described as the 'line of no cut and no fill' can be defined by joining the points where, between adjacent fill and cut grid points, the existing and new level is the same. It is also possible to define areas of cut and fill separately on plans on which new and existing contours are superimposed without reference to a grid of levels. This is done by joining up the points at which equal contours intersect and this method may be used merely to demarcate areas of cut or fill or, in conjunction with other methods of measurement, to quantify the movement of material.

The use of the grid of levels with defined areas of cut and of fill enables the designer to establish:

(1) The excess or shortfall of material on a site as a result of his design.
(2) The additional quantity of material which is required to be moved from place to place within the site.
(3) The different distances, as far as they can be defined by the separate areas, that different volumes must be moved on a site, to redispose them according to the plan.

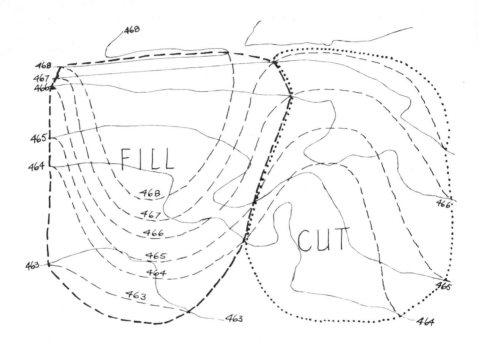

Fig. 2.6. Plan of old and new contours with areas of fill and cut defined. These can be determined with reasonable accuracy by joining up points where proposed contours divert from or join existing contours. Where a new contour line runs parallel to an existing one the extent of the earthmoving should usually be assumed to be the mid-point between them. The lines obtained by joining up these points are known as lines of no cut and no fill.

In some cases the rehabilitation of derelict land involves no more than the general regrading of exceedingly broken terrain to a new, comparatively smooth profile of land. Instances such as this may divide up into a large number of discrete areas of cut and fill of small size and irregular outline and there is little or no advantage in defining the areas of cut and fill separately. In these cases the movement of material is usually limited both by depth and distance and the extent of the problem can easily be gauged.

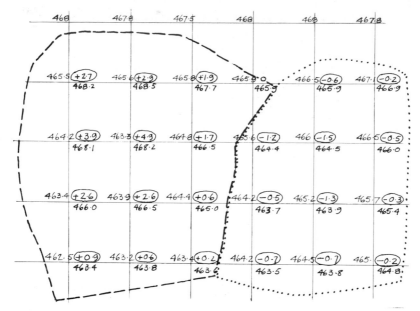

Fig. 2.7. Areas of cut and fill. These can also be determined by use of the grid of levels, the outline of the areas being attained by determining all the points on the grid where either there is a change between cut and fill or between a point at which levels change and one where there is no change. These can be joined up to give lines of no cut and no fill, containing either areas of cut or areas of fill. These areas will be different from those obtained by relation to the contours but both methods should give a reasonable approximation for volume calculations. If a reasonably accurate average change in level can be obtained for areas whether of cut and fill, by relating the number of points to the total area, the measurement of the area by planimeter multiplied by the average depth will give the volume of material.

Individual spot levels

By taking measurements of individual spot levels which delineate squares, rectangles, or triangles and from the measurement of which the volumes of prismoids or similar solid figures of either cut or fill can be calculated earth-moving volumes can be ascertained by the use of individual measurements. This method is suitable for small scale operations, and at a larger scale where simple shapes involving even grades are involved. In addition to the method of level surveying already described in this chapter, the use of a self reducing tacheo-meter, a development of the theodolite, which can be used for quick gauging of height and position of a series of points in relation to the instrument station has been adopted for this work. It has the advantage that because it relies on the measurement of angles rather than sighting horizontally it can be used from a single position despite great changes in level between different measurement points. It has been found to be particularly useful during the progress of works when, in order to establish volumes of material moved for interim certificates for payment to contractors, or for other purposes, it can provide a reasonable approximation which is relatively easily obtained. Although its application has so far been principally limited to this sort of situation where stage measurements not demanding a high degree of accuracy are required, it is also suitable for the measurement and definition of finished topography. As most regraded sites conform to simple shapes the use of this method may well be the most appropriate in many cases.

Computer application

The use of methods in which the mathematical drudgery is lightened has been developed in conjunction with the computer. The design of motorways and other large scale earthmoving operations has been the subject of a good deal of research and development and this has resulted in the evolution of a number of techniques by which the calculation of measurement can be undertaken

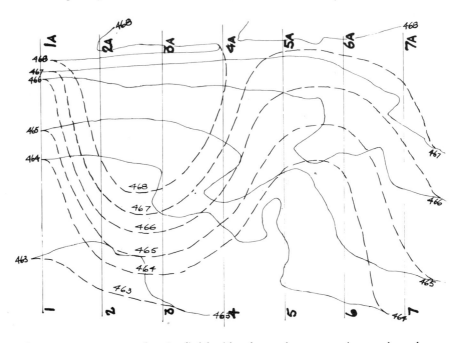

Fig. 2.8. New contours for the finished levels are shown superimposed on the existing contour plan. From these can be interpolated new grid levels which can be used in the calculation of volumes of material to be moved to achieve the new landform. The extent of areas of cut and fill can also be defined from this plan.

with the aid of computer programmes. A number of so called digital ground
models have been devised and these, including some from abroad, have been
under scrutiny by the Transport and Road research laboratory in recent years.
Most of these have been devised for use with the traditional cross-section
method for computation of volumes, which is the standard preferred method
for highway purposes. Despite this, they may consist of a regular grid, random
points, or triangles, all of which can be adapted to this method. Some attempt
has been made with certain of the methods to make use of the computer programme to provide design solutions for cut and fill, relying on programmed
instruction to limit the vertical relationship of adjoining grid points to within
certain specified tolerances. In the same way that the success of certain methods
of digital ground model is limited because of the very large computer storage
space they require, so this would seem to be a problem where design levels
depend on a series of complex relationships. An attempt of this kind was made
in the reclamation of an open cast coal site at Acorn Bank in Northumberland
in 1965, and subsequently in the use of computers to reduce earthmoving cut
and fill in the design of vertical road alignment. Designs which conform to
vertical alignment criteria laid down are produced by the computer and these
are then tested again by the computer to establish the minimum earthmoving
requirement. Such programmes as the Transport and Road research laboratory
PRELUDE, VENUS and MEDUSA programmes are all used in this way.

CROSS-SECTIONS
The use of cross-sections to determine the volume of earthworks has developed
as a result of the linear form of the road, the railway, or even the canal with
which the majority of calculations of volumes have been concerned. It is often
described as being ideally suited for the assessment of volumes of heaps of overburden or of pits, both of which are commonly rectangular in form. A series
of cross-sections is drawn, usually at regular intervals and the area of cut and fill,

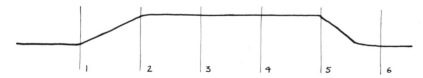

LONGITUDINAL SECTION OF SPOIL HEAP WITH CROSS-SECTION LINES

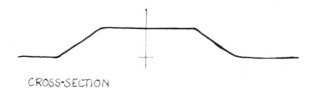

CROSS-SECTION

Fig. 2.9. Diagram to show cross-sections along a heap of spoil at regular intervals.

depending which is involved, is calculated. By the use of the prismoidal formula, the volume of material between the two cross-sections can be calculated.

The prismoidal formula is derived from the fact that a prismoid, being a solid with its two end faces in parallel planes, can be divided into a number of prisms, wedges and pyramids all of which are the same length. For accuracy it is necessary to know the mid-point area of the figure as the relationship of the mid-point area to the basal area in prisms, wedges and pyramids is different in each case. However, the volume can be expressed in the same way for each figure, namely;

$$V = L/6(a + a_2 + 4m)$$

where V = volume; L = length between end areas; a and a_2 = end areas; m = mid-point area (in the case of wedges and pyramids, the end area a_2 is zero, a line and a point respectively).

This formula is thus adopted for the prismoid and it is usual to use alternate sections as the mid-point resulting in the instruction usually given that these should be an odd number of sections drawn if this method of calculation is to be used. A slightly less accurate method of arriving at the volume of cut or fill with cross-sections depends on the application of the 'Trapezoidal' formula, some times known as the end area method. This assumes an average cross-section derived from half the sum of the two end areas and results in a figure which is generally above the real volume.

The formula used is

$$V = [L(A_1 + A_2)]/2.$$

It is frequently advantageous to record the volumes between cross-sections individually as giving a clearer picture of the volume and distance of material movement from one part of a site to another, but where this is not the case an application of the prismoidal formula is known as Simpson's rule can be used to calculate the volume between any uneven number of cross-sections. This is expressed as follows:

$$V = 2L/6(A_1 + 4A_2 + A_3 + A_3 + 4A_H + A_5 + \ldots + 2A_n - 2 + 4A_n - 1 + A_n)$$

where L is the uniform distance apart of all cross-sections.

While ideal for sites which are linear in form, cross-sections can be used for different shapes and the interval to be selected will depend on the nature of the ground shape and the regrading proposals. Intervals are usually chosen for ease

of calculation and to provide regular cross-sections. Where a computer programme can make an allowance for irregularly placed cross-sections this can
be done if the topography warrants it. Where more traditional methods of
calculation are adopted it is perhaps advisable to follow the rule of reducing
the variables which might give rise to calculation error, by spacing the cross-
sections at regular intervals. The choice of cross-section positions and intervals
may depend on the original method of obtaining information on the existing
site topography. Where a contour plan based on an air survey is used they may
be drawn with a fair freedom of choice. Where a grid of levels has been used as
the basis for information then this should normally be made the module for the

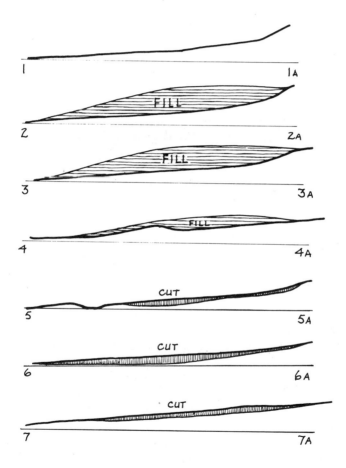

Fig. 2.10. Cross-sections obtained from a contour plan of existing and proposed
contours, and shown in elevation. From these drawings the areas of cut and
fill in cross-sections can be measured with a planimeter, and the volume between
adjoining cross-sections calculated by use of the trapesoidal or the prismoidal
formula.

cross-sections, making use of direct measurements rather than interpolation.
· While the number of variables involved makes the recommendation of cross-
section intervals difficult without reference to a particular site, surveying textbooks recommend distances apart of 20 m on broken ground and up to 100 m
on gently sloping land. Intervals will ideally reflect the significant changes in
topography. The same criteria will apply to the selection of spot levels along the
cross-section lines from which the ground shape along the cross-section line can
be determined, and from which the area of cut and fill can as a result be calculated. Calculations of these areas may be undertaken in a number of ways
including dividing the area into triangles (whose areas can be calculated),
counting squares of known area, use of the planimeter or the application of a
formula. The last method is appropriate where, as on a road, a large number
of cross-sections of uniform shape occur over a reasonable distance: on short
lengths and small jobs the use of the planimeter is preferred. For 'level across'
sections, that is sections in which the ground level is flat across the face of the
section the following formula can be used to determine the area of an embankment or cutting cross-section with uniform sloping sides.

Area = vertical height (formation level + height x m width).

In this m is the number of horizontal units per 1 vertical unit for the side slope;
for the expression 1 in 8, m equals 8. The formation level is the width of the
section measured at the top of an embankment or the bottom of a cutting.

On major earthmoving exercises in road works the development of quite
sophisticated techniques arising from this basic method have occurred. These
have involved the use of computer programmes to achieve a preferred vertical
alignment in which the balance of cut and fill along suitable lengths is ensured.
This has made use of volume information to determine the formation level of
sequences of cross-sections, by dictating the end area of the sections. The
Transport and Road research laboratory is preparing a suite of programmes
under the umbrella title of the Highway Optimization Programme System
(HOPS). The aim of this system is to minimize new road costs, principally
by the most economic possible arrangement of the layout to reduce earth
movement to the minimum compatible with design standards for alignment.
This extends, or is intended to extend in the future to both vertical and
horizontal road alignment.

A less ambitious method has been adopted on a number of reclamation
sites where a road programme which is not specifically a design tool, but
a means of measuring the volumes of material moved, has been used. This
has been described in the volume *'Landscape Reclamation'* (1971). The programme in this case consisted of a package devised for and in use by Sir Robert
MacAlpine and Sons Ltd. This enabled a series of cross-sections to be measured,
and the information produced included the volumes of cut and fill between

Table 2.2 Computer ground point data sheet records the levels at chosen points on each cross-section to reflect vertical changes of ground shape. In each case the offset from a centre line is recorded as well as the height.

Section	Offset	Level	Offset	Level	Offset	Level	Offset	Level	Offset	Level	Offset	Level	Soil depth

Table 2.3 Computer data sheet for finished levels. This information is fed into the computer with the ground points data. The same section must be used but the offsets can be quite unrelated reflecting the vertical changes in the new ground shape.

Section	Offset	Level	Offset	Level	Offset	Level	Offset	Level	Offset	Level	Offset	Level	Offset	Level	Cut slope	Fill slope

Table 2.4 A computer print out is obtained from the information provided in Tables 2.2 and 2.3, when this is supplied to a computer programmed with the appropriate road programme. Stations, as the section lines are sometimes described, are frequently shown by numbers representing their spacing. In contrast to aritthmetical means thare is no reason why the sections should be at regular intervals for computer calculations. Cut and fill areas are those in the vertical cross-sections. Cut and fill volumes are those between cross-sections, and accumulated from the first, through to the last cross-section. Other information, on soil depth for example may also be available from the programme.

Station	Cut volume (m^3)	Fill volume (m^3)	Acc. cut. (m^3)	Acc. fill (m^3)	Cut area (m^2)	Fill area (m^2)
$A - A_1$	531	2524	531	2524	482	196
$B - B_1$	824	1768	1355	4292	297	763
$D - D_1$	3240	163				
$E - E_1$						

adjacent sections together with accumulated totals. It is also possible to measure topsoil removed separately, based on an assumed average depth. While this is not usually relevant on derelict land and industrial reclamation sites it may be very useful on other sites where extensive earthmoving is involved. Because of the very high cost of the development of programmes a choice has to be made between the use of one which is readily available and writing a new one.

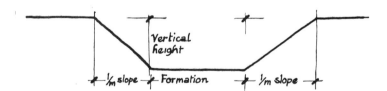

Fig. 2.11. Diagram to show the dimensions given in the formula for determining 'level across' section areas.

The resultant choice, which is often between that of adopting an existing programme with some severe limitations and preparing a purpose made new programme. will depend on circumstances but it is only when extensive opportunities of operating a new programme can be foreseen that the expense involved can be justified. In a great number of cases the availability and convenience of having a ready made programme make its selection the more likely. In the case of the MacAlpine programme the limitations consisted of being able only to accept a maximum of eighteen offset measurements on each cross-section.

Another was that the maximum linear measurement that could be accepted on each side of the centre line was 999.99 units. This was measured in feet at the time of the use of the method referred to, but could be adapted to measure in metric units. Both of these limitations derive from the fact that the programme was devised for the calculation of highway designs involving a linear form of development with relatively narrow cross-section and standard finished cross-sectional design. On a thin linear site the information about the disposition of cut and fill between sections, which can be set down in tabular form in such a way that it can quickly be seen where excess cut can be placed with the shortest length of carry, can be most valuable. It may not be quite so useful on a wider site, where lateral movement cannot be so easily gauged.

It is, perhaps, worthwhile mentioning the fact that although some use of computers has been tried in reclamation work, which is the largest area of 'earthworks' operation in which landscape architects are normally involved, the majority of local authorities appear still to favour older manual methods of calculating volumes of material.

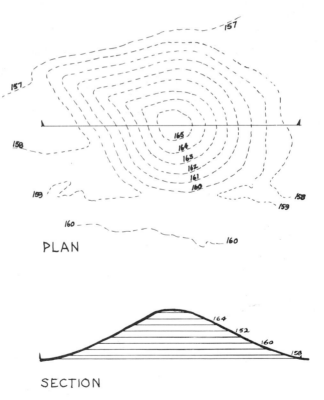

PLAN

SECTION

Fig. 2.12. A simple shape, a cone, for example, as shown here in a plan and section, is very suitable for the application of the contour method of calculating volumes.

CONTOUR LINES

The third method of calculating changes in volume is by the use of contour lines. This is a method which is rather limited in its application, depending for its convenience and ease of application on the shapes of the ground being simple both before and after regrading. A simple example of the convenient use of this method might be where a conical heap of shale was to be removed or reduced in height. The method of assessing the volume might be to determine the area of successive horizontal sections of the heaps from which the volume of the 'slices' between chosen contour lines could be calculated. The advantage of the method, which is ideal for use with a planimeter depends on the fact that the contours can be measured straight off the plan. The more complex the topography encountered the less significant is this advantage until the point is reached where the measurement of either grid points or cross-sections may provide an easier approach.

The use of the planimeter

The measurement of areas which have an irregular shape on a very uneven outline can be undertaken accurately by the use of a planimeter. This provides a very easy means of establishing end areas which can be used in the calculation of volumes on the basis of cross-sections, and can also be used to determine the areas contained by contour lines as described in the previous section. Alternative approaches to the determination of areas involve calculations based on the principles of triangulation, and these may be appropriate, used as they are when a computer programme is available to undertake the sheer drudgery of the arithmetic. Otherwise the process is slow. long-winded, time-consuming and costly.

Instructions for the use of planimeters are provided with most machines and it is only necessary to say here that the machine consists essentially of two bars hinged together. A measuring wheel records the area of any shape, no matter how irregular, drawn on a piece of paper when a pointer on the free end of the instrument is moved in a clockwise direction around the outline of the shape. The other end of the instrument remains fixed. The movement of the bar following the outline of the shape to be measured rotates a wheel on the freely moving bar, near the hinge. According to the direction of movement of the bar, the wheel turns quickly or slowly and forwards or backwards but its rotation is dependant on the actual area enclosed and this can be measured by the calibration of the wheel. By the introduction of a refinement, measurements at different map scales may be undertaken; this involves varying the length of the fixed bar. Different methods of calibrating the measuring wheel will allow for measurement in metric or imperial measure at different scales. Care should obviously be taken in the use of this apparatus, for example it should always be used on a horizontal surface, and the surface must be smooth and even, so that the free movement of the wheel is not impeded. The fixed end of the apparatus should be placed outside the boundary of the area to be measured and in such a position that the perimeter can be traced around without any difficulty. It may, in some cases, be necessary to subdivide an area for the purposes of measurement. It is, finally, most important that the instrument is read before and after measuring rather than making any attempt at zeroing, which is difficult to achieve and may actually result in inaccuracies in working the instrument. It is common practice to take several readings of an area, often three, and average these. If there is a wide disparity between readings it may be advisable to take additional readings to try and establish if an error has occurred in one or other.

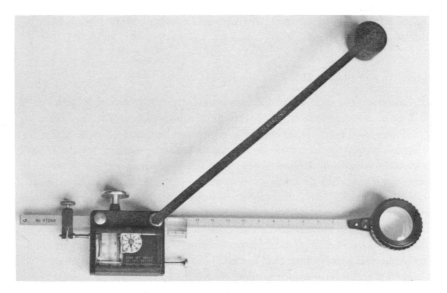

Fig. 2.13. The planimeter is a most valuable instrument enabling one to measure the dimensions of irregular shaped areas. The illustration shows a typical planimeter manufactured by Clarksons and incorporating a zero setting device which is not found on the majority of models (photograph by Clarkson Lord and Co. Ltd., Cramlingon, Northumberland).

A very high degree of accuracy has been claimed for the use of the planimeter provided the instrument is used as it should be. When the limitations inherent in the use of paper plans, the inaccuracy of prints and the thickness of lines on scale drawings are taken into account the errors are less attributable to the apparatus than to these other factors. In addition to this a number of other matters affect the accuracy of predictions that can be made about the movement of volumes of material which mean that a very high degree of accuracy is superfluous.

VARIATIONS IN VOLUME IN TRANSPORTED MATERIALS
The excavation and transportation of materials from one place to another may
result in quite dramatic changes in the volume of that material, and designs
which involve earthmoving should allow for changes which may take place.
This includes attempting to assess what sort of changes are likely to occur.
This may frequently be an extremely difficult task, particularly as is sometimes
the case when it is not possible to control all the variables which could result
in changes. Changes in volume result from three basic things: the nature and
particle sizes of the material to be moved; the degree of compaction or consolidation of the material in the site; and the degree of compaction that can be
achieved when the material is placed in its new position. Of these the third
is perhaps the most difficult to predict, unless special requirements can be laid
down as part of a contract procedure. This can usually only be required where a
structural need dictates a high degree of supervision and careful handling. Otherwise the additional costs of working at a slower and more deliberate speed
and one at which the level and uniformity of compaction is high may be difficult to justify.

Regrading of different materials has given rise to widely varying results,
sometimes to the confusion of the designer, it may be said. Some early schemes
in the reclamation of colliery waste sites were based on assumptions about
volume changes similar to those which apply in the excavation of natural ground
for such things as opencast or strip mining, with unfortunate results. Natural
ground is well and uniformly consolidated and material excavated from it will
increase in bulk when it is replaced. Material moved in opencast or strip mining
is normally assumed to increase by over 10% and this figure is often used as the
anticipated change in level after excavation, removal of coal and return of overburden, using a drag line. In other words if a depth of 100 ft of material was to
be removed consisting of a few feet of coal and the remainder of overburden,
the material replaced would amount to a depth of 110 ft. This contrasts tightly
packed material *in situ* with loosely packed replaced spoil. The opposite often
obtains in the case of colliery spoil regrading. Here the waste material is found in
heaps which have been deposited quite loosely from overhead bucket lines, or
from trucks tipping from the extremities of inclined planes. The consolidation
which has taken place is haphazard and limited. The material in most modern
operations is moved by heavy scrapers and this means that it is deposited in
comparatively thin layers and that the machinery passes over the deposited
material layer by layer. The result of this is that a high degree of consolidation
is often achieved over a very large proportion of the area in question, although
the consistency and uniformity of compaction necessary for structural
requirements cannot be guaranteed without special supervision.

Nevertheless a high degree of consolidation does result and this means that
the volume of the material will decrease quite dramatically and by up to 20%
as a result of this sort of operation. It may then be said that a range of changes

in volume between −20 to + 15% or more may be commonly encountered as
a result of regrading works. It is usual to undertake a basic range of tests prior to
earth or spoil moving on all but the smallest operations and these may include
tests to establish the bulk density of the material *in situ* as well as particle size
analysis. From this sort of investigation the first two of the three listed categories of the factors giving rise to changes in volume can be answered. The third
depending on the method of compaction to be used is, as has already been indicated, rather less easily predicted, short of specifying precise methods of laying
down of material as previously discussed. Designs for new land form will make
allowance for anticipated changes in volume, although it will be appreciated
that these cannot be accurately predicted. Designers should be prepared for
this and should arrange to proceed with works so that the whole impact of
the design undertaken is not vitiated either by a shortage or an excess of
material, which can often only be seen towards the end of an earthmoving
contract.

Angles of slope of material

Angles of slope need to be considered carefully in the design of new landform.
It is unusual to find that one's designs are dictated by the angles of repose
of materials met in earthmoving operations, nevertheless there are particular
circumstances in which these can be the most critical factor. Safe slopes for
materials are affected by whether material has been newly deposited or
excavated from existing ground and in the latter case it is often possible to work
at slightly steeper angles than would be acceptable for newly deposited and
inconsistently consolidated material. A table of slopes in rock formation
given in B.S.C.P. 2003 makes a distinction between the safe slope in the
excavation of cuttings and the angle of repose in the construction of embankments, with the former in the majority of cases many degrees steeper than the

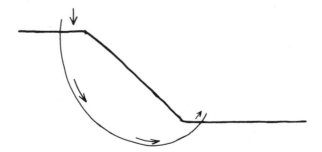

Fig. 2.14. Failure in banks: at critical slopes, the material of any bank could
result in failure of the bank, either by rotational slip in collodial soils along the
arc shown, or by slumping at the surface.

latter. The angle of repose of rocks will usually be found between 33 and 42°, while materials with a smaller particle size will generally be in repose at lower angles, wet clay at an angle of 15°. Other materials are stable at angles between these. The stability of slopes is a product of what is known as the shear strength of the material involved, which is the force required to separate the material on a given plane. Soil and rocks are held together by friction and in the case of small particle colloidal soils by cohesion, which is the grip exerted between particles by a film of water enveloping adjoining particles.

This particular phenomenon gives rise to the familiar mechanical failure of embankments which arises, either as a result of undue loading at the top or weakness at either bottom or top, in the case of cohesive soils known as 'rotational slip'. This is where loading on an embankment or cutting has exceeded the shear strength of a cohesive soil, with the result that a line of slip forms an arc and the combination of small particles and the colloidal nature of the soil maintains the surface of the arc as a smoothly polished surface. The remedy for such a problem is in the construction of buttress drains or some other method of construction which reduces the load and ensures that the bank is supported by some other means than the polished arc. Buttress drains consist of a series of vertical trenches filled with compacted stone rubble and extending below the line of the arc into solid ground. Placed at intervals of between as little as 3 and 5 m, and 10 m these break up the solid volume of an area of rotational slip and provide an additional solid frictional support against any further movement. Particularly in urban areas where lands are scarce and expensive the economic use of sites demands the use of banks at the maximum acceptable angle, in many cases, of course, use requirements may be even more stringent and call for retaining walls and structures, but these are specialized and expensive. Where banks at their most critical angles are required the greatest care is necessary, and the particularly vulnerable areas of the shoulder and toe of the slope need to be properly protected from anything which might result in weakness.

The excavation of a drainline at the shoulder of the slope might separate the weight of the bank from frictional support where it was critical and might allow entry of water with a further weakening effect. The same might be true of excavations for some structural purpose at the base of the bank when the ground at the base formed the principal support for the weight of the bank. In both cases the result would be a failure in a bank at a critical angle and where this did not result in a rotational or deep seated slip, it might still give rise to a surface slip, which would result in only marginally less serious problems.

In the majority of cases, however, designs are dictated not by the mechanical requirements of the maximum slopes physically attainable but by the limitations of land use requirements, or even aesthetics. Where, for example the restoration of dereliction attempts to reproduce the natural landscape pattern of an area and 'blend in' the newly regraded area, a careful analysis of the angles of slope of the existing topography is called for. It was this 'aesthetic' consideration

Fig. 2.15. Grass and concrete mixed surfaces using precast concrete slabs are not always ideal for covering banks.

in addition to other functional and practical reasons which resulted in Durham County Council reclamation team deciding that slopes on reclamation sites in that county should not exceed 1:5; this being the maximum slope commonly met, with some notable exceptions, in the county. Other decisions might be taken in different areas with different geological conditions. In the discussion of criteria for land form design earlier in this chapter reference is made to the minimum and maximum slopes compatible with free drainage on the one hand and prevention of erosion on the other. This is clearly most important where sites will depend on surface drainage only. Where provision can be made for comprehensive underdrainage topographical requirements are less critical. It is suggested that at slopes of 1:80 or less the free drainage of surface water does not take place and in these circumstances land will become unfit for use because of standing water or damp patches. At slopes in excess of 1:30, on the other hand, the possibility exists of the erosion of particles of surface soil and this accelerates with the increase of the slope. It is also subject to the nature and intensity of any rain storm, the cover or lack of it on the soil surface, and the length of slope along which the water may collect. Within this range of angles of slope the majority of uses can be accommodated. Some require more shallow ground (bowls and other sports demand this) and accordingly require special provisions for drainage. At the other end of the scale a great deal of land in its

Fig. 2.16. Stabilizationof the bank by creating lines of support, which also retain moisture, in this case constructed with chicken wire and building paper. Planting is in the soil cultivated above the lines.

natural state is at greatly steeper angles of slope. Where this is so the limitations of use of a site may be those imposed by the use itself, as is the case with various sports, or limitations resulting from the use of machinery as in the case of agriculture. A number of critical angles of slope both maximum and minimum are set out in Fig. 2.16. In the case of what may be described as a developed site, limitations of use may result from the process as in industrial premises which generally require development on a single level. Alternatively limitations of use combine with those of ease of construction, for example it is possible to develop sites for individual specialized and thus high cost housing, on sites which are much steeper than can be accepted for standard housing for the mass market.

ESTABLISHMENT OF STEEP BANKS
It is important to consider here what treatments are available for the establishment of banks which are unavoidably steep. A great deal of detail on this subject is set out in the volume *Landscape Development of Steep Slopes* (Hackett, 1972). In this volume the word steep is used to denote angles of slope exceeding $30°$ (which can also be expressed as 5% or 1 inch in 1.732). Problems occur, however, in much shallower conditions than this and 1:30 which is less than $2°$ has

already been underlined as a critical angle at which erosion can be detected. Particularly acute changes in level call for structural solutions such as the construction of retaining walls or covering the surface of the bank with hard surface material, the latter known as 'pitching'. There are many situations where this sort of treatment is not necessary and is neither desirable visually nor acceptable on grounds of cost. In these cases a number of techniques may be adopted by which the establishment of vegetation which will stabilize the surface can be accelerated.

Alternatively the use of methods to reduce the possibility of movement of the surface of the soil until the development of a suitable vegetative cover can be established may be used. The principal problem is the movement of soil as a result of the action of water. The solution to this may involve either the reduction of the distance that soil can move, or the limitation of the extent of build up of volume of water which is permitted or both of these. Another solution may be to apply some surface binder which will help to hold the soil in place. Some methods involve a combination of these activities. It can be argued that because the latter approach is the most direct in relation to the actual problem it is likely to give the most satisfactory results. It is also true that there is likely to be some inclination away from the methods which generally operate on the former principle as these tend to involve a good deal of labour and materials and the labour element in particular results in high costs.

Fig. 2.17. Line stabilization by laying down lines of turf which will be pegged in place in most cases.

Drainage ditches

The simplest solution to problems of this sort may involve only the excavation of drainage ditches filled with rubble which deflect surface water before it has accumulated into too great a build up. This is a common practice on highway and railway banks, as a permanent solution. The same solution is adopted in different circumstances on regraded land at much lower angles of slope, where storm conditions may be anticipated before the development of a vegetative cover. In these cases, as described elsewhere, the excavation of a series of parallel channels almost precisely at right-angles to the line of the maximum fall will cut off the collecting storm water and divert it in such a way as to keep the volume reasonably small and not likely to cause serious erosion damage (see Seelye, 1953).

Structural solutions

A common solution to rather more intractable problems in earlier times was the construction of a framework of timbers placed on a bank in a grid either with the grid set into the bank or with soil put in place in the square apertures. This would clearly be a method particularly favoured where it was necessary to attempt to establish topsoil and plants on an otherwise bare bank. The grid squares might vary in size from ½ m across to 1 − 2 m depending on the conditions. The structure would prevent the extensive movement of soil over the surface and would dissipate and to some extent divert the force of water. In practice this method was often supplemented by the use of chicken wire laid over the ground surface which provided a further element of stabilization and enabled the growth of youg vegetation to take place. There are very few circumstances where the application of a method so laborious can be justified nowadays. A variation on this method of timber construction might be the laying of turf to form a similar framework although this technique might be limited in application to sites which were not excessively steep. In some circumstances it may be necessary to peg the turfs, in accordance with usual practice for turfing on banks. An alternative method of supporting the stability of banks structurally is the use of lines of material placed horizontally along the face of banks at regular intervals. These may be designed to create a series of shallow terraces, or they may simply be intended to break the flow of water and hold up soil particle movement.

One of the principal functions of such features may well be the retention of moisture so that vegetation becomes quickly established along the topside of the lines, where it is held. This enables the progressive establishment of vegetation and stability of the bank to be achieved provided that nothing occurs to disturb the system such as human intervention or an exceptionally severe storm. The traditional materials used for this method are fascines which are bunches of faggots laid horizontally. A series of horizontal platforms are excavated on which the fascines are laid with their ends projecting from the bank at right-angles. The excavated earth is then replaced over the fascines, being consolidated as well as possible. The fascines are often laid with a slight upward thrust out of the bank and this allows moisture to percolate more easily back into the bank and be held above the solid shelf below the excavation. Where flat terraces are created these may be used for tree or shrub planting, otherwise seeding or turfing may be undertaken and a variation of this technique may be used involving the use of cuttings of willow or poplar species, so that

Fig. 2.18. An embankment drain which is similar in appearance to a buttress drain although not in this case serving the same function.

these growing elements form the initial structural framework. In these circumstances they are laid singly and not in fascines.

In the University of Newcastle steep slopes research project (Hackett, 1972) three methods were tried. The first consisted of brushwood trenches at 1.8 m intervals, the second involved vertical strips of double thickness chicken wire 0.15 m wide and the third used strips of turf, laid inverted and held in place by wire stretched between pegs at 1.8 m intervals on either side of the turf. In both the latter cases the distance between trenches was 2 m. In the experiment, results were seriously affected by damage due to vandalism, however, it is beyond doubt that the third method involving turf was very successful and it appears that the turf, as well as the seed which supplemented it, had grown very luxuriantly. The conclusion that, in areas where vandalism can be anticipated, methods which are inconspicuous should be used, is unavoidable. It may be that where other planting is ultimately required the establishment of ground cover such as grass should be attempted as a preliminary to random planting of other species.

The third method used in the Newcastle steep slopes project was a variation on the use of turf already described. In all these cases the materials used, although some of them were live and growing, were all being used in part structurally. In the cases described the methods have all been intended to reduce the movement over the surface and establish planted zones where plant growth has more favourable opportunities, with the intention that this should result in the ultimate spread of plant cover and surface stability over the whole site. The alternative to this has been mentioned previously, namely to provide some structural cover over the whole slope. Experiments using polypropylene netting were undertaken in 1969, previously matting had been used although this had proved too dense for satisfactory use. The netting proved to be very successful allowing establishment of grass and preventing erosion, and following this work has been developed quite extensively for commercial use. Perhaps this method can really only be justified in limited areas with particular erosion problems.

Turf pegging is another method of achieving complete cover of the bank to be treated. Like the previous method described, it suffers from the high cost and the labour necessary to prepare and lay the material.

Other new solutions revolve around the spraying on of materials which help to bind the surface of the ground and/or improve growing conditions particularly for germinating of seeds. One of the earliest of these used was bitumen applied in a thin coating which retained heat and moisture and so long as it was not too thickly applied, permitted grass to break through on germination. Grass seed would be spread sometimes embodied in a mulch of, say, peat, incorporating nutrients, prior to the spraying of the bitumen. Other workers have experimented with the use of PVA (polyvinyl acetate) to accelerate germination. This forms a colourless film over the ground easily penetrated by grass seedlings but protecting the surface.

The materials used most extensively in Britain, in the last 15 years or so and first developed in the United States are hydromulches. These consist of a mixture containing seeds, fertilizer, and a mulching material which helps to bind the ground surface, all suspended in water. This mixture is sprayed under pressure so that inaccessible banks can be covered and the spray can be projected 30 or 40 m, if required. In this way banks which would otherwise be difficult and costly to deal with can be treated quite quickly. As with all techniques which involve expensive capital equipment the area to be treated needs to be reasonably extensive to make the work economic. Very dry conditions at the surface are a frequent problem of much embankment material and the application of water and the mulch to retain a proportion of it, until such time as germination has begun, and with it the ability to retain other precipitation, is an important aspect of this method. A number of commercial firms offer this service and have their own formulae for the spray and mulch. It has been found possible to spray a number of seeds other than grass and this method has been used successfully in a wide variety of situations. It has already been indicated that the treatments outlined in the previous section are necessary where circumstances force the designer into creating very steep slopes. In the majority of situations such slopes should be and are avoided by the designer. He will be guided by the functional requirements of different land uses when designing regrading, as already indicated and will also be limited to some extent by the limitations of machinery operation.

Fig. 2.19. Spraying a seeding mulch (photograph by E.F.G. (New Lands) Ltd.).

The use of earthmoving machinery

Reference was made at the beginning of this chapter to the advances which had resulted from the introduction of modern earthmoving equipment. In the nineteenth century the railways were created with the pick and shovel, earth was moved in osier baskets on the backs of mules, and miles of embankments were raised and cuttings excavated. The change from those times to the present is very remarkable, although some are inclined to regret the fact that the ease with which material can be formed into embankments, has made the creation of bridges and viaducts across the full width of valleys no longer an economic possibility. In the days before the development of the petrol engine a limited number of machines were developed depending upon the power of steam, but it was the internal combustion engine which ushered in the new age of earthmoving.

It may be useful to think of earthmoving machinery as fitting into one of two types, those that dig and those that push. A brief outline of some of the types available will explain this classification. In the 'digging' category are face shovels, draglines, and excavators, while in the pushing category are blade dozers, graders, and scrapers, each of these pieces of equipment being specialized in its use. In the former category the movement of material by the machine itself is usually limited to the length of swing of the arm of the machine as it is unusual to operate it other than when stationary. Transport of material for any distance is only achieved by the use of additional machinery and this usually implies further handling problems at the point of unloading. Where material is excavated, moved, and deposited within the compass of the machine this usually necessitates some further handling which could be limited to surface grading but might also involve attempts at consolidation. One of the major differences, and in fact advantages, of the machines in the second category is that within their own particular terms they tend to be self sufficient in completing regrading.

FACE SHOVEL

This is one of the earliest methods of digging soil or clay or any soft rock and consists of a digging bucket on a hinged arm. By a series of pulleys the principle of leverage is employed to raise the bucket upwards and away from the body of the machine, on the end of the outer segment of the hinged arm. The leading edge of the bucket digs into the face of the material and this falls into the bucket where it is held until moved to where it is to be dropped. In the latter position it is released by allowing the bottom plate of the bucket to open. From the description it will be appreciated that the face shovel, or shovel as it is sometimes described is most commonly used for the excavation of heaps of material, or banks, or cliff faces (although obviously not solid rock), where the material to be excavated is higher than the machine. The rigid nature of the arm enables the machine to excavate without serious deflection in quite hard material

and to pick up solid lumps of rock and similar objects if required. Shovels range
in size quite considerably, most common being those with buckets of the range
between ⅜ — 3½ yd³ (0.282 — 2.7 m³). A number of larger versions are in use
notably in the American opencast or strip mine coal areas and these include
bucket sizes in excess of 100 yd³ (76.5 m³).

DRAGLINES

A number of manufacturers produce the same basic body and engine to which
the appropriate sized face shovel equipment and dragline arms can be attached as
alternatives. This may be extended to other equipment of a similar nature,
such as cranes, and clam shells, or pile drivers. In spite of this use of a common
basic machine, the operation of the two types of equipment of the shovel
and the dragline are almost totally opposite. Whereas the shovel acts outwards
and upwards the dragline bucket is operated by first being cast out, but is
filled by being drawn back towards the machine itself. The bucket in this case
is not held rigidly but is attached by wires to a boom which is used to lift
and place the bucket prior to filling and to move it around to the point of
emptying. The wires attaching the bucket to the front end of the actual machine
are the primary means of filling the bucket by drawing it along the surface
of the ground so that the cutting edge digs into the surface and so is gradually
filled. The dragline thus works above the area to be excavated and towards the
machine. This sort of operation is unsuitable for very hard material or material
with large lumps as the bucket is less easily controlled than it would be were it to
be rigidly held. It is on the other hand highly suitable for use in sand and gravel
excavations particularly in wet pits where it can operate from the bankside.
The sizes again vary in common use from ⅜ — 3½ yd³ (0.280 — 2.7 m³). Here
again in both Great Britain and the United States to name only two areas, the
extraction of open cast or strip mine coal has led to the construction of
mammoth examples of this equipment to deal with the huge volumes of overburden it is necessary to handle. In the North East of England, 'Big Geordie'
and in the heart of the Ohio coal field, the Ohio Power Company's 'Big Muskie'
have an almost unbelievable ability to move, in the latter case with a bucket
capacity of 350 tons.

GRABBING CRANE OR CLAM SHELL

This is a machine of limited value in the removal of volumes of material. It
depends on the vertical force of the bucket dropping to penetrate into the
material to be excavated, the jaws of the bucket being then brought together
to form an enclosed volume. Its successful use depends on material being soft
and without large rocks or other features. It is commonly used in water; wet
sand pits or the dredging operations in harbours and river channels are its
most appropriate application. Otherwise it is only useful where loose sand or
similar material is to be excavated.

UNIVERSAL EXCAVATORS

The introduction of hydraulic controls and linkages has enabled the development of a range of excavators which can be operated with great precision. The advantages are chiefly limited to small scale work where accuracy, as in digging trenches, is valuable and enables the machine to compete in this respect with hand digging methods. A wide range of machines of this type is available and they may simulate the movement of either the shovel or the dragline. They do not add significantly, however, to the mechanics of bulk earthmoving.

All the machines so far discussed are in the first category suggested earlier, and will need to be operated in conjunction with additional transporting machinery; trucks, wagon ways, or conveyor systems for example, to dispose of the excess material to other sites or to distant parts of the same site. As these additional machines do not incorporate the means of spreading and consolidating the material satisfactorily at the point of deposition, this implies the involvement of yet more equipment, a high capital involvement and a wasteful use of manpower, as with the exception of conveyor systems and possibly sophisticated automatic trans, all these other processes need individual operators.

PUSHING MACHINES

The use of 'scrapers' as they are known, machines which remove material from the surface of the ground and pick it up into a bucket in the machine, carrying the material to a point where it is again deposited in a shallow layer, is an extension of the principle incorporated in the bulldozer or the blade grader.

DOZERS

These machines can be used to push material which is relatively loose or can be reasonably easily loosened. Thus heaps can be spread with a bulldozer, or areas of ground which are too high can be reduced and the excess material spread within a short distance.

GRADERS

The blade grader is a specialist application of this principle and is used for fine grading of such things as games pitches, airport runways, and road bases, which call for very critical surface falls. The blade of the grader is set so that areas which are too high are scrapped off and the material pushed along until a low point on the profile is reached when the fact that the surface is lower relative to the blade enables some of the material to be laid down with the blade passing over it. As a number of passes are quite commonly required to achieve the desired affect of grading, the wheels of the machine may be relied upon to attain a reasonable degree of compaction.

Fig. 2.20. A dozer with blade to push loose material (photograph by H. Leverton and Co. Ltd.).

Fig. 2.21. A blade grader used to attain accurate surface grading (photograph by H. Leverton and Co. Ltd.).

SCRAPERS

It is generally accepted that the scraper is the ideal machine for earthmoving in most circumstances. Coming in a range of sizes, the machine consists of a cutting blade which takes off a thin layer of the surface, which is successively pushed back into the 'box' of the scraper. When the machine has been filled up the box is lifted hydraulically to bring the scraper blade away from the ground surface and the material is carried to the point of deposition. The box has a moveable plate at the back and this is pushed forward so that material is spilled out frontwards. According to the height of the blade so a layer of a certain thickness is laid down until the back plate has moved forward to its extremity and the box is empty. Scrapers consist of independent boxes towed by crawler tractors, or motorized scrapers with their own power units and running on very large pneumatic tyres. Although there are a large number of the former in use and they are much favoured by small operators and for particular

Fig. 2.22. A motorized scraper used for hauling material within sites (photograph by H. Leverton and Co. Ltd.).

uses, they are not at the time of writing, being manufactured. It is argued that the sort of work for which they are suitable can be more efficiently handled by small motor scrapers. Certainly, the latter can travel at far greater speeds, the top speed attained by a Caterpillar D8H being 6.4 mile h^{-1} (10.25 km h^{-1}), whereas the top speed of a motorized scraper may be between $22 - 45$ mile h^{-1}.

The use of an 'elevator scraper' incorporating an elevator device which picks up material off the cutting blade, breaking down the solid masses of clay soils in particular and depositing it at the back of the box adds to the use of operation. For the first consideration, the breaking up of the solid mass as it enters

Fig. 2.23. A caterpillar 613 elevating scraper showing the elevator which enables the machine to load easily and without any aid from a pushing machine (photograph by H. Leverton and Co. Ltd.).

the box makes the material easier to spread in relatively thin and more easily controllable layers. It also has the advantage that this method of loading reduces the power necessary to fill the box in comparison with standard machines. This is because the standard machine has to overcome the inertia of the whole of the volume of material already picked up, which must be pushed back and upwards into the box to accommodate additional material. When the filling cycle is nearly complete this requires very considerable power and for this reason it is usually necessary to operate scraper loading with the assistance of a crawler tractor which, by pushing from the back, provides the necessary additional power. In the case of elevator scrapers the machine can be worked without this assistance and this is regarded as representing a considerable operational advantage.

Limitations on the use of scrapers are the slopes upon which they can work and the distance of haul. In regard to the first the limit of operation of fully loaded machines is sometimes given as an angle of slope of about 12½% (1 in 8); at steeper slopes the load carried by the machine would have to be reduced. Some machines are said to be able to operate fully loaded although in bottom gear at slopes up to 22% (just over 1 in 5) but this is slow and costly as an operation. Maximum operating speeds can only be attained where the gradient is 1% (1 in 100) or less. These figures refer of course to uplift hauls.

Only at the shallowest gradients can the top gear and highest speeds of travel be attained and steeper slopes call for lower gears and a loss in both speed of operation and fuel efficiency, which substantially adds to the cost of work.

Loading which depends not only on the maximum power of the machine but
also on additional thrust from a pushing vehicle must be undertaken on the
flat or preferably downhill. The organization of the haul road must provide a
flat run which is smooth and clear if maximum efficiency is to be achieved. It
used to be considered that operating distances of this type of machine were very
critical. Scoular (1966) gives the following recommendations: that tracked
vehicles could be used economically only up to 400 m (¼ mile) whereas motorized scrapers on rubber tyres could be used up to a mile. On large operations
the use of the biggest machines with a large capacity, and attaining speeds of
up to 45 mile h^{-1} (72 km h^{-1}) may extend this distance considerably, depending
on the nature of the haul road that can be provided.

In the United Kingdom circumstances in which lengthy haul roads of this
nature are found are perhaps more unusual, and are likely to be complicated by
additional hazards such as highway crossings or the need to construct bridges
over streams, all of which must enter into the consideration of methods of
earthmoving to be adopted for a particular site. The use of motor graders to
ensure that haul roads remain smooth and even, and do not develop ruts is
regarded as a very worth-while operation by civil engineering contractors and
this demonstrates the importance placed on the satisfactory condition of haul
roads by those who need to achieve the best financial return by improving the
efficiency of operations. The need to give assistance at the loading stage to all
but elevator scrapers results in the practice of working scrapers in teams
usually of three machines which can be assisted by the pushing machine in turn
and which will result in this not being idle for anything but short periods. In
some circumstances this ratio of numbers may be varied and as many as five
machines may operate with the same pusher.

Influence of machines on the design of landform

Earlier in this chapter a list of criteria for earthmoving designing was set down
and this included reference to the understanding of the ways of operating
earthmoving plant. Although there will be circumstances where either the
functional requirements or the aesthetic purposes result in the need to create
designs of a particularly strong geometric shape, there are many instances when
this is not the case.

Knowledge of the operating cycle of scrapers enables the designer to prepare
proposals which will not result in complex movements of machinery which
give rise to high costs. In the same way the implications of creating platforms
which are, perhaps, narrower-than the width of this type of earthmoving equipment need to be borne in mind. It may be necessary because of problems of the
site, or because of the specialized nature of the design, to do this, but if it is
not the case then the design should take this into account and allow for the
most economic approach to the completion of work in the design. The box

scraper lays down soil in relatively thin layers over a fairly extended distance, building up the level of the surface and compacting it reasonably well as it goes. It works most efficiently when it can move in an unbroken cycle, being able to turn in a single movement, and when steep inclines, especially on the loaded part of the cycle, are avoided as far as possible. Steeply angled banks and sharp geometric shapes are much more expensive to create than smooth flowing curves with relatively easy grading.

Summary

This chapter has attempted to cover in general terms the process of designing a new landform, including the criteria which should influence the approach to design. These consist both of the criteria which dictate the landform in terms of land use and maintenance as well as limitations of construction brought about by our present technological methods and abilities. Also the methods of preparing the design of new landform improvements have been considered, and last but certainly not least in importance, some indication of the way in which instruction and information must be provided to enable the contractor to carry out his work quickly and efficiently.

INSTRUCTIONS TO CONTRACTORS

The importance of providing clear and precise instructions which can be easily followed by any contractor must be obvious. It is also true that, as in other aspects of landscape construction work, the more clearly and accurately the extent and complexity of the work which he is going to be asked to undertake is explained to the contractor, the more chance there is for him to produce a reasonable quotation, or estimate of price. It is only common prudence, when the full extent of a job or part of it is slightly obscure, to make allowance in any cost estimate for the worst possible situation or the most difficult operation. The basis of the information to the contractor will be a contour plan based normally on the air survey base, including existing and proposed topography. Care must be taken to ensure that levels are related to an established point, in Great Britain a bench mark or spot height measured by the Ordnance Survey whose height is known and which will remain in place following the completion of work. This will be required as a constant reference point during operations. In addition to the plan the contractor should be supplied with a set of cross-sections of the proposed area of the works, at an appropriate scale and suitably annotated. The contractor will adopt his own method of setting out the proposed works, involving what is sometimes called boning rods, set into the ground in a predetermined relationship to the finished level. The contractor may well make use of the sections for this purpose or for making his own calculations about the movement of material from one part of the site to another. If it is possible, as is done in some computer programmes, and as shown

Table 2.5 A table of cut and fill volumes between sections to show how the material may be disposed without excessive haulage may be used to help contractors in arriving at most economic pricing.
This sort of table is usually provided for information only. Figures in m^3.

Total cut Apportionment	Total fill Apportionment		Quantity	Rate	Amount
Section A − A_1/B − B_1 $\underline{531 - AA_1/BB_1}$	From AA_1/BB_1 531 From BB_1/CC_1 824 1169 2524	m^3	2524		
Section $\underline{BB_1/CC_1}$ 824 − AA_1/BB_1	From CC_1/DD_1 1768	m^3	1768		
Section $\underline{CC_1/DD_1}$ 3240 − 1169 to AA_1/BB_1 − 1768 to BB_1/CC_1	From CC_1/DD_1 163	m^3	163		
Section $\underline{DD_1/EE_1}$ etc.	From CC_1/DD_1 140 etc.	m^3	140		

in Table 2.5 to provide the contractor with detailed information about the volumes of material in different parts of the site and the quantities and distances of movement which will be necessary to achieve the finished result this can provide further valuable guidances and enable the contractor to provide a keenly priced and competitive quotation. Materials of different types and with different handling qualities should always be specified separately. Table 2.6 (see pages 78 − 79) gives a table of weight and bulk of a number of materials.

Table 2.6 Bulk/weight of some common materials

Material	Weight in bank		Percentage swell	Swell factor	Loose weight	
	$kg\ m^{-3}$	$lb\ yd^{-3}$			$kg\ yd^{-3}$	$lb\ yd^{-3}$
Clay (dry)	1360	2300	25	0.80	1090	1840
Clay (light)	1665	2800	30	0.77	1280	2160
Clay (wet or dense)	1780	3000	33	0.75	1330	2250
Concrete	1920 − 2480	3240 − 4185	40	0.72	1380 − 1060	2330 − 1780
Concrete (wet mix)	−	−	−	−	−	−
Earth (dry)	1665	2800	25	0.80	1330	2240
Earth (wet)	2000	3370	25	0.80	1600	2700
Earth with sand and gravel	1480 − 1780	2500 − 3000	30	0.77	1140 − 1425	1920 − 2310
Granite	2610	4500	50 − 80	0.67 − 0.56	1490 − 1780	2520 − 3000
Gravel (dry)	1930	3250	12	0.89	1720	2900
Gravel (wet)	2130	3600	14	0.88	1900	3200
Loam	1600	2700	20	0.83	1330	2240

Table 2.6 (continued)

Material	Weight in bank		Percentage swell	Swell factor	Loose weight	
Mud-dry-close	1280 – 1760	2160 – 2970			960 – 1460	1790 – 2460
Mud-wet-packed	1760 – 2080	2970 – 3510	20	0.83	1460 – 1730	2470 – 2910
Rock hard	2370	4000	50	0.67	1530	2680
Sand-dry	1930	3250	12	0.89	1720	2900
Sand-wet	2130	3600	14	0.88	1900	3200
Shale	1780	3000	33	0.75	1330	2250
Slag – sand	1000	1670	12	0.89	880	1485

(After a table prepared by Clark Equipment Ltd)

References

B.S.I. (1959). Code of Practice, *Earthworks* B.S.C.P. 2003.

Clark, D. (1949). *Plane and Geodetic Surveying* 4th Edition Revised and Enlarged by Glendenning, J. Vol. 1. Constable and Co. London.

Hackett, B. (1964a). Landform Design and Cost Factors. *Landscape Architecture* Vol 54 July 1964 Louisville, U.S.A.

Hackett, B. (1964b). *Land Modelling* paper presented to Public Works and Municipal Service Conference 1964.

Hackett, B. (1972). Landscape Development of Steep Slopes. Oriel Press: Newcastle-upon-Tyne.

Hackett, B. (1967). Earthworks and Ground Modelling, in Weddle, A. *Techniques of Landscape Architecture*. Heinemann: London.

Middleton, R. E. and Chadwick, O. (1955). *A Treatise on Surveying* (6th Edn.). Vol 1. E.&F.N. Spon: London.

Roberts, H. E. and Stothard, J. N. (1968). Use of Computers for Road Design *Journal of the Institute of Civil Engineers.* paper no. 7133. I.C.E.: London.

Scoular, J. D. (1966). The use of heavy earthmoving machinery and plant. Landscape Reclamation Seminar: University of York.

Seelye, E. E. (1963). *Design, Data Book for Civil Engineers.* John Wiley: New York.

Tschebotarioff, G. P. (1951). *Soil Mechanics, Foundations and Earth Structures.* McGraw Hill: London.

University of Newcastle-upon-Tyne (1971). *Landscape Reclamation*. Vol 1. I.P.C.: London.

Whyte, W. S. (1969). *Basic Metric Surveying.* Butterworth: London.

3 Drainage

Introduction

The landscape architect will be called upon to make proposals for drainage in a wide range of conditions and situations in the course of his professional work. He may be involved in large scale exercises which involve land drainage provision over many hectares or square miles. He may also be concerned with the design of playing fields or recreation areas requiring elaborate provision of drains over a less extensive area. The drainage of areas of hard surface and the proper design of these areas is another aspect of the work which the landscape architect would expect to undertake. In addition to this he should have a working understanding of agricultural drainage and also of the problems of specialized sites: reclamation of industrial waste land, for example.

For all this it is necessary to understand some basic facts about rainfall and the way this is affected by the ground conditions where it falls.

RAINFALL

Basic statistics about rainfall which give average rainfall for years, seasons or months provide only a limited picture of rainfall. It is important to know whether rain is likely to fall in a pattern of short sharp showers or long steady downpours or a mixture of these. It may be that there is a seasonal variation in the pattern of rainfall, although this may not necessarily be significant from the drainage point of view.

A series of tables of frequency of rainstorms in which the duration and intensity of rain are factors has been prepared by the Transport and Roads Research Laboratory (Young, 1973). This information is critical to the design of drainage systems to remove storm water. Intensity of rainfall has traditionally been measured in inch h^{-1}, but metric formulae have more recently been prepared in which the equivalent unit of mm has been adopted. Some general statements on the nature of rainfall may be made which will help to illustrate the topic. It can be said that very intense rainfall most commonly only falls for a short duration, longer periods of rainfall are usually very limited in intensity. Very intense rain storms are in fact infrequent in occurrence, and it is likewise true that very long rain storms are also infrequent.

In both these cases the frequency of the occurrence is almost in inverse

Table 3.1 Variation in rate of rainfall with duration and frequency in UK (after Young, 1973)

Frequency (one in n years)

Duration (min)	1 year		2 year		5 year		100 year	
	mm	in	mm	in	mm	in	mm	in
2.00	69.2	2.72	85.8	3.58	107.8	4.25	181.5	7.15
3.00	61.6	2.43	76.5	3.01	96.5	3.80	165.5	6.52
5.00	50.8	2.00	63.5	2.50	81.0	3.19	143.9	5.67
10.00	35.9	1.41	45.7	1.80	59.8	2.36	114.1	4.49
30.00	18.2	0.72	23.2	0.91	31.5	1.24	70.5	2.78
60.00	11.6	0.46	14.6	0.58	19.7	0.78	47.8	1.88
2 h	7.3	0.29	9.2	0.36	12.3	0.48	30.2	1.19
24 h	1.3	0.05	1.6	0.06	2.2	0.09	5.2	0.20
48 h	0.8	0.03	1.0	0.04	1.3	0.05	3.2	0.12

From this it will be seen that anticipated intensity is reduced with long duration. A storm lasting 5 min and with an intensity of 81 mm h^{-1} (3.19 in h^{-1}) may be expected not more than once every 5 years. A storm lasting 24 h would only be likely to attain an average intensity of 5.2 mm h^{-1} (0.20 in h^{-1}) once every 100 years. Young gives a great number of intermediate figures.

proportion to either the intensity or the length, or both. A very long, very intense storm will thus be a most rare phenomenon. It will be possible to count in years the likelihood of a storm of a particular length or duration occurring in a neighbourhood, and this will be important for the design of drains, water courses or sewers. For many purposes it is perfectly satisfactory to take a standard value for the likely rainfall and assume that this will cover adequately any likely eventualities. In the case of extensive drainage projects it may be necessary to take a more precise line and arrive at drainage proposals as a result of accurate calculations. Even when this is done, however, it is common practice to take account of the worst conditions that might be expected only within a predetermined space of time. Although a storm of great severity could be expected, say, once every 80 or 100 years, to design a system, at great cost, which was capable of dealing with the results of that storm could not really be justified. Instead a calculated risk is taken and the designer, having decided what sort of risks are acceptable, designs a drainage system which would be capable of coping with the worst sort of occurrence that would be expected over X years, without damage. Should a worse storm subsequently occur, it may result in some minor flooding, and slight inconvenience for a short period of time and this is regarded as an acceptable risk. Tables given by Seelye (1953) for the United States, illustrate the range of maximum rainfall variations which might be anticipated. This varies from the North East of the country which is driest, to the South East, the wettest. Once in 2 years a rainfall amounting to 0.25 inch (6.3 m) could be expected in the far North West whereas in the same period 2.25 inch (57 m) would occur in the South East. In 5 years the variation would be from 0.5 inch (12 mm) to 3 inch (75 mm), whereas in 25 years the maximum 1 h rainfall would be from 0.75 inch (18 mm) to 3.75 inch (93 mm). Once in every 100 years a maximum rainfall amounting in the North West to 1 inch (25.4 mm) and in the South East to as much as 4.50 inch (113 m) could be expected. Britain is in many respects comparable with the North Eastern United States where in a 10 year period the worst storm might be expected to vary in intensity and duration from 1.25 inch (32 mm) per hour in the north to 2.50 inch (63 mm) per hour further south. Once every 100 years the same area would show values from 2.50 inch (63 mm) to 4.00 inch (100 mm). For limited areas in England the design maximum of 2.00 inch (50 mm) per hour is recommended, in the British Standard code of practice for Building Drainage (B.S.C.P. 301:1971). Seelye recommends an expectancy period of 5 years for American conditions.

NATURE OF GROUND
The second factor which must be taken into account when designing a drainage system to handle the volume of water resulting from precipitation is the nature of the ground or other surface upon which it falls. Some water runs straight off the surface into streams formed originally as a result of the collection of the flow of surface water, or artificially created water courses, ditches or drains, or collects to form temporary or permanent pools or lakes. Other water permeates the material upon which it falls and entering the ground percolates through to emerge at a lower level in the form of springs or join the drainage pattern of an area. It may alternatively, remain trapped in the ground. Some proportion of the precipitation may evaporate, but account is not usually taken of this in dealing with designs for drainage.

Different materials, it will become obvious, have widely differing charac-teristics when it comes to the penetration of moisture. Seelye (1953) gives a range of values which are very detailed and range from metal roofs to parks and golf courses, comparable values were given for British conditions by the Ministry of Housing and Local Government (1967). From these it is clear that the range is from building roofs, where the surface water run off will be 9/10 or more of the water falling, which needs to be immediately taken care of and carried away in drains if flooding is be avoided. At the other end of the range the run off may only be 1/10 of the rain fall, the other 90% percolat-ing into the soil of such areas as parks or golf courses, similar values being found for established woodlands. Table 3.2 (see page 84) sets out these values, com-paring those which are commonly used.

CONCENTRATION OF DRAINAGE WATER
Because the drainage of surface water run off is concerned with coping with the

Table 3.2 Values of impermeability factor = run off/rainfall (principal values from Seelye, 1953)

Total precipitation shown as 1.0

Surfaces	Values Seelye Min.	Max.	British Standard
Roofs	0.90	1.00	0.95
Pavements:			
Concrete or asphalt	0.90	1.00	0.75 − 0.90
Bituminous macadam open and closed	0.70	0.90	(Roads)
Gravel, all grades	0.25	0.70	0.50 − 0.75
			(Paths)
Railway yards	0.10	0.30	
Earth surfaces:			
Sand − uniform grain size to well-graded			
Bare	0.15	0.50	
Light vegetation	0.10	0.40	
Dense vegetation	0.05	0.30	
Loam from sandy/gravelly to clayey			
Bare	0.20	0.60	
Light vegetation	0.10	0.45	
Dense vegetation	0.05	0.35	
Gravel from clean to sand gravel mix (no silt or clay) to high clay content			
Bare	0.25	0.65	
Light vegetation	0.15	0.50	
Dense vegetation	0.10	0.40	
Clay from coarse sandy or silty to pure colloidal clay			
Bare	0.30	0.75	
Light vegetation	0.20	0.60	
Dense vegetation	0.15	0.50	
Composite areas:			
Central city areas	0.60	0.75	
House residential areas	0.50	0.65	
Suburban residential areas	0.35	0.55	
Rural districts	0.10	0.25	
Parks, golf courses, etc.	0.10	0.35	0.10
Woodland etc.	0.10		0.10

peak flows resulting from rain storms, the time that the water will take to flow across the surface of the ground before reaching the actual drain will be the third of the critical factors in designing an adequate capacity for the system. The capacity of drainage pipes can be determined very accurately according to material, age and condition, and gradient. If the amount of water in $ft^3 \ s^{-1}$ ($l \ s^{-1}$) which has to be carried away from a particular area can be determined, then it is a very easy matter either to select a pipe size to accommodate this volume, or determine whether an existing system will be able to cope with the additional volume or not.

Formulae for the calculation of run off

Two formulae are frequently used for the calculation of the run off of surface water and both depend on knowledge of the three factors already mentioned. The first of these and perhaps the most familiar in use is what is known as the rational formula. In this the peak discharge or run off (Q) is the product of the area drained (A), in acres, the coefficient of run off (c), as a decimal of a whole number, and the intensity of rainfall (i) in inch h^{-1}. Thus $Q = Aci$, where Q is in $ft^3 \ s^{-1}$.

An alternative approach is the empirical one of the Mac math formula. This amends the rational formula to take account of the slope of the ground of the area of the watershed and is expressed as $Q = Aci^5 \ S/A$ where S is the average slope in ft 1000^{-1}. This factor of slope clearly will affect the speed of concentration of the water quite markedly and may, therefore, be important in calculations.

The British Standards Institution have made recommendations for the assessment of peak flow and designing to cater for this. These are contained in British Standard Code of Practice 2005 (1968). They include formulae for determining rates of rainfall; the Ministry of Health Formula, the Bilham Formula, and the Norris Formula. A table of rates of rainfall is also given in this code of practice from which either with rational formula or the Mac math formula can be used to provide an assessment of the run off which is to be designed.

Removal of surface water

Having decided, for the area to be drained, what provision is necessary to carry away the anticipated peak flow it is necessary to see whether this can be undertaken by the use of existing drains. At worst, it may be necessary to build a new main surface water sewer to a treatment plant and natural outfall, at best it will be possible to connect into an existing surface water sewer. Another alternative may be that the existing sewer has inadequate available capacity, and in this case the design may make use of what are known as storm water bunds. These are dry ditches, the capacity of which will vary according to the

Fig. 3.1. Main drains laid in trenches supported with timbers braced with jacks, thus enabling the minimum excavation of material.

requirements but which will hold the water up at times of peak flow. In this way the effect of any flooding is limited to these bunds and the water is allowed to drain away at a slower rate, in fact quite quickly, after the inundation. Designers tend to regard these bunds with some disquiet as a source of danger, and the alternative of actually providing the additional drain capacity is frequently preferred. The use of 'balancing' ponds or lakes is a further alternative possibility frequently adopted for larger scale operations. The new town of Killingworth, Northumberland provides a good example of this feature. When the town was first planned it was realized that available sewers for the disposal of surface water could not cope with the surface water run off which would arise as a result of the proposed development. Accordingly a low lying area,

resulting from mining subsidence and liable to standing water was selected as
the site for a lake. Around this as a central feature the town has been created
and the lake is designed to have adequate spare capacity to hold storm water,
which can be released to the main sewers at a rate they can accept. The laternative
of building additional surface water sewer though the built up Tyneside con-
nurbation, either to the Tyne or the sea, would have been an undertaking of
great magnitude, expense and difficulty.

FLOW IN PIPES

The capacity of pipes is, naturally, dependant principally on their diameter.
However, this is not the only factor and the angle of fall of pipes can make
a significant difference to the flow capacity of those of the same diameter.
Additionally the material and its age and condition may be taken into account
where really accurate estimates of flow need to be attained. The Hydraulics
Research Station of the Department of Scientific and Industrial Research has
published a volume of charts (Ackers, 1963) which give the discharges for pipes
of different cross-sections according to gradient and the roughness value. But
roughness and the temperature and nature of the fluid which is to be carried
in a pipe are additional factors which will need to be taken into account for
accurate assessment of capacity or discharge. For pipes which are not circular
in cross-section, a measurement of what is called hydraulic radius is used. By
the use of these charts an accurate assessment of the capacity of an existing
pipe, or the provision it is necessary to make for the removal of a known volume
of flow, can be made.

The design of drainage systems and the removal of surface water are not
solely a matter of the maximum capacity of the pipes. Two other factors must
be considered. These are concerned with the more normal flow rates which are
encountered an involve designing to ensure that flows in the pipe system will be
brisk enough to keep the pipes properly cleansed with regularity, but at the same
time avoiding a speed which would result in scouring of the internal surface
of the pipe by silt or debris.

A graph giving the capacity for pipes of from 100 mm (4 inch) to 300 mm
(12 inch) was produced in the appendix to the Ministry Handbook *'Landscaping
for Flats'* (1967). This is reproduced here (Table 3.3) (see page 90) and shows
the gradients at which pipes of particular diameters are self cleansing. It is worth
noting that the use of oval pipes which have the same capacity as round ones for
large mains has some advantage when smaller volumes are flowing. The rate
of flow in these is greater than would be the case with round pipes, because of
the more restricted lower part of the cross-section. This can have advantages
in terms of self cleansing in times of reduced flow. Some authorities recommend
designing to a minimum velocity of flow in the pipes which can be regarded
as a constant with different volumes of water and pipe dimensions. A velocity
of 750 mm s^{-1}, is regarded as the minimum for self cleansing flow and this would

allow a minimum gradient for a 100 mm pipe of 1:80. It is recommended practice to design foul sewer systems on the basis of their flowing at a maximum capacity of 90% of their volume. Maximum velocity of flow is achieved when the pipe is 4/5 full in terms of depth. The 100% use of the table reproduced will

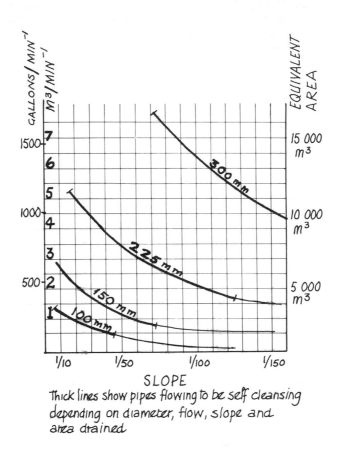

Thick lines show pipes flowing to be self cleansing depending on diameter, flow, slope and area drained

Fig. 3.2. This figure shows the relationship between area to be drained and flow in pipes in the selection of pipes to flow without causing scour or sedimentation according to gradient. Modern opinion now tends to discount scour as a serious problem (After a D.O.E. original).

be adequate to allow for the provision of drains for an area equivalent to an impermeable drainage area of 120 000 ft² (11.50 m² approx) or for a series of such areas. When they are connected and a main sewer is required to take away the flow from a whole system, then it may be necessary to have recourse to the more complex hydraulic design charts.

FLOW IN CHANNELS

Similar constraints apply to the problem of flow in channels as are found with pipes. One of the main problems of channels which apart from the minor danger of scour does not cause any serious concern in relation to pipes is that of erosion. It is, of course, possible to construct channels in reinforced materials, and a variety of materials may be used for this purpose. They may be built out of concrete or made with masonry walls, they may be reinforced with walls of gabions and in this way erosion can be prevented. In a great many cases, however, this sort of approach is too expensive and tiresome, and an approach to design, in which the rates of flow are calculated to be within acceptable limits of the natural material of the ground, is adopted. The use of open channels where the function is solely the movement of water from one point to another is less frequent as a solution than piping. In agricultural areas open ditches which have no collection function are being replaced on the advice of the Ministry of Agriculture, by piped drains. The latter, it is argued, take up less room both as far as manoeuvring machinery and crop growing are concerned. They do not present the hazard that open ditches do, and they are much less demanding of maintenance. It is only, it seems, where there is some special reason, usually aesthetic, that the use of open channels for the movement of water in this way can be justified.

Where open ditches are used the need for them to be set at gradients which will not result in erosion of the bed or walls means limiting the gradient to approximately a minimum of 1:80. The sides of the drains should be constructed to slopes not exceeding 1:1½ and the dimensions will be between 1 and 3 m across at the top and from 0.25 to 1 m in depth (Fig. 3.3) (see page 91).

Seelye (1953) gives a table showing velocities of flow which, taken as a mean, will not result in the erosion of channels. This is given in feet and inches and is reproduced with metric measurement equivalents (Table 3.3) (see page 90). From this it will be seen that there can be quite a wide range of flow variation between different types of soil. It will also be noted that channels tend to become more stable as a result of what is known as 'ageing'.

This is obviously a fact that must be borne carefully in mind when designing the layout of a ditch drain system. The design of channels which will contain the necessary discharge of water can be calculated by reference to the maximum rainfall selected for design purposes and the area of land to be drained using the rational (Kutters) formula for the slope of the ground. The cross-section of drain, and the longitudinal fall necessary to attain the requisite discharge, will then be obtained using the Hydraulic Flow charts already mentioned (Ackers, 1963).

An alternative is to use the Scobey chart and the hydraulic radius (the area of the cross-section of the ditch divided by the wetted perimeter distance) to obtain the discharge and the velocity. This also works the other way so that if the velocity and discharge are known suitable values for the slope and the hydraulic radius can be selected to provide adequate drainage. This chart is

Table 3.3 Mean velocities which will not erode channels after ageing (after Seelye).

Material in channel bed	Velocity			
	$(ft\ s^{-1})$ Shallow	$(ft\ s^{-1})$ Deep	$(km\ h^{-1})$ Shallow	$(km\ h^{-1})$ Deep
Fine sand or silt	0.50 – 1.50	1.50 – 2.50	0.55 – 1.65	1.65 – 2.75
Coarse sand or silt sandy loam	1.00 – 1.50	1.75 – 2.50	1.10 – 1.65	1.90 – 2.75
Silty or sandy loam	1.00 – 1.75	2.00 – 3.00	1.10 – 1.90	2.20 – 3.30
Clayey loam or sandy clay	1.50 – 2.00	2.25 – 3.50	1.65 – 2.20	2.45 – 3.80
Fine gravel	2.00 – 2.50	2.50 – 5.00	2.20 – 2.75	2.75 – 5.50
Colloidal clay or gravelling (not colloidal) loam	2.00 – 3.00	3.00 – 5.00	2.20 – 5.00	3.30 – 5.50
Colloidal, well graded gravel	2.25 – 3.50	4.00 – 6.00	2.45 – 3.85	4.40 – 6.60
Pebbles, broken stone, shales or hardpan	2.50 – 4.00	5.00 – 6.50	2.75 – 4.40	5.50 – 7.10
Turfed gutters	3.00 – 5.00	—	3.30 – 5.50	—
Cobbled gutters or bituminous paving	5.00 – 7.50	—	5.50 – 8.20	—
Stone masonry	7.50 – 15.00	—	8.20 – 16.45	—
Solid rock or concrete	15.00 – 25.00	—	16.45 – 27.45	—

Ageing of channels

Seelye notes that resistance to erosion increases with deposition of silt and cementation of colloids improves the density and stability of the channel bed. For new channels temporary check structures may be used to reduce velocity. Permitted velocity should be reduced where flow is less than 100 mm (6 inch) and where abrasive material is likely to be frequent in water.

Fig. 3.3. Open ditches used to cut off the flow of surface water over open land, particularly where a high rate of surface water run off occurs with disturbed land or land that is unvegetated.

published in Seelye's 'design' (1963). The slope, which it will be obvious has a very close relationship with velocity, will conform to the values given ın Seelye's table mentioned above (Table 3.3). The Forestry Commission (Henman, 1963) recommends not exceeding 1:30 as this slope or anything steeper will give serious dangers of erosion on all but the most stable soil. Most other authorities tend to recommend a much shallower gradient as the maximum [Conover (1953) suggests 2% maximum gradient in USA conditions]. The minimum slope recommended is 1:400 although there are some grounds for suggesting that flow may be satisfactory in some cases on shallower slopes than this.

Where there is some danger of erosion it may be desirable to use check dams along the length of the ditch, and in this way the general longitudinal fall can be reduced except at the dam itself. The design of dams can vary quite considerably from very simple small checks created by placing bushwood bundles across the watercourse held in by stakes, to quite elaborate constructions in stone

Table 3.4 Different surfaces need minimum falls to shed water and leave a dry surface. This usually relies on falls in two directions where only one is available this should not be less than the figure specified for each material.

Materials	
Slab paving	1:70
Rolled asphalt	1:40 − 1:48
Hot rolled asphalt	1:48
Tarmacadam	1:40
In situ concrete	1:48
Engineering bricks	1:50
Concrete blocks	1:50
Granite setts	1:40
Cobbles	1:40
Water bound macadam	1:30
Gravel	1:30
Hoggin	1:30
Uses	
Airfields	1:50 to 1:80 (maximum)
Vehicle parking	1:60 (minimum)
Tennis courts (hard porous)	1:240
(hard not porous)	1:80
Other courts	1:60
Footways (maximum)	1:20
(minimum)	1:40
Cycle tracks	1:40

or concrete. A number of these are illustrated by Conover (1963). The smaller check dams, brushwood for example, will not allow for anything but quite minor changes in level. One of the primary purposes of the use of check dams is the retention of suspended soil particles which might flow on down a fast flowing stream but which are deposited when the water is held up behind a check dam. These features are required to be included in a drainage provision of reclaimed opencast or strip mining areas in a number of States in the USA. The problems of silting and turbid water are a major difficulty in water quality control in these areas in relation to land reclamation. For this reason, it will be clear that adequate sized pools must be provided up-stream of check dams when these are installed and allowance made in the provision for maintenance to clean out the pools when they become excessively silted. It is also important to ensure that the bed of the stream and possibly the banks are adequately strengthened against the likely erosive force of water where it will fall immediately below the dam. An apron which is at least 1½ times the height of the dam is necessary to prevent erosion of this downstream section. The cross-section of these ditches is important and a V-shaped section should always be avoided, the preferred section for the ditch having a flat bottom or being broadly U-shaped.

It has already been suggested that the use of open ditches will be avoided

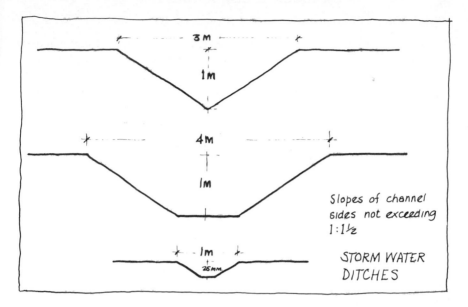

Fig. 3.4. Drain cross-section.

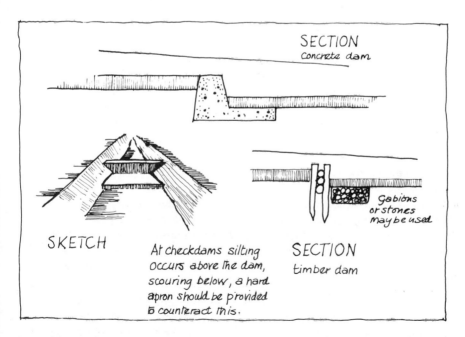

Fig. 3.5. Illustrations to show dams with reinforcement of bed and banks approximately 1½ times height.

if possible and that their use is not recommended in current agricultural practice. This being the case, it follows that the use of such drains is likely to be limited to such occasions as when they have a dual function or provide a temporary remedy to a drainage problem. Some appropriate situations are discussed in the following section.

Drainage of fields and open spaces

When considering the drainage of areas of agricultural land, or woodland or open space it is not only the question of the rapid collection of surface water which it is necessary to consider. Land drainage fulfils a number of functions, the principal one of which might be said to be the maintenance of a proper level of soil moisture for the optimum growth of vegetation. This may consist of trees, or arable or fodder crops or may be ornamental plants or ground cover for recreational purposes. Water in the soil is generally thought of as being of three kinds.

(1) Hygroscopic water — this is water actually absorbed into soil particles and thus unavailable for plant use.

(2) A film of water around the soil particles — this provides all the necessary water for crops and most plants. It is held up by the soil particles and is not susceptible to drainage.

(3) Excess water filling the interstices between the soil particles, these interstices are known as pore spaces and if these are filled with water the soil becomes waterlogged.

   The aim of land drainage is to remove the excess water, or category three above, from the rooting zone of the plants. The behaviour of soils, as a result of the action of water and the availability of both moisture and nutrients, is a subject which is of considerable complexity and has been dealt with in some depth by pedologists and hydrologists. It is sufficient for our purposes to make some simple generalized statements and to refer to the water table of a soil as defining the vertical transition between a zone at the surface with no excess water and a zone beneath it where there is excess water available. It is, then, the aim of the land drainage to retain the water table at an acceptable level below the ground surface. There is also an upward movement of water from this zone into the higher zone so that the water film around the particles can, under most circumstances, be replenished. This upward movement is sometimes referred to as capillary attraction. As has been suggested, in this complex subject the behaviour of soils of different types and consistencies vary very considerably. The natural level of the 'water table' will also vary very considerably according to the nature of the soil and the relevant geology and topography. As sand and gravel soils tend to drain away sharply in contrast to clays and heavy loams there is generally less need on the former for elaborate drainage provisions. There may, however, be a very high 'water table' with these sand

and gravel soils as a result of their relative positions. Retaining the water table at an appropriate level is most critical for crop production and areas of intensive recreational use. It may be perfectly possible, where land is used only for grazing or casual recreation, to rely on natural drainage, particularly on light soils, or to limit the drainage provision to the use of field boundary ditches. Given reasonable frequency and small field sizes, and the presence of adequate natural falls over the ground surface, the worst effects of precipitation can be

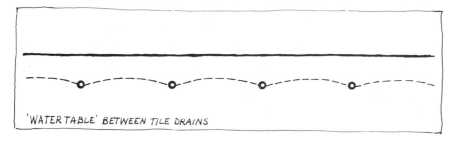

'WATER TABLE' BETWEEN TILE DRAINS

Fig. 3.6. Sketch to show shape of water table between drains. Water table between drain lines is not level but forms a vertical curve with the highest point of water midway between drains.

dealt with. Nevertheless the point should be made that there are very few situations of this sort that would not be improved by proper drainage provision.

One of the problems of dealing with the reduction of the water table is that the influence of a ditch or drain is limited in extent. The introduction of a ditch, or a drain, into an area of high water table will depress the water table over a limited area on either side of the line of the ditch itself. Beyond the lateral zone of the influence the level of the water table will be unaffected. The transition will obviously be gradual and so the water table will not be flat but will be sloped upwards from the zone of maximum influence of the ditch to the zone where the ditch ceases to have any effect. This effect varies according to the nature of the soil, heavy clay soils being less susceptible to the influence of ditches reducing the water table than light sandy soils. Boundary ditches alone are unlikely to create conditions which are the best for crop growth and some other means must be sought. Study of the publications of the Ministry of Agriculture, Fisheries and Food relating to drainage shows that poor drainage can be responsible for a range of ills in crops. Among these are poor germination, crop diseases, poor response to fertilizers, drought which can affect plants with shallow root systems, and patchiness of cropping. In addition, of course, poorly drained land is subject to soil damage by tractors and other machinery, which are in any case difficult to operate on wet land. Animal diseases and shallow rooted weeds flourish on poorly drained land. Other benefits of drainage are the increased aeration of the soil that results from the removal of water from the soil interstices and the consequent rise in temperature of the soil. Where there is excess water in the soil there is a loss of water by evaporation when the atmospheric temperature rises, which process keeps the temperature of the soil depressed. This is one of the causes of what are known as 'late' soils, which respond only slowly to the warmth of spring.

There are many soils and large parts of the world where conditions of excess soil moisture do not arise, and the discussion is particularly directed to British conditions. In these Islands it has been found necessary to provide means of 'underdrainage' firstly for agricultural improvement and more recently for the creation of recreation areas particularly for winter games. Underdrainage has been part of British agriculture for something over 300 years in one form or another, although prior to this, cultivation of open fields relied on the ridge and furrow shape of the strips to shed surface water and take the excess from the ridge of the strip into the boundary furrow. A great deal of agricultural improvement occurred in the 19th century, but the major period of activity was the 18th century, when thousands of acres of heavy land were brought to a reasonable level of fertility as a result of underdrainage.

MATERIAL FOR UNDERDRAINAGE

There are two types of drain in common use. The first is the traditional porous clay ware pipe drain which comes in short lengths of 450 mm (18 inch). The bulk of the system will consist of small bore drains in the case of porous clay ware 75 or 100 mm (3 or 4 inch) in diameter with mains which may rise from 150 to 225 mm (6 to 9 inch) in diameter, 100 mm (4 inch) pipes are most commonly used for submains which have a dual function of removing water from lateral drains as well as draining their own area.

The alternative is the use of perforated PVC piping. The latter is much lighter and has advantages both for handling and use as a result of this. It can be used in lengths of 3 — 4 m or in longer rolls. This means that because of the longer lengths and method of joining, the problems which are so real with clay ware of differential settlement or unevenness in laying which can result in silting and blockage are not a problem with PVC to the same extent. The greater smoothness of the surface of the PVC allows a higher rate of discharge through pipes than is the case with clay ware and the equivalent PVC will have a smaller bore than clay ware. It is usually reckoned that a 50 mm (2 inch) PVC pipe is the equivalent of a 75 mm (3 inch) clay ware.

PROCEDURE FOR DRAINAGE

For any area the first necessity is to have a survey of the topography of the area, which on small sites is likely to be obtained by field survey involving a grid of levels. The distances between measurement points on the grid will depend on the topography encountered but will likely be between 10 and 50 m apart (see Chapter 1). With this information it is possible to determine the best drainage pattern for the ground. For this, of course, it is necessary also to know the position and height of suitable outfalls into streams, rivers or public sewers.

Drains are commonly laid out in more or less standard patterns, which
have been described as falling within the following types:

Herringbone pattern   Grid-iron pattern   Parallel pattern (Fig. 3.7)

(a)

Fig. 3.7. Drainage patterns.
(a) Grid-iron drain layout
(b) Herringbone drain
(c) Random drain layout

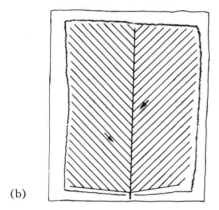

(b)

(c)

They may also be laid in more random fashion to suit particular situations and
topography.

The arrangement of pipes should be laid out to take advantage of the natural
falls of the ground. For minor drains or laterals, the falls will need to be at a
minimum gradient of 1:250. For mains, something lower can be adopted but
1:600 is probably the lowest gradient than can safely be adopted. The disadvantage with very low gradients is that if the water in the system 'backs up' or is
held up, it affects a very large area. Drains should be laid in straight lines and to
an even gradient so that there is the least opportunity for them to be obstructed
or fouled, and the junctions between laterals and mains should be at an obtuse
angle so that the flow of water is not impeded. For individual laterals the maximum advisable length is generally taken to be 65 m.

Both the depth of laterals and the distance apart is dependent on the type
of soil in which the drains are to be constructed. The minimum desirable depth

Fig. 3.8. A machine to dig and fill in ditches for the setting in of drainpipes.

for drains to avoid damage from surface traffic is generally regarded as 750 mm. This depth is selected as the depth for drains in heavy clay soil. In medium soils this is usually measured to 900 mm and in sandy soils a depth of 1.2 m is common. Naturally it is necessary to have the laterals closest together in heavy soils and a spacing of 5 m is adopted for laterals in this condition. In the medium range of soils this may be increased from 7 to 7.5 m and in light sandy soils up to 15 m.

Drains are laid either by hand or by machine. It is unusual nowadays to encounter the use of hand methods for the whole operation except where only very small excavations are involved. An additional length of drainage to deal with the problem of a damp area might be a case where the excavation and pipe laying could still be undertaken by hand. Although the presence of tree roots implies some danger to drains, there may be circumstances in which the line of a drain is close to trees and excavation by hand is necessary to prevent damage to the roots. Depending on the age, condition and species of tree involved it may be necessary to protect the drain and probably only a sealed pipe to carry water away would be sited in this sort of position. Where the soil is particularly stony, and some soils may include quite large boulders, it may be very difficult to operate using machines and hand work in part or whole may be necessary.

It is quite common to lay both clay ware and PVC pipes by hand when the excavations have been carried out by machine and in this case a universal digger with a specially shaped bucket to excavate the minimum necessary width should be employed. It is important that the base of the excavation should be smooth and even, and that it should be solid. In the event of excessive excavation resulting in the need to fill back before laying pipes this must be fully consolidated to prevent any danger of uneven settlement.

The most efficient method of laying drains is by the use of a drain-layer. These can be used to lay both clay tile drains and PVC lengths. The design of a layout which enables simple operation of the machinery is important. It may be possible, for example, to produce a grid iron layout in which the lines of one section of the grid while being separate drains are nevertheless continuous, allowing for continuous operation of the machine along a single line. The clay tile drain layer excavates, places the tiles in the ditch bottom and replaces the soil in a single continuous operation and can also eliminate much of the labour of transporting and laying out of pipes, which is associated with less sophisti- cated methods as a supply of pipes can be carried on the machine. PVC pipes are laid commonly by an adaptation of the principle of the mole plough which forms a circular channel in the soil. This draws the pipe behind it and is used with the type of PVC pipe which comes in lengths rolled on drums.

It is important that the junctions between laterals and submains or mains are properly designed and constructed, particular care being taken that the angle between the two drains is less than a right-angle. An angle of 60° is frequently adopted as being a good compromise which achieves a satisfactory layout of mains and laterals without restricting the flow too seriously at junctions.

It is also important that the method of forming the junctions is one that will not result in constrictions, deflection or turbulence. Although field practice has resorted on occasion to breaking main pipes to introduce the laterals or bringing the laterals in above them, there is no really satisfactory alternative to properly cast junction pipes.

Mole drains

An alternative to piped underdrainage in heavy clay soils is the use of the mole plough. The 'mole' is drawn along underground and is shaped very much like an artillery shell. The system depends on the cohesive nature of clay soil which will compress together to form a virtually glazed wall as a result of the com- pression and polishing action of the mole as it is drawn through the soil. The actual dimension of the mole is traditionally between 60 and 100 mm in diameter. They are drawn in parallel lines at quite close intervals, commonly 2 or 3 m apart (the Ministry of Agriculture gives 3 m as the maximum distance). The fall is given as an optimum of 1 in 400. Generally moles are expected to last no more than about 12 years, although this will vary with the soil. In cases where moles drain into ditches it was accepted practice in times when labour costs were not so prohibitive, to set six or so tiles into the outfall end to improve stability. It is questionable whether this could be justified now. The minimum depth for mole drains is 525 mm (21 inch) and where moles are used in conjunction with piped mains these must obviously be put in prior to mole drainage.

Drainage in special situations

The foregoing has been concerned with the design and layout of general land drainage for extensive areas by means of underdrainage. In some circumstances the use of extensive underdrainage measures may not be considered to be fully justified. This might be as a result of the soil, the land use or the topography of

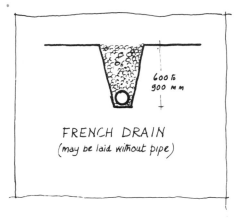

Fig. 3.9. A French drain with pipe set beneath fill material of open stone to within 25—35 mm (1—1½ in) of surface ground.

the area, or a combination of these factors. In such circumstances the use of a French drain, in which a pipe in a ditch is combined with filling the ditch with permeable drainage material may be appropriate. This will control the ground water table in the vicinity of the French drain but can also accommodate the results of surface water drainage which may collect, and need to be dispersed, quickly. For this reason French drains are frequently placed at the base of embankments, in low spots and across anticipated lines of flow of surface water. On many areas used for casual recreation and the like where the surface is sufficiently angled to throw the water off, a French drain may be adequate to disperse the collected water. They are similarly used to protect the soft landscape areas beside major roads and motorways.

Another method of controlling and containing the surface water flow is the use of shallow channels, sometimes called diversion ditches. These may be only 100 — 250 mm in depth but 1 — 3 m in width, planted with vegetation and able to hold the surface water flow resulting from conditions of sudden storm to be released into a piped system at the capacity of the pipe. Most of such

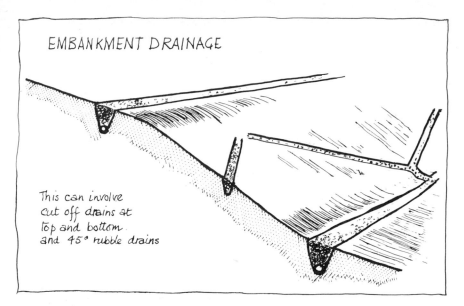

EMBANKMENT DRAINAGE

This can involve
cut off drains at
top and bottom.
and 45° rubble drains

Fig. 3.10. Embankment diversion and cut off.

channels will hold standing, or slow moving water, but where water will move
at any speed along the channel and there is any danger of erosion, the bed
of the channel may need to be reinforced in some way (see Table 3.3).

Alternatively, plants which will have the dual effect of slowing down the flow
of water and binding together the soil may be introduced. Either this sort of
diversion ditch or a French drain may be introduced at the top of an embankment which might be subject to erosion damage. In either case, however, care
must be taken to ensure that this is not placed so as to cause the danger of
weakening the bank in the case of clay soils where rotational slips could occur.
In other soils weakness could develop through water entering at the top and
perhaps emerging in the form of springs.

The control of water is particularly important in steep banks and it is
common practice on railway and highway embankments to remove ground water
which might otherwise issue in springs with resultant weakness and erosion
by the use of hill 'grips' or rubble drains which are set at 45° to the slope of the
embankment. These drains which may or may not be piped at the base lead
the water in a more gentle and controlled manner to the base of the embankment where it is disposed of into the system. These are rarely used in a regular
pattern, being more commonly needed to take care of the 'issues' which are
brought to light as a result of earthworks.

A very specialized, and expensive form of embankment drainage used when a
rotational slip has taken place is the buttress drain (see Chapter 2). This consists of a series of deep excavations cut below the line of rotational slip. The

ditches thus created are back-filled with well packed stone work. The individual buttresses are not necessarily piped but the water is led to the drainage system at the base of the embankment by sloping the base of the buttress, which may even be stepped. Not only is the water removed from the embankment very effectively but the mass of the embankment, weakened along the line of the rotational slip, is broken down into a number of smaller masses and the material is held in place by the frictional force exerted laterally by the stone of the buttress. Because it represents a very considerable engineering exercise this technique is not usually undertaken except where a failure has already taken place.

Some constructional situations call for the inclusion of drains to remove excess ground water and prevent its affecting the stability of the structure much in the same way that interceptor drains may be required in relation to embankments. It is necessary to provide this sort of interceptor around many major buildings. Major roads also require the inclusion of drains along the immediate verge of the road to ensure that the road base and sub-base are kept free of excess moisture, whether it percolates through from the surface or rises from the ground below. Such cut offs also prevent the lateral movement of soil moisture under roadways.

When earthworks are to be undertaken it is sometimes necessary to provide under-drainage where the land is to be built up, prior to the building up. Damp spots or spring lines may be evident and before more material is spread over these, provision must be made in the form of French drains, or something similar, for the control of this situation by the removal of excess moisture.

Another situation in which it is important to control ground water is where retaining walls are to be constructed. It is important that water is not allowed to build behind a retaining wall in such a way that it could result in it becoming unstable or damaged. It is common practice to lay tile drains along behind retaining walls and lead them to the main drainage system. In this way the area behind the retaining wall remains dry and stable. The pipe is placed at the base of the back fill of open drainage material usually put in this position. In many cases of present concrete walls, current practice is to build a loose wall of open 'breeze' or other blocks which act as a drainage medium behind the wall. Some designers follow the practice of placing weep holes at the base of the wall. This has a number of disadvantages, the weep holes consist of narrow pipes which often project from the face of the wall and become broken by vandals. This may not be a major disadvantage but frequently the flushing of water into paved areas used by pedestrians, with the accompanying silt and in some cases staining of the surface, is undesirable.

Forestry drainage

The benefits of drainage through improved soil conditions in commercial forestry have long been appreciated. It is clear, however, that tile drains are an inappropriate method in any area where they would be likely to be affected by the presence of tree roots both for this reason and because open ditches being a great deal cheaper to provide, do not cause the same inconvenience in wooded areas as in open land where they would interfere with land use and cultivations.

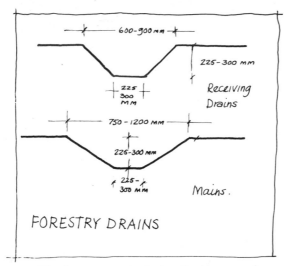

Fig. 3.11. Forestry drains dimensions etc.

The Forestry Commission (Henman, 1963) recommended an arrangement of drains parallel or as near parallel as possible to the contours, with falls not more than 1:30 nor less than 1:400 in lengths of between 100 and 200 m connected to mains within the same range of gradients. The dimensions of receiving drains should be 600 − 900 mm across the top and 225 − 300 mm across the base, and the depth should always be at least as great as the width. The mains themselves would be similar but with a width of between 750 and 1:200 mm across the top.

Because the purpose of receiving drains is to control, principally, the ground water the distance between these drains can be increased as the slope increases. This is in contrast with contour drains used to control surface water drainage on steep banks where the distance apart will be reduced in diverse relationship to the angle of slope. An example of this is the use of contour drains on reclaimed land, which will be discussed in a later section. The Forestry Commission suggests that the spacing of receiving drains on banks should be: angle of slope 1:20, 1:14 and 1:10; distance between drains 20, 30 and 40 m respectively.

In many soils used for forestry planting which may have a high moisture content, either because of the soil texture or because of the water retentive qualities of peat, the technique of ploughing the turf to form ridges is often

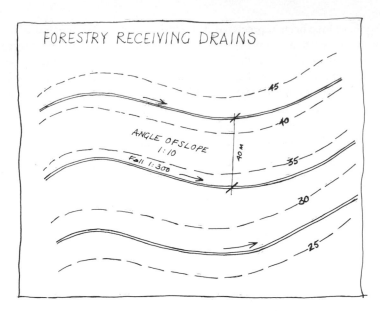

Fig. 3.12. Forestry receiving drains.

undertaken: this has the result of providing local drainage particularly desirable for the development of young trees. It is usual practice to plough up and down the hill slope at an angle of between 45° and 90° from the receiving drain.

DRAINAGE PROBLEMS OF RECLAIMED LAND

The principal problem of the drainage of reclaimed land stems from the fact that much waste material regraded by earthmoving equipment has the characteristic of allowing a very high rate of run off in proportion to rainfall. This characteristic is only maintained in the period before the development of vegetation, which is usually completed in one or two seasons. It does mean, however, that special precautions must be taken during this time. Recent practice has tended to rely on contour drains on embankments with cut off drains at the shoulder and toe of these features. These are usually left as open ditches for the first season at least, and filled with approved rubble, probably 30 − 75 mm pieces, with a pipe of porous clay or concrete laid in the bottom as the permanent solution. If the rubble is placed in the ditch before the vegetation has developed properly and the surface water run off has reduced, this very rapidly becomes clogged with silt and is impossible to clean, and of course is useless as a means of drainage. It is also important that the ditches are cleaned and shaped up properly before the laying of pipes in the ditch bottom.

A major problem in this kind of work is that of erosion and particular care must be taken to ensure that these dangers are minimized by keeping slopes reasonably shallow and avoiding too great a concentration of volume of water in unprotected channels. Conducting water down slopes requires particular attention and it has become accepted practice to install closed pipe systems in glazed clay ware with man-holes at the top and the bottom of the slope to ensure that the flow of water is properly controlled, and contained. This is obviously a very expensive practice, although it is justified by the erosion damage that can so easily be sustained as a result of the failure of less reliable methods. If the temporary drainage provision can be so designed to be used as the drainage system for the future development of the site this would be an ideal solution.

DRAINAGE OF PLAYING FIELDS

The drainage of open spaces used for recreation generally conforms to the arrangement of patterns of under drainage already discussed. Some specialized areas, however, may call for particular treatment to ensure an especially high standard of drainage. Among these are bowling greens and cricket tables.

Bowling greens may be either flat rink or crown green, the latter being raised in height to a central crown some millimetres above the level of the edge of the green. In both types of green a porous layer of material usually 125 mm in thickness is laid down immediately below the turf to allow sharp drainage. On flat rinks it is normal practice to lay down field drains in diagonal lines across

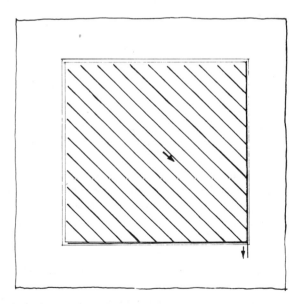

Fig. 3.13. Bowling green drains. Bowling greens are drained by the use of drains laid diagonally across the green to lateral down either side. These are beneath open ditches which extend around the whole green.

the green at 4.5 m centres. These, which should be 75 mm in clay ware, will
connect to 100 mm pipes placed in a rectangle around the link in the bottom of
a peripheral ditch which is filled to within a 150 — 200mm of the porous
gravel material. All corners, junctions, or bends in this sort of system should be
laid down in glazed clay ware pipes. With crown greens it is not usually necessary
to provide the diagonal pipes, the surface slope of the ground giving a sufficient
shedding of the water, in contrast to the horizontal surface of a flat rink.

Similar treatment is often adopted for cricket squares in which case a number
of authorities advocate the ommission of field drainage pipes beneath the
square in case of settlement or uneven drying. A drainage layer should be
provided and a pipe placed around the square to remove the water from this
layer and connect to the field drainage pattern. Corners and junctions of these
pipes should be in glazed ware, the whole in 100 mm diameter pipe.

Running tracks consist of hard surface material which is usually highly permeable. Porous tracks may vary from cinders, which are the traditional material,
to a range of non-resilient all-weather porous materials. Although these are
porous some surface water will be shed, particularly when rain of any great
intensity is experienced. The requirement that falls on tracks should be very
slight makes the use of a porous material desirable. The A.A. specification for
tracks requires that there should be no longitudinal fall on a track and a cross
fall of not more than 1:100. This necessitates the use of a perimeter drain to
ensure quick drainage, around the track, consisting of a French drain with a
4 inch pipe laid at a fairly shallow depth of 450 —500 mm. The ratio of run off
to percolation will obviously vary with the intensity of the storm and the precise
nature of the material. It may well be in a comparable range with the gravel in
Seelye's chart of the coefficient of run off, in which, depending upon the particle
size and proportion of different sizes, the run off would vary from 25% to 70%
of rainfall. While standard hard porous surfaces will require falls of about 1:150
to ensure surface drainage it is possible by the use of the non-resilient all-weather
surfaces to reduce the falls to about 1:400. This is because they consist of
washed stone with no fine concrete, beneath a proprietary surface layer. The
open nature of the base ensures free drainage. Impervious but resilient surfaces,
such as the 'Tartan' track which has been much used recently for major stadia,
can be laid down to falls of 1:100 and used successfully. Where porous material
is used for surfacing the perimeter, drains should be supplemented by the
provision of a series of short laterals under the track at about 75° to the
perimeter drain and at intervals of between 5 — 8 m. Where impervious material
is employed this arrangement of laterals will not be necessary, and either the
type of French drain already described or a shallow concrete channel connected
to a pipe carrier drain system should be employed to carry away surface water.
In many stadia used for sports or cycling the external perimeter drain will need
to have the capacity to carry away the water falling down from the external
banking and this must be taken into account in calculations of capacity.

Drainage of paved areas

The ratio of surface water run off to percolation on hard surfaces establishes the
need for these surfaces to be laid with sufficient slopes or falls on the surface
to lead rainfall, which would otherwise lie on the paving, to positions from
which it can be led away, quickly and conveniently into a surface water drainage
system. The falls which are chosen are usually the minimum of water across
the surfaces and must allow for unevenness in the surface. Fine asphalt surfacing is subject to some minor irregularities from a plane even when skilfully
laid; Arnison (1967) specifies that for dense tar surfaces on roads, an accuracy,
measured with a straight edge of ¼ inch in 10 ft should be required. This can be
expressed proportionately as 1 in 480, and will allow quite gentle falls to be self-
draining. Other surfaces are subject to greater irregularities and those, such as
granite setts and cobbles, which consist of small units may hold water, either
as a result of the variations in level of the surface units, or because of the level
of the 'grouting' of mortar or other material between them. This means that
some paving materials must be laid to quite pronounced falls if the surface water
is not to be trapped. As a generalization it can be stated that the smaller the
paving units involved, the steeper will it be necessary for the falls to be. Quite
apart from the obvious inconvenience to users it is important that the surface
water is not allowed to stand because in winter conditions, freezing and drying
of water will have a very damaging effect on the materials of the surface.

QUICK REMOVAL OF SURFACE WATER
Drainage of surface water thus becomes a major factor in the design of paved
areas. This is particularly critical where formal open spaces, which are intended
to have the appearance of flat planes, are concerned. The number and position
of drainage gullies becomes an integral part of the pattern and design of the
paving, and many designs are dictated more by this than by the limits of
capacity for flow of gullies or pipes. Take as an example a 100 mm glazed pipe
connecting a small gully, such as would be used for paved pedestrian surfaces.
Depending on the gradient of the pipe, it would have the capacity to drain
between 3000 and 6000 m² approximately, assuming a maximum rainfall of
75 mm h⁻¹. Thus each gully and pipe, if the drainage were to be laid out with the
gullies on a grid system, could be set out at a distance of just over 54.7 m from
the next, at the lowest gradient and pipe capacity. At the highest pipe gradient
this would be just below 78 m apart, in each direction. If we assume that paving
is laid to fall evenly from a high point mid-way between the two gullies, and in
the two directions we can then see what falls will be involved, depending on the
materials. For brick paving, for example, falls of 1:25 might well be adopted as
an appropriate means of clearing surface water and such falls would mean that
between the high point and the gully on the grid, a distance of 27 − 35 m, there
would be a change in level of over 1 m. This sort of change, if repeated would

result in a very undulating appearance, greatly removed from the flat plane which the designers wish to simulate. Gullies in flat, or apparently flat paving are set much closer and might commonly be at 7.3 m (24 ft) centres as was the case for the brick paving on the west front of Newcastle-upon-Tyne civic centre, where a fall of 1:48 could be adopted in brick paving to give a difference of only 75 mm (3 inch) between low and high points. This sort of variation is usually perfectly acceptable where a more pronounced cranking would not be. This spacing represents a much less critical capacity than might be dictated by the limitations of pure drainage design. The actual area for each gully would be 53.29 m² (570 ft²) in this case, and this is just over 1/66th of the maximum area that the drain size could deal with. Of course, the reduced area means that the time taken for the over ground flow of water from the extremities to the gullies is minimized, although this may not be very significant on pedestrian areas. It may be a factor, in some circumstances, in the design of highways where perhaps adequate falls cannot be easily achieved.

Recommendations for the falls on highway surfaces are given to take account of the requirements for quick drainage of surface water necessary for these surfaces. There is clearly a need, in the case of surfaces where a film of water might result in aquaplaning of vehicles, to remove this surface water as rapidly as possible and for this reason recommendations for surfaces on highways are for quite steep gradients. Public footways are usually laid to quite steep falls with the water being drained to the roadside gullies. In B.S.C.P. 2006 a fall of 1:24 is recommended for these pavements, usually 2 m approximately in width. Table 3.4 gives a number of recommendations for crossfalls. Less formal areas of hard surface and roads which are on sloping ground do not present the same design problems as have already been described and the areas to be drained can be related precisely to the capacity of pipes and gullies as long as some allowance is made for partial blocking of the gullies by debris. It may be desirable to adopt the design criteria usually applied to foul drains which involves designing on the basis of 90% of the capacity of the pipe, although it should be said that this is not regarded as necessary in most standard texts. The problem of design which achieves adequate falls on flat sites is, of course, not limited to formal pavement, or pedestrian areas, but may apply to roads and other hard surfaces. So far the discussion on design has been limited to the use of individual gully gratings which may vary in size from the common pedestrian area size of 225 × 225 mm to roadside gullies which could be 1.0 × 457 mm. These involve drainage to a series of points. The alternative to this which is suitable, particularly where it is difficult to get satisfactory longitudinal falls is to use long gullies which may be of several types. The advantage of these is that the water can be thrown laterally off the ground surface and collect in a channel or gully which can be laid at a comparatively low gradient. These may be as simple as a dished concrete channel with only a shallow section, or may be a sunken half round channel with a grating cover or alternatively a precast

Fig. 3.14. Surface water drainage by a concrete channel and 'Safeticurb' patent drain. The open channel disgorges into a gully, the grating of which has been removed by vandals.

rounded channel with longitudinal slots connecting the surface to the drainage channel. All these types may be laid at comparatively shallow angles and falls of between 1:20 and 1:240. This may provide an ideal method of drainage for flat areas.

The spacing of road gullies depends on the criteria of pipe capacity and gradient, and can be calculated on the basis of the area of watershed for each gully. This should include, obviously, the area of footway and roadside verge, and an allowance, certainly in residential or other developed areas, for water which is likely to run off driveways and other adjoining surfaces. Roadside gullies will commonly be found at distances of 40 − 60 m apart and this sort of distancing will usually be found much more than adequate to cope with most normal rainfall conditions. The most important thing is to ensure that surface water is not allowed to stand or build up in volume over the highway surface.

Where small areas of hard surface are involved, there is a temptation to shed the water from these surfaces to adjoining soft areas to obviate the need for drainage provision. This practice should be followed with caution as it may cause problems of excessive water in the soft areas, leading perhaps to the need for providing tiles drains for them. Areas of grass, of course, are usually laid to levels of say 15 mm above adjoining hard surface for ease of maintenance,

Fig. 3.15. Surface water drainage by 'Safeticurb' patent drainage used in conjunction with slab paving in an historic setting. This material makes a strong visual contribution in many situations (photograph by Charcon Products Ltd, Derby).

and so that water cannot physically be shed from hard surface to grass, unless a special detail is employed. As a general rule it should be assumed that water should not be shed from one surface to another but dealt with as it falls. If water is shed from grass or planted areas on to a hard surface, for example, this will be likely to result in washing of silt on to the hard surface. Sometimes when tree pits and areas of shrub planting are set within surrounding hard surface areas there is a need to get water to the roots of the plants and the falls on the

Fig. 3.16. Surface water drainage by 'Safeticurb' patent drains in an industrial area, contrasted with bituminous surfacing (photographs by Charcon Products Ltd, Derby).

paved surface will be designed to ensure that this is achieved. It is important, then, to ensure that not only is the supply of water adequate, but that it is not excessive. This may mean the provision of an under drainage system within the soil of the tree pit or planted area. Water from the surface can be allowed to percolate through the surface soil supplying the plants with their requirements, but any excess is carried away by a tile drain system which prevents water-logging and in effect creates and controls an artificial 'water table'. It is important that when surface water is shed from vehicular areas into tree and shrub pits, there should be some means of intercepting the flow of surface water to avoid contamination of the soil by petrol or oil, or at certain times by salt.

MAINTENANCE OF DRAINAGE SYSTEMS
When dealing with drainage both of fields and open areas of soft landscape, and hard surfaces it is important that adequate provision is made for the maintenance of the drains. It is also important that noxious substances are not permitted to enter natural drainage systems, water courses or rivers, or to pollute sewage processing plants. For these reasons drainage systems are

Fig. 3.17. A system of surface water drainage feeding from open channels into silt chambers connecting into tree pits. This is also illustrated in Fig. 3.18.

provided with a series of access and cleansing points at appropriate intervals to enable a reasonable level of maintenance to be undertaken.

Chambers on sewer lines

On sewers less than 0.9 m in diameter the B.S.C.P. 2005 recommends that on straight runs man-holes should be placed at intervals of not more than 90 — 110 m. This is the maximum distance at which drains can be rodded to remove blockages. Where there are changes in direction, or junctions or a change in pipe size it will be necessary to provide a man-hole. This does not apply in the

case of laterals leading from gully gratings in areas of hard surface where rodding
can be undertaken down from the gully and cleansing of the laterals, if necessary, achieved in this way. Where the top end of a sewer does not lead directly
from a gully, it may be provided with a means of access called a rodding eye.
Vehicular area drainage will necessitate the inclusion of petrol and oil traps
as well as silt traps in some circumstances and these items are described and
illustrated below. It is usually recommended that main sewers should be laid
at not less than 1.2 m (4 ft) under hard surfaces, roads etc, and 0.9 m in areas of
soft landscape under cultivation.

For field drainage it is not usually considered necessary to provide access to
the laterals for regular cleaning but the junctions between sub-mains and mains
and changes in direction of these drains may necessitate the provision of access
chambers, which may be described as inspection or junction chambers. These
may need to be provided also when a marked change in vertical direction occurs,
at the head and foot of a bank for example. In a field drainage system a reasonable
number of these chambers should be silt chambers to ensure that this is properly
controlled. A chamber at the top of a bank, where the main is to be taken down,
should be a silt chamber to collect this material before it can be carried down
and deposited in the drain at the point below the bottom of the bank where the
reduction in velocity of water would result in the deposition of the silt.

Junctions between closed drains and water courses

Drainage of open areas may involve depositing water from underground pipes
into open water courses, or even taking surface water flowing in open ditches
into piped sewers. When this sort of junction occurs it is important that it is
properly and strongly constructed as this is the kind of point at which problems
of erosion are likely to arise. The same is true where sewers are permitted to
discharge into rivers. It should be noted that the provision of this sort of outfall
can only be undertaken with the approval and supervision of the local water
authority on most rivers and streams. Even where the stream and outfall do not
fall within the jurisdiction of the water authority proper precautions should be
taken.

The level of the outfall should be at least 150 mm above the normal flow
of the stream. It should be fitted with a cover to prevent water backing up the
pipe from the stream in times of spate. There should also be a grating across the
mouth of the pipe to prevent the entry of vermin. The construction should be
such as to prevent any danger of erosion of the stream. The pipe should be set
in a wall of brick or concrete and may be recessed from the stream with wing
walls. An apron of concrete should be provided where the surface water might
splash down on to the base of the stream. It may also be necessary to provide
a grating to protect the mouth of the pipe from becoming clogged with debris.
Attention should be paid, where pipes discharge laterally into narrow streams,

to the need that may arise to protect the opposite bank from erosion. Similar forms of construction will be needed, particularly a grating to collect debris, where water from an open ditch is to flow into a sewer pipe.

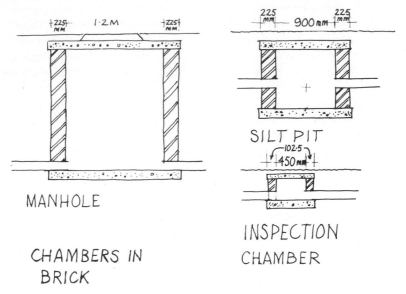

Fig. 3.18. Chambers in brickwork, man-holes, silt pits and inspection chambers.

Man-holes

These are chambers large enough for a man to enter and work; for this reason the dimensions will not be less than 1.2 m (4 ft) x 0.76 (30 inch) internally, with a minimum height at the full width of 1.2 m (4 ft) to give adequate working space. It is important that this full height is available with man-holes constructed on deep sewer runs where access to the man-hole may be through a thinner vertical shaft. Man-holes are usually constructed in brick in which case they are rectangular and the dimensions above apply or in precast concrete segments usually between 900 mm (3 ft) and 2400 mm (7½ ft) in diameter, which are set on a concrete base and placed one upon the other.

Brick man-holes are built on an *in situ* concrete base, using a 1:3:6 concrete mix. Depending on ground conditions this base may or may not require to be laid upon a sub-base of hard core blinded with ashes. The concrete base is likely to be 150 mm in thickness, and upon it will be built the walls of the man-hole in 225 m brick. The brick selected should be reasonably impermeable and for this reason second class engineering bricks are often specified. An alternative, or additional, refinement of specification to ensure that the man-hole remains watertight may be to require that the man-hole walls are rendered with cement rendering on both the inside and outside. Normally rendering is only required on the inside faces, and for a thickness of 15 mm (½ inch). Where second class engineering bricks are used this is unnecessary. Man-holes may be straight through, or single or multiple junction man-holes, with the drain-pipe set just above the base so that the fall of the pipe is continuous although the section passing through the man-hole itself will consist of a half round channel. All junctions or changes in direction will then occur within the man-hole. Man-holes will be finished with concrete slabs which may be precast or *in situ* but will be reinforced and with standard man-hole covers in cast iron. The finish of man-hole covers is discussed later.

Back drop man-holes. Where there is a need to change the level of sewer pipes, for example, when entry has to be gained into an existing deep sewer and the new work can, for the most part, be set at a higher level, a back drop man-hole can be used. This will reduce the depth of excavation that might otherwise be required. A back drop man-hole consists of a man-hole excavated to the level of the lower pipe run with a vertical pipe turning at the lowest part to enter the man-hole horizontally, set in concrete outside the wall of the manhole itself. This vertical pipe is connected to the higher

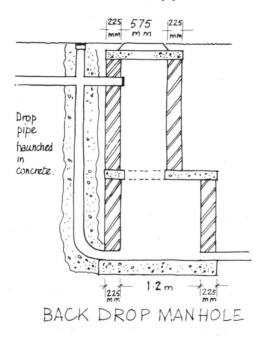

Fig. 3.19. Back drop man-hole.

level and allows water to pass from the higher pipe to the lower through the man-hole. There are usually access points and connections to the upper pipe in the man-hole wall and a cover at ground level to the vertical pipe.

Both of these which are normally closed and waterproof provide access for cleansing the system.

Interceptors

Petrol and oil interceptors are particularly necessary in vehicular areas. A standard pattern consists of three adjoining chambers built in the same manner as a brick man-hole, the walls being 95 mm thick and the chambers connected by inverted U-shaped pipes. Each chamber is 0.9 m x 0.9 m x 0.9 m (3 ft x 3 ft x 3 ft). The oil and water remain floating upon the surface of the

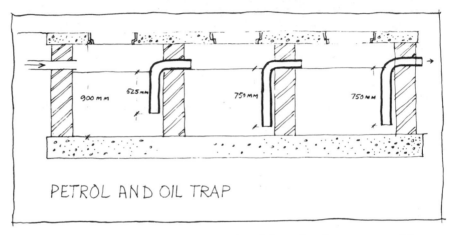

PETROL AND OIL TRAP

Fig. 3.20. Petrol and oil interceptors consist of three chambers connected by vitrified bend pipes beneath the surface of the effluent in the chambers, as petrol and oil float on the surface they will not be transferred through the system. Petrol will evaporate off the surface of the water and the chambers should be ventilated to allow dispersal with the atmosphere.

water in the chambers when the flow from chamber to chamber is from the lower depths of the chambers. The petrol evaporates from the surface and for this reason a ventilating grill is provided. Oil remains floating on the surface and may need to be periodically removed.

Silt traps

Many surface water gullies are designed to trap silt by virtue of having a deep sump with the outflow pipe existing above the base of the sump. Many such gullies are supplied by iron founders as standard units and roadside gullies might have internal measurements of 500 x 400 mm with a depth of 600 mm (or 19 inch x 15 inch x 24 inch). Pavement or yard gullies would be smaller in dimension, and these frequently will incorporate removable silt buckets for easy cleansing.

Silt pits

These are constructed in the same manner as man-holes except that the base of
the pit should be at least 300 mm (1 ft) below the invert level of the pipe.
The base of the pit should be reinforced concrete and the cover usually consists
of reinforced concrete bars with lifting rings. In open land the top of the pit
will be 150 mm (6 inch) below the surface of the ground with soil placed over
it. Dimensions across the pit will usually be 900 x 600 mm (3 x 2 ft). Brick work
may require to be rendered for waterproofing.

Inspection chambers

Occurring in straight runs or at bends or junctions these will be constructed in
the same manner as silt pits except that the internal dimensions will need to be
no more than 250 x 450 mm (10 x 18 inch), and the depth will be that of the
pipe outlet. Because of the smaller dimensions, the cover only needs to be constructed of 75 mm reinforced concrete and the walls need only be ½ brick
width, 102.5 mm (4½ inch).

Soakaways

In some circumstances where it is not possible for one reason or another to
provide a full drainage system, problems of wet land or standing water can be
alleviated by the provision of soakaways. These consist of pits constructed like
man-holes with 150 mm concrete (1:3:6) base and 225 mm (9 inch) walls. The
walls are built of perforated brickwork. Soakaways may be connected to short
lengths of pipe and to a limited number of gullies on hard surface areas. The
soakaway should be built with a capacity equivalent to the depth of 12 mm of
rainfall over the area of land to be drained. This water which can be collected
from the surface and upper layers of the soil can be released slowly into the
lower layers of the ground. Precast concrete soakaways are manufactured by
Mono Concrete Co., Ltd, from 900 mm (3 ft) to 2400 mm (7½ ft) diameter
with, for special conditions a larger size of internal diameter.

Summary

(1) Drainage of areas of soft landscape is aimed primarily at ensuring the
removal of excess water from the top layer of soil to promote the health
and good growth of plants, and enable the use of the land.
(2) Drainage is not in this aspect an exact science; rule of thumb methods of
drainage may be followed frequently with complete success but one should
always be prepared to amend a drainage system designed in this way to take
account of special circumstances.

(3) It is important that adequate provision for maintenance, collection of silt and cleansing of the system are provided.

(4) Pipes must be laid at suitable gradients and solidly bedded and all danger of obstruction by sinking or poor junctions avoided.

(5) Both for sub-soil drainage and surface water drainage with glazed pipes designs should aim to provide the shortest system of drainage runs and the simplest in terms of flow. This is important both for initial cost and for subsequent maintenance.

(6) Surface water and sub-soil drains must be laid at gradients which are self-cleansing and will not result in scour on the pipes.

(7) Special precautions are always required when there is any change in direction, or junction of water courses or where water flows into or out of a pipe.

(8) Consideration must always be given to the protection of structures from ground water.

(9) On hard surface areas the capacity of pipes may not be the only criteria for the layout and frequency of gullies. This may be dictated by the design requirements of the paved area or the need to remove surface water very quickly for safety reasons.

(10) Although very accurate calculations can be made for the design of drainage systems these are always based on a calculated risk in accepting the highest rate of rainfall that can be expected in a period of X years. Because of this, while it is obviously important to calculate reasonably accurately for the drainage of a large area, most small drainage designs can be designed using more crude, rule of thumb methods.

British Standards

The following British Standard Codes of Practice and British Standards relate to drainage and should be consulted.

B.S.C.P. 2005:1968	Sewerage.
B.S.C.P. 301:1971	Building drainage. Drainage of roofs and paved areas.
B.S.C.P. 65 and 540	Clay drain and sewer pipes including surface water pipes and fittings. 1. Pipes and fittings.
B.S.C.P. 497	Cast man-hole covers road gully gratings and frames for drainage purposes.
B.S.C.P. 556	Concrete cylindrical pipes and fittings including man-holes inspection chambers and street gullies.
B.S.C.P. 1194	Concrete porous pipes for under drainage.
B.S.C.P. 1196	Clay ware field drain pipes.

References

Ackers, P. (1963). *Charts for the Hydraulic Design of Channels and Pipes.* Hydraulics Research Paper No. 2, D.S.I.R. Hydraulics Research Station. H.M.S.O.: London.

Architects Journal (1969). *Handbook: Building Services and Circulation, Section 4.* A.J.: London.

Arnison, J. H. (1967). *Roadwork Technology.* 3 Volumes. Iliffe Books: London.

British Standards Institution (1971). BS Code of Practice 301: 1971 *Building Drainage.*

Conover, H. S. (1953). *Public Grounds Maintenance Handbook* T.V.A., Tennessee: U.S.A.

Cooper, T. (1965). *Practical Land Drainage* Leonard Hill: London.

Department of Education and Science (1966). *Playing Fields and Hard Surfaces.* Building Bulletin 28. H.M.S.O.: London.

Henman, D. W. (1963). *Forest Drainage.* Forestry Commission Research Branch. Paper No. 26.: London.

Kendall, R. G. (1950). *Land drainage* Faber: London.

Ministry of Housing and Local Government (1967). *Landscaping for Flats.* 2nd Edn. H.M.S.O.: London.

Seelye, E. E. (1953). *Design: data book for Civil Engineers.* John Wiley: New York.

Tandy, C. R. (1972). *Handbook of Urban Landscape.* Academic Press: London.

Weddle, A. E. (1967). *Techniques of Landscape Architecture.* Heinemann: London.

Woolley, L. (1971). *Drainage Details in SI metric.* Building Trades Journal: London.

Young, C. P. (1973). *Estimated Rainfall for Drainage Calculations in the United Kingdom* D.O.E., Transport and Road Research Laboratory. Report No. LR 595.

4 Surfacing

Introduction

The aim of laying down artificial materials over the ground is to ensure that the surface of an area is stable and remains so in the face of continuing use. Some surfaces will be laid down with the positive aim of deterring use and others may be found on slopes which are too steep for the maintenance of natural surfaces. Neither of these uses of hard surface are provided to cope with the wear on the surface, but they are exceptions. In the temperate areas of the world the surface of the ground is maintained in a generally stable condition by the growth of vegetation, although a statement such as this can only be made if the effects of the cycle of denudation, transportation and deposition of natural geological materials classically described in the textbooks of geology, are discounted. Two situations occur where the normal condition of surface stability of natural ground become threatened. The first, already mentioned above, is when the angle of the slope is so steep that the material will not stay in position but will be liable to fall under the influence of gravity, particularly if this effect is assisted by such agents as wind and water. In these cases the natural result is that the process continues until an angle is reached at which the material is in a stable condition in most circumstances. The second situation is when the use of the ground in question by animals, including humans, results in damage to the vegetation, which may be followed or accompanied by damage and disturbance to the surface layers of the ground. This then becomes susceptible to the action of other agencies.

Hard surfacing of banks

Something of the problems of the former case has been discussed in the previous chapter on Earthworks. One solution to the maintenance of such slopes is to cover them entirely with hard surface material. The decision to adopt such an approach should be very carefully considered and will only be justified in particular circumstances. It should be emphasized at the outset that every attempt should be made to avoid the need to maintain steep banks as part of a design. Such features have too many attendant problems. The dangers of rotational or deep seated slips, and subsidence, or surface slides, are well known, and have already been discussed. The maintenance of vegetation on steep banks is a constant battle which is exacerbated by the effects of human or animal trespass. The covering of banks with hard surface materials is costly, and the operation far exceeds the normal costs of laying similar materials on more level

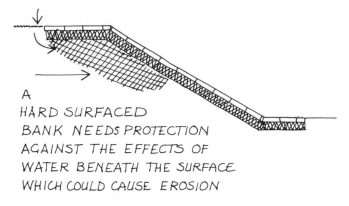

A
HARD SURFACED
BANK NEEDS PROTECTION
AGAINST THE EFFECTS OF
WATER BENEATH THE SURFACE
WHICH COULD CAUSE EROSION

Fig. 4.1. Protection against erosion.

sites. From an aesthetic point of view the appearance of such slopes is harsh and usually dull, although this criticism may, in appropriate circumstances be remedied by the use of ornamental materials or panels. It need hardly be said that such treatment will add further to the costs involved.

When this method of stabilizing the surface of banks is undertaken, additional precautions are required to ensure that the passage of water is not permitted behind, or beneath, the surface layer. This may result from the entry of water at the top of the bank, the presence, or development of springs in the face of the bank, or the penetration of water through the hard paved surface, finding its way between the surface and the underlying layers. In cases such as this the erosion of the bank material may result in the development of a void and the ultimate collapse of the surface material. It follows that the use of such techniques should be coupled with careful attention to drainage provision. The use of some of the more recent techniques which combine grass and concrete, with a framework of concrete and soil filled interstices, is subject to the same objections. These techniques may consist of precast or *in situ* concrete construction. In either case their contribution to the embankment stability in any substantial way is extremely dubious. Their use must be limited to the stabilization of the surface in which they seem to have little advantage over cheaper, more easily maintained and aesthetically pleasing alternatives. Where properly used, the advantage of this technique is that the presence of the concrete is largely concealed by the development of grass in the interstices. A green appearance is achieved over areas, say, of the occasional car park. This effect is largely dependent on the fact that most areas such as these are seen in perspective, and at an angle. When the material is presented, in tilted up plan form, on the side of a bank the effect of concealment is very much less complete. This technique will be discussed at greater length subsequently.

PURPOSES OF HARD SURFACING

The use of artificial surfaces provides a stable condition which will be maintained for a reasonable period of time in the face of the use of the ground for some purposes. The two most important criteria for the design of such hard surfaces are the surface characteristics of the material to be used and the strength of the supporting layers of the structure. The latter will vary according to the weight and frequency of the loads to be applied, and the former will be influenced by the type of use which is contemplated and the relative duration of wear which can be achieved, depending on the level of initial capital outlay. Two examples may help to illustrate this.

A major road which carries a high volume of heavy traffic will have a very thick overall construction capable of supporting the weight of heavy and continuous traffic movement without the road being damaged or disturbed. The surface will consist of a fine bound finish of asphalt or tarmacadam which is both waterproof and hard wearing. The most expensive finish, which is totally waterproof will be justified in this sort of case, where long trouble-free life is called for. In contrast a casual footpath in a remote rural area where there are few passers by will need only a relatively thin layer of material, which will probably require little attempt at stabilization and be quite pervious to water, to provide a surface which will cope with the demands placed upon it. The strength for which it is necessary to allow in the actual structure of the hard surface itself will depend on the nature of ground conditions, as well as upon the extent of use of the surface.

GROUND CONDITIONS

The strength of ground to withstand loads varies considerably from solid rock which can support heavy weights, to soft, weak clay and peat soils which are unable to support any but the lightest loads. This ability to support loads is sometimes spoken of as the bearing capacity, and depends on the type of soil, its moisture content, its state of compaction and its fine structure. One commonly used method of assessing the strength, or bearing capacity of a soil is the use of the California bearing ratio (C.B.R.). This depends on the measurement of the result of the application of a standard weight, in the form of a plunger, on to the soil to be measured.

The differing loads required to cause penetration of the plunger into a standard sample of crushed stone to different depths are taken as a standard. The results of the tests with individual soils are compared with this standard, the weight required to penetrate any soil to a particular depth being stated as a percentage of the equivalent load required to depress the stone sample to the same depth. The C.B.R. is used primarily for the design of 'flexible' pavements as described below where the construction depends directly on the strength of the actual ground on which they are laid, the approximate values of different materials are shown in Table 2.6, where the subject is also discussed.

FLEXIBLE AND RIGID ROAD CONSTRUCTION

The design of roads is usually thought to be divided into two principal approaches. These distinguish between 'flexible' roads and 'rigid' roads. The former consists of materials which transmit the load on the surface directly down to the ground beneath. Such materials as hoggin, gravel, asphalt and even quite fine dense tar are in this category as although there may be some small and incidental lateral transfer, the principal effect is for the weight to be exerted vertically downwards and spread over only a narrow area, being more dependent on depth for its dissipation. Heavy loads may result in deflection of the surface, which may be only temporary, but which is all too likely to be permanent, when these loads are excessive for the bearing capacity of the ground beneath the road surface.

Rigid roads are designed on the principle that a solid structure in the form of a slab is laid down and this enables the weight of a load applied at a particular point to be spread laterally over the whole of the slab. In this way the

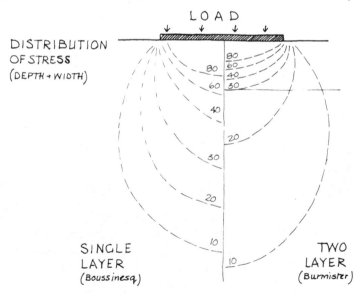

Fig. 4.2. Relation of sub-base depth required to C.B.R.

impact of loading on a rigid road is very much less significant in relation to the strength, or bearing capacity, of the soil beneath. For this reason the use of

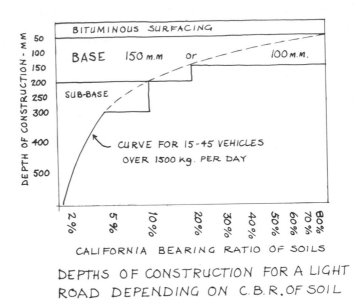

DEPTHS OF CONSTRUCTION FOR A LIGHT
ROAD DEPENDING ON C.B.R. OF SOIL

Fig. 4.3. Depths of construction for a light road depending on C.B.R. of soil.

Fig. 4.4. A concrete road in the course of construction, this concrete surface is laid with reinforcement on a sub-base of lean mix concrete.

the C.B.R. is only suitable for the design of flexible roads. It is, in any case, limited in its application because test methods are difficult to apply to many of the wet cohesive soils found in this country. The method of calculation of structural thickness for flexible roads provides variations in the depth of road bases and sub-bases according to the C.B.R. of the ground. If applied to rigid roads this method would result in considerable overdesign of the structures. In a volume prepared for the Asphalt and Coated Macadam Association in London (Lowe, 1971) the author reproduces a diagram showing the distribution of stress into the ground laterally and demonstrating that the effect of a load applied vertically reduces according to depth. Zones of stress have been worked out mathematically by Boussinesq for cases where a uniform layer is involved and by Burminster, where two layers of road material are used and both are cited in *Modern Flexible Road Construction*. The latter circumstance is more common, and it is on this basis that the chart (Fig. 4.3) relating the depth required of the sub-base for roads, to the C.B.R. of the soil encountered, was prepared. It will be obvious that loading levels will be important in this calculation and for this purpose anticipated levels of traffic are assessed within certain ranges of tolerance. Fig. 4.3 shows two design levels for comparatively lightly trafficked roads.

In practice the 'flexible' road consists of a number of layers above the 'subgrade' or natural material upon which the structural layers are placed. Engineers refer to this sub-grade as soil, but it is important to establish the difference in nomenclature that the landscape architect will meet between engineers and

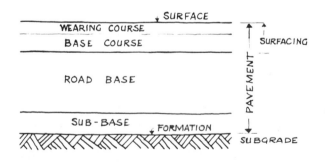

TYPICAL SECTION OF FLEXIBLE ROAD

Fig. 4.5. Typical section of flexible road.

horticulturalists. As he is likely to be dealing extensively with both types of specialist he needs to realize that the term 'soil' in their respective vocabularies covers widely different materials.

Sub-grade and formation level

The engineer will insist on the need to remove all 'vegetable' soil prior to laying down road material. He may further require the application of a total weed killer to ensure that no living roots remain and that no dormant seeds can develop and grow through the structure. For this purpose a weed killer based on 'Simazine' is usually specified and in addition it may be suggested that some method of sealing the sub-grade should be adopted either using bitumen, or chippings, or even building paper. The first two materials may be suggested to provide a protection if the sub-grade is to remain exposed for any length of time or to be subject to any wear by contractors or others. It is important that the 'formation level', as the surface of the sub-grade is described, is firm and even. Department of the Environment (Ministry of Transport) specifications call for formations to be within 25 mm of the levels specified on any drawings. It is not only for structural reasons that it is important that accuracy in this direction is achieved. Costs could be greatly increased by the need to augment volumes of material to make up levels everywhere to the acceptable minimum, when formation level was very variable.

Pavement

Above the sub-grade the flexible road traditionally consists of three layers of materials which themselves may be further divided. A typical cross-section in which these materials are shown is given in Fig. 4.5. It is also worth emphasizing that engineers refer to the entire structure of a road or similarly constructed surface as a 'pavement'. This is another term which the layman may find conflicts with his understanding of the word.

Sub-base

The layer of material next to the sub-grade is known as the 'Sub-base'. This layer of material is only required to be of comparatively low structural strength, as is obvious from the diagram of the distribution of structural stress reproduced above (Fig. 4.2). Specified for this purpose may be clinker; shale from quarries, coal waste and spent oil; and hoggins, or other similar materials. The minimum C.B.R. of the material should be 15%. It is important that the materials should be chemically tested, particularly those from colliery excavations, to establish freedom from soluble sulphates which could react with other elements of the construction. The typical layers of the pavement construction are shown in the Department of the Environment chart of construction depths. From this chart it will also be seen that the provision of a sub-base on lightly trafficked roads is unnecessary in all but the weakest range of structural soils. This is not the case with general highway construction, but since landscape designers are likely to deal unaided only with minor roadways, it may be a point worth mentioning.

Base (or road base)

Immediately above the sub-base is laid the base of the road. This is the main load bearing layer of the road, and is expected to have a greater strength than the sub-base. It is selected from materials which conform to the full standard, or 100%, C.B.R., these include hardcore, properly blinded to fill the voids, lean concrete (1:15 or 1:20) crushed stone or slag (nominal sizes either 38 or 68 mm) or even coated macadam. The use of 'pitching'; large stones laid by hand in a single layer, interspersed and covered with a further layer of smaller stones, is now completely discontinued although it was to be found frequently specified even after the Second World War. It is, of course, laborious and costly and quite out of tune with modern practice, but structurally provides a very suitable road base.

Surfacing

The uppermost layer of the pavement is known as the surfacing. The function of this is to provide an even surface for the traffic that needs to be carried, and one that is durable and proof against the effects of weather. This is important not just for the maintenance of the surface itself but also for the protection of the entire structure of the road. Although a few little used roads and farm tracks may be constructed of 'unbound' material, the use of a 'bound' material, a mixture of aggregates with, usually, a bituminous liquid binder is the most common surfacing material. This may be laid down as a single layer, but is very frequently put down in two. In the latter case the opportunity arises to differentiate in size between the 'wearing course' as the upper layer is called, and the 'base course' below it. Greater structural strength is created in the latter by the use of larger components in the aggregate. The base course may be from 38 – 76 mm in thickness. The wearing course, varying from 13 – 38 mm in thickness, consists of much finer material resulting in a more impervious surface. The use of a single course of material limits the extent to which the material can be mixed to provide either strength or impermeability, without affecting the performance in the other direction.

Bound surfaces

The classification of bound materials according to the nature of the binder involves two broad categories. These are asphalt and coated macadam.

   Asphalt. Asphalt is a mixture of liquid binder and fine aggregate which sets very hard, and forms a strong mortar. It is often heated for ease of laying and for this reason it is recommended that it should not be used in cold weather, when setting is likely to be very rapid. Asphalt may be obtained as a naturally occurring substance or as a manufactured mixture. Its essential qualities are that it is dense and generally permeable, and that it adds its own significant strength to that of the aggregates used in the construction of pavements.

Coated macadam. In the case of coated macadams, the aggregates used are coated with a binding material which is a liquid, either tar or bitumen. This is simply a coating, and the entire spaces between the individual pieces of the aggregates are not filled up. A high proportion of voids are found and the strength of the mixture is principally dependent upon the inter-locking of the particles of the aggregate, and not on the binder, as is the case with asphalt. The structural properties of certain mixtures of different sized aggregates were first observed by the Scottish engineer John Macadam in the early nineteenth century. The material is often quite porous. A list of the main categories of 'flexible' road paving surface material and their principal uses, is given in Table 4.1 (see page 129). The appropriate British Standards in which they are described is also given by number. The complexities of specification of these materials are best followed by reference to some of the publications of the Asphalt and Coated Macadam Association, and the standards for paving prepared by the British Standards Institution.

The subject, however, is one which is full of traps for the unwary. The discovery that cold asphalt is classed under the heading of coated macadams, and is often laid hot, is an example. This is a material used as a wearing course, laid as a thin layer, and having a broad range of applications; its use is set out in B.S. 1690:1962. One finds similarly that dense tar surfacing, for which there is no British Standard, is usually placed under the classification of coated macadams, although its characteristics are more similar to asphalts, in the way in which its strength depends very considerably on the mortar. Dense tar, as its name implies forms a dense and impervious mixture as a result of the proportions of the aggregate filler and tar used. There are a number of limitations in the use of materials, as might be expected. These may relate to the suitability of materials for specific purposes, to their cost, or to their compatibility one with another. Generally speaking the more durable materials are more expensive and this may be seen as the reason to make use of cheaper materials with short-term savings in mind. Table 4.1 indicates the uses to which the various specifications commonly used can be put. The following notes illustrate some of the factors which affect the choice of materials.

Bitumen macadam (B.S. 1621:1961) is suitable for roads, footways, cycle tracks and playgrounds. Some authorities do not recommend it for use on car parks although this use is included in the literature of the Asphalt and Coated Macadam Association Ltd. This material is usually more expensive to use than tar macadam (B.S. 802). B.S. 2040:1953 provides an alternative

Table 4.1

Uses of bound surface materials (listing the main materials covered by British Standards, and in common use).

		Footpaths	Games areas	Cycle tracks	Parking cars	Parking lorries (under 5 ton)	Parking heavy lorries	Housing estate cycling ways	Private roads	Main roads	Motor racing
Bitumen macadam (crushed stone or slag)	B.S. 1621:1961	X	X	X	X	X	X	X			X
Tarmacadam (crushed stone or slag)	B.S. 802:1967				X	X		X			
Tarmacadam (gravel aggregate)	B.S. 1241:1959	X	X	X							
(rock or slag)	B.S. 1241:1959		X	X	X						
Cold asphalt	B.S. 1690:1962	X	X	X	X			X			
Rolled asphalt	B.S. 594:1961	X	X	X		X	X	X		X	X
Dense tar						X	X	X		X	X
Mastic asphalt (natural rock)	B.S. 1446:1962						X			X	
(manufactured)	B.S. 1447:1962						X			X	

Table 4.2 Common specification for the use of bound surface materials (measurements in mm but figures in parentheses are in inches)

Material	Wearing Course		Base Course		Base	Notes
	thickness	nominal size	thickness	nominal size		
Bitumen macadam B.S. 1621:1961	19 (¾)	9 (⅜)	51 (2)	38 (1½)	150 (6) hardcore for car parks or 125 (5) dense coated macadam	A.C.M.A. Ltd recommend total construction thickness for vehicle parking as follows:
Tarmacadam B.S. 802 B.S. 1241:1959 B.S. 1242:1959	19 (¾) 13 (½)	9 (⅜) (single course 62.5 (2½)) 6 (¼)	51 (2) 38 (1½)	38 (1½) 25 (1)	For footways dense coated macadam may be at 75 (3) or hardcore at 100 (4)	Private Cars
Fine cold asphalt B.S. 1690:1962	19 (¾)	13 (½)				Medium Lorries
Hot rolled asphalt B.S. 594:1961	25 (1)		51 (2)		125 (5) Asphalt used as a road base for vehicles	Heavy Lorries

A.C.M.A. Ltd recommendations (Notes column detail):

	Clay	Loam	Gravel
Private Cars	300–250 (12 – 10)	250–200 (10 – 8)	200–150 (8 – 6)
Medium Lorries	600–375 (27 – 17)	375–300 (15 – 12)	300–250 (12 – 10)
Heavy Lorries	675–425 (27 – 17)	425–350 (17 – 14)	350–300 (14 – 12)

specification for use with gravel aggregates, on all but the most heavily used roads.

Tar macadam (B.S. 802: 1967). Both this material and bitumen macadam, discussed previously, are composed of aggregates of crushed rock or slag. A number of hard rocks are acceptable and these are listed in British Standard 812:1967. Slag may be from blast furnaces or steel or electric furnaces. In all cases the requirements include minimum crushing strength, resistance to impact or abrasion, and water absorbtion. The degree of resistance to polishing by traffic is an important consideration in the case of the use of aggregates in wearing courses. Tar macadam is usually recommended for the surfacing of car parks as it is generally considered to be more resistant to the softening effect of spillage of oil and petrol than other materials. This applies also to tarmacadam as specified in British Standard 1242:1960, for crushed rocks, or slag and B.S. 1241:1959 for gravel although this standard is primarily devised for footways, games areas and cycle tracks, and as such is a relatively limited specification.

Cold asphalt (B.S. 1690:1962). This is a specification for a wearing course which may be one of two grades, either fine or coarse, according to the texture of surface required. It is used frequently as a means of resurfacing existing roads or surfaces, and may be used as a surface in a wide range of situations.

Dense tar surfacing (for which there is no British Standard Specification) is another wearing course material. This is an impervious material, and is particularly resistant to oil droppings. As the binder weathers, the result is to increase the surface texture, and improve resistance to skidding. For these reasons it is suitable as a surface material on heavily trafficked roads.

Hot rolled asphalt (B.S. 594:1961). This material is laid hot like tense tar. Together with dense coated macadam it displays better load spreading properties than most materials previously used on road base construction, and those described above. In addition it is regarded as one of the longest lasting materials in use and may be expected to provide a serviceable surface for up to 20 years. It is used for a wide range of purpose, although it may be necessary to include a surface dressing of chippings of gravel to add to the roughness of the surface. This material, in common with others laid hot, needs to be laid in a reasonably high ambient temperature otherwise it will set before it can be properly laid, rolled and consolidated. This limits its use in Great Britain, effectively, to the summer.

Mastic asphalt (B.S. 1446:1962, natural rock asphalt or B.S. 1447: 1962, manufactured asphalt). This is a material used as a road surfacing which can be laid when warm by means of a float. Although it is fluid in this condition it hardens under normal temperature conditions to form an impermeable, voidless mass. It provides a very good wearing course for heavily trafficked roads, although chippings need to be incorporated to provide resistance against skidding.

Each of the specifications mentioned includes a number of alternatives according to the purpose for which it is to be used, the thickness of the layers and the size of aggregates, and these should be selected for the job under consideration according to advice from engineers or the publications of the Asphalt and Coated Macadam Association, already quoted.

A number of general points, however, should be made. It is generally the case that tar preparations are less expensive to use than those based on bitumen. For this reason tar is frequently used as the road base material. Where this is used in conjunction with a bitumen or asphalt surfacing, the latter should not be superimposed until the tarmacadam has weathered for a period of time, or preferably has been used by traffic. This is because fresh tar can react chemically with asphalt and damage will result to the structure.

It is most important, particularly with open textured mixtures, that adequate compaction is achieved, especially where the use of the surface will not contribute to continuing the compaction. This is true particularly for surfaces used only by pedestrians: footpaths, play areas, etc. It is not only the opening up of the surface in this way which needs to be guarded against. These materials are liable to spread as the result of traffic, and particularly when rises in temperature cause softening, and for this reason it is important that they are kept in place by an adequate edging. This is important to the process of compaction, otherwise during rolling the surface may be compacted and at the same time the material may be spread out.

The choice of bound surfaces is almost governed by functional considerations. Although there is perhaps little to object to in the appearance of bound surfaces, there is at the same time less to kindle a real spark of enthusiasm for the material, in aesthetic terms. Its advantages are that it provides a range of reasonably durable and functional surfaces. Generally black in colour it ranges from a completely smooth textureless surface to one in which quite a rough texture may result from the selection of large aggregates. The use of chippings in connection with the finer textures is not simply intended to provide an improved surface for traction, it is also frequently specified to give some visual relief from a close grained black surface. For this purpose white or interestingly coloured chippings may be specified. Additionally the colour of the binder may be varied from black, although this is usually an expensive variation. Some speciality wearing course surfaces are available commercially, providing a wide range of colours.

One of the advantages of this type of material is its use where hard wear is met in what is basically an informal situation. Thus a path or cycle track which passes over undulating ground or meanders through an informal green space may be laid in bound bituminous surfacing. While many would argue that this is not quite as appropriate aesthetically as the more informal loose or water bound finishes it is perfectly acceptable, particularly if used with coloured aggregate, chippings or coloured binder.

Wearing qualities of bound surfaces

It is generally accepted that, apart from the particular advantage of tar being less subject to softening by petrol or oil, bitumen is more durable than tar. A tar-macadam surface might last in good condition for five years, compared with six or seven years for an equivalent bitumen. Cold asphalt surfacing is a comparatively short life material used sometimes as a stop gap where a road needs temporary repairs. As it is now considered normal practice to reconstruct the whole pavement, of a well used road after about 20 years of use, this method might be adopted in the last few years before reconstruction. Hot rolled asphalt may be expected to give satisfactory wear for 15 years or more, and dense tar and mastic asphalt may last for the duration of the pavement's life. Durability will be dependent on reasonable compaction of the material and this involves the use of a sufficiently heavy roller. In the case of roads this will be 6 – 10 tonnes. For footpaths the weight of roller must be limited to a weight that can be supported by the construction of the pavement and this has in the past been quoted as 3 tonnes. More recent specifications have quoted the same weight, where possible, as used for road bases. The Asphalt and Coated Macadam Association Ltd give a minimum weight of 2.5 tonne, for a roller to have any useful effect.

Unbound and water bound surfaces. Many designers object to the use of bound surfacing with its black finish in many circumstances, where they feel that this sort of finish has too much of the character of the urban park, and generally too great an air of formality. For this reason they prefer the use of some other material and accept that this may mean more frequent repair and reconstruction of the surface.

Some unbound and water bound materials are more commonly used for road bases than as the surfacing. Some materials are also referred to as dry bound, and this usually means a mixture of even sized stones, into the interstices of which is vibrated a mixture of fine material.

Dry bound macadam. The Asphalt and Coated Macadam Association Ltd give a specification for dry bound macadam with aggregates of nominal size either 35 or 50 mm laid in compacted layers of 75 or 100 mm. Fine material (from 5 mm to dust) is vibrated into each successive layer. Subsequent compaction should be undertaken with a roller of between 8 and 10 tonnes.

Materials which are spoken of as water bound depend on an appropriate water content as well as the right mixture of particle sizes. One of the best and frequently most economical of these is hoggin.

Hoggin. This is a naturally occurring product found principally in the South East of England. It is predominantly gravel, but with sufficient clay particles to achieve a considerable degree of density and impermeability when properly compacted. Because hoggin and similar gravels are laid as they are found naturally, they are frequently referred to as self binding. It should be noted

Fig. 4.6. A rural road made with water bound materials is an appropriate use of material for the setting.

that the water content level is an important ingredient in the success of the construction. Hoggin and other self binding gravels are ideal as surfacing materials both structurally, and by reason of their appearance.

Fig. 4.7. Gravel surfacing around the plane trees along the Mall, London.

Water bound macadam. The original 'water bound' material was water bound macadam. This consisted of broken stones not more than 68 mm (2½ inch imperial dimension) laid in layers between 75 − 125 mm (3 − 5 inch). A binding layer of fine material was watered into the top surface. Broken stone of this kind may be used as both a road base, and as a surfacing material, whether 'dry bound' or 'water bound', for such purposes as rural car parks not subject to intensive use, or farm roads, or tracks.

Gravel

The choice of gravel surfaces is limited to a small number of circumstances. It may be appropriate for pedestrian paving or for vehicles when these are light and infrequent. Loose gravel is inappropriate in most public situations or where the gravel can be flung about by vehicles or other means and cause damage, the least of which might be to grass cutting equipment. Gravel is usually laid on 100 mm hard core for pedestrian use, or 150 mm for vehicles. The gravel is

Fig. 4.8. 'Construction' of a rural car park may consist of no more than laying a surface of local stone chippings. (A car park in the Lake District.)

laid in two courses, the lower of 50 mm of fine gravel and hoggin, and the upper of 25 mm with gravel or chippings which pass a 20 mm mesh. Adequate rolling is important and as with hoggin the moisure content should be correct at the time of rolling.

Sealed gravel. A slightly more durable surface may be achieved by the device of laying a fine gravel on a base of stone chippings or gravel. The fine gravel, usually 10 mm nominal size, is sealed with bituminous emulsion after rolling and a further, finer course of gravel or chippings, nominal size 6 mm laid. A period of time, usually at least fourteen days is allowed between the consolidation of the gravel and stone base and the application of the bitumen and the surface dressing. For vehicles the stone base will normally be 150 − 200 mm, laid on a well consolidated sub-base, whereas for pedestrians this may be reduced from 100 to 150 mm. For pedestrians the application of the sealing coat of bitumen and the 6 mm gravel or chipping surface may be duplicated to give a better wearing surface in the face of the random nature of pedestrian wear. Some days should be allowed to elapse between applications of emulsion.

Soil cement stabilization. The technique of stabilizing soil with cement to provide a road base has also been recommended for the provision of farm roads. The basic process involves breaking up the soil to create a fine tilth. For this a rotary cultivator has been recommended, cultivating to an original

depth of 150 mm which would result in a final depth of loose soil of 200 —
225 mm. All stones are required to be removed, and the cement mixed with
the cultivated soil at rates between 33 m² of road per tonne of cement for
sandy gravel and 37 m² per tonne for light clay. It may or may not be necessary to spray the surface with water depending on conditions, but in any
case the surface needs a final compaction. These roads are of limited value
being very subject to damage by cattle droppings and urine. In addition,
traffic which is liable to cause damage, virtually anything other than vehicles
with rubber tyres, must be avoided. For the protection of the surface a coat
of bitumen is recommended and this will normally be supplemented by a
covering of chippings or grit. The presence of organic material may interfere
with the successful setting of the cement, although this can sometimes be
corrected with the addition of lime to the soil. While this method has been
shown not to have the range of applications that may have been expected of
it a number of years ago, it should not be entirely neglected as it may in some
circumstances provide the right level of investment for a road where the
nature and density of traffic does not justify any greater expenditure.

Gravel. Loose gravel, which is the only surface material that can truly be
described as unbound has only limited application. It is really only suitable
when there is no traffic at all or at the most, pedestrian use of an area. Unlike the
other surfaces in this category it has no structural strength and, therefore,
needs to be laid on a base of hard core or similar material, for pedestrian use
this will usually be 100 mm in thickness. There are some self binding gravel
mixtures which are commonly used in the same way as hoggin. A number
are sold under proprietary names.

Proprietary surface mixes for games etc. Many of these are prepared to give
a fine surface texture and require to be laid on a base of larger aggregate
dimensions. When this is done a common specification is the use of a surface
layer of 50 mm of the product laid on a standard hard core base. The surface
needs to be compacted by rolling and may require watering to help bind the
surface. In the case of most water bound surfaces it is necessary to provide
for rolling at infrequent intervals. Some manufacturers, for example, advise
rolling games surfaces before use after conditions of frost because the surface
will tend to heave as a result of its action. Gravels in this category are
frequently composed of dolomitic limestone which is subject to chemical
binding action.

Dolomite. The products of dolomitic limestone quarries are frequently
used as a surface dressing for surfaces such as hard pitches for hockey, net-
ball, etc. These are bound chemically, solidifying by the action of water to
form a largely solid mass, and provide a reasonably firm and stable surface
for such uses. The material however, is really only suitable for a surfacing and
needs to be underlain by a base of hard core to the usual thickness specified
for pedestrian use of 100 mm. Some manufacturers recommend a reduction

of this to 75 mm with a surface dressing of a little as 32.5 mm although the more usual, and desirable, specification is for a 50 mm surface layer. It is important for porosity that the base material is free draining and that an adequate drainage system is laid down, also that the size of particles of the gravel itself is carefully controlled so as to avoid fines or dust that would restrict drainage. A nominal aggregate size of 10 mm has been recommended for this surface. Treatment for the maintenance of the surface involves raking and rolling occasionally, and watering is only likely to be necesary in exceptional circumstances.

Rigid roads

The foregoing has been concerned with flexible surfaces, used by vehicles and in a number of other situations. The rigid method of construction is almost exclusively used where traffic consists of heavy and continuous wheeled vehicles' movements. Alternatively it may be a solution to a particular problem where difficult ground conditions are met and need to be overcome in providing a hard

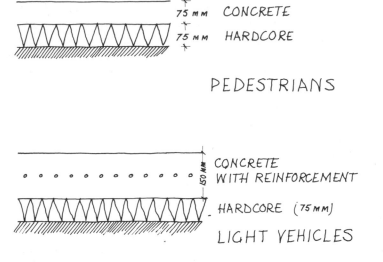

Fig. 4.9. Comparative depths of concrete required for pedestrian or light vehicular use.

surface for less demanding traffic. The principle of this method is the use of a structural form which spreads a point load over the whole of the structural element which makes up the section of the surface upon which the load rests. It may be that this is spread over an even more extensive area.

Reinforced concrete. The main method of constructing a rigid surface is by the use of a reinforced concrete slab. For major highways the thickness

of concrete and the weight of reinforcement will be calculated according to
the particular conditions and loading to be faced. A slab will not usually
be less than 150 mm in thickness and the concrete reinforcement will usually
consist of mesh steel with a weight of 3.80 kg m^{-1} for lightly trafficked roads
(those with between 45 − 150 commercial vehicles per day). For roads with

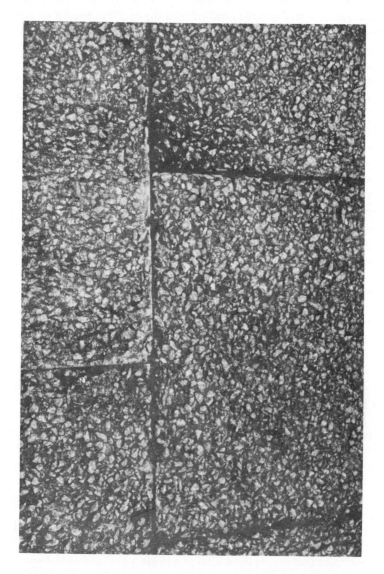

Fig. 4.10. Precast concrete paving with exposed aggregate finish provides an
interesting texture, which may be valuable as a non-slip surface.

less than 45 vehicles per day the slab thickness may be reduced to 130 mm
and the reinforcement to 2.71 kg m⁻¹. In fact, it is the lower part of the slab
which is placed under tension by the imposition of any load on the surface
and the function of the reinforcing is to add tensile strength to the concrete
slab. The usual method of setting in the reinforcement to ensure that it
remains in the right place is to lay the concrete in two layers, with the
reinforcement placed and the remainder of the concrete poured on before the
first layer has had any chance to set so that a proper union is achieved
between the two layers of concrete. It is important at the same time to
ensure that the reinforcement is properly encased in concrete and is not
subject to the action of the atmosphere and any penetration of water which
might result in its corrosion. It is for this reason that placing at the top of
the slab is commonly specified. The effect of reinforcing on the structural
strength of concrete slabs is not very great, and its main purposes are to hold
them together. It has been found, that the best practical results are obtained
by placing the mesh in this position as long as adequate cover is maintained.
In some cases it may be necessary to use two layers of reinforcement.

In situ concrete (reinforced). For areas of pedestrian circulation, *in situ*
concrete may be laid without any reinforcement, and for this purpose a thickness of 75 mm may be quite adequate. This may be compacted by hand
tamping to give a satisfactory plain finish or may alternatively be treated to
create an ornamental surface. If an aggregate with varied and interestingly
coloured stones is used, the surface may be brushed first before the concrete
has set, when it is 'green', so that the aggregate is exposed on the surface.
Another technique which may be used is the application of a crimping roller
which impresses a regular pattern of indentations on to the surface of the
concrete to create an interesting surface.

In the case both of reinforced and unreinforced concrete the provision of
a base of hard core is desirable except on gravels or similar natural soils which
can be well compacted. As the structural strength of concrete pavement is much
greater than that of flexible paving materials the base needs to be no greater than
75 mm in any situation. This will consist usually of well consolidated hard core
which is 'blinded' with ashes to fill in all interstices into which concrete might
otherwise penetrate, resulting in waste. *In situ* concrete slabs must be laid to
allow for expansion and contraction; amd this means providing joints at regular
intervals where the area of the slabs to be laid warrant it. Where heavy reinforcement is used the distance apart which is the maximum that can be permitted is
much greater than where light reinforcement or none is used. For lightly
reinforced areas the expansion joints may be a maximum of 12 m apart. This
sort of distance may coincide very well with the need to lay the concrete in
separate sections that can be dealt with as a single 'pour' and can be accessible
at a particular time. Frequently, too, the desire to achieve a pattern in the
treatment of the surface may result in the making of a decision as to the placing

Fig. 4.11. Paving consisting of panels of *in situ* concrete textured with a crimping roller, brick lines to form a pattern and cobbles laid flat around a plinth.

of expansion joints. Sections of *in situ* concrete on pedestrian areas may be delineated with lines of bricks or slab paving.

Other paving. In addition to the homogeneous surface described above there are a number of unit paving surfaces commonly in use. These may consist of interlocking or non-interlocking units.

Interlocking paving blocks. The advantage of interlocking units is that the weight of traffic is spread from the unit upon which it directly rests to those

Fig. 4.12. Interlocking paving on an estate road at Westhill, Highgate (photograph by Mono Concrete Ltd).

adjoining. This is the principle upon which the design of road bases has been developed from Roman times, the method of setting even sized road base stones by hand to form a layer of abutted stones, known as 'penning' (previously mentioned) also illustrates this principle. The 'pave' surfaces of the Continent consist of hard stone, principally granite setts, and in latter years concrete blocks, laid to form an interlocking surface by the process of laying the setts with tightly abutting sides.

Fig. 4.13. Traditional patterns in granite setts, in this case picked out with lines of whinstone setts.

More recently the technique has been reintroduced to this country with a range of concrete blocks manufactured with standard interlocking shapes which provide the necessary lateral support one to another. Some measure of the significance of the development of these materials is the formation of the Interlocking Paving Association, at 60, Charles Street, Leicester. This manufacturers' association aims to promote the products and ensure adequate standards of manufacture and user specification. A number of manufacturers supply these products in a range of colours and shapes and they are suitable for uses including quite heavily trafficked urban roads, although not for design speeds over 30 − 40 mile h⁻¹ (48 − 64 km h⁻¹). The important points in the construction of these interlocking surfaces are to ensure that, with rectangluar blocks, a herringbone or similar pattern of laying which will give the maximum interlocks between units is adopted. It is also important that the paving surface is laid tightly up to a firm edge so that there can be no lateral movement and relaxation of the interlocking effect. The blocks themselves are laid by hand on a laying course of sand which is 50 mm in depth, in turn laid on a sub-base. After laying, the blocks are bedded in by the use of a vibratory compactor which consolidates the laying course of sand and actually forces some of this between the

Fig. 4.14. Re-used granite (pale) and whinstone (dark) setts mixed in paving. These have been laid in this case with wide joints some of which appear to have been mortaced, giving altogether a patch finish.

blocks to increase the interlock. In this way a very stable surface is achieved. The design of the sub-base itself is governed by ground conditions and the standard recommendations are that the same depth criteria as for bound finishes should be adopted for this material.

Granite setts. Granite setts may be laid to take advantage of the interlocking principles and as has been mentioned this is a common method on Continental roads. In these cases they will usually be laid on a dry bed of sand of

Fig. 4.15. Brick paving laid to throw water towards the trees. The bricks will be motar jointed for most of the paved area but need to be loosely set in around the trees to allow percolation and to allow removal as the trunk expands.

Fig. 4.16. 'Pitching' on a roadside slope using rectangular whinstone setts laid with wide joints. This provides a stable surface.

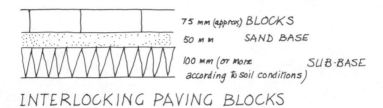

75 mm (approx) BLOCKS

50 mm SAND BASE

100 mm (or more   SUB-BASE
according to soil conditions)

INTERLOCKING PAVING BLOCKS

100 mm x 100 mm GRANITE SETTS

50 mm SAND BED

150 mm SUB-BASE

GRANITE SETT PAVING

Fig. 4.17. Cross-sectional diagrams of paving construction.

Fig. 4.18. Interlocking paving is perfectly suitable for heavy traffic. Monolok at Watford Gap on the M1 (photograph by Mono Concrete Ltd).

25 mm approximately and well compacted. They will be laid on anything
from a sub-base of hoggin, where only light or pedestrian traffic of a sporadic
kind is anticipated, to a base course of consolidated hard core or even 'lean'
mix concrete (1 part cement to between 15 and 20 parts aggregate, depending
on conditions). When laid dry it may be necessary to fill in the interstices
between the setts with sand or with a 'dry grout', a mixture of sand and
cement brushed over the surface in an absolutely dry condition. This is most
important, as is the need to ensure that none of the grout is allowed to
remain on the surface and mar the appearance of the stone.

Fig. 4.19. Granite setts laid with wide joints which may be filled with asphalt
or bitumen.

The surface may be watered after brushing to ensure the setting of the mix, and incidentally to wash off any final traces of grout. In some situations the ornamental use of granite setts may call for the use of joints which are not grouted up to the surface of the paving. Such recessed joints are sometimes sealed with bitumen after the setts have been placed in a cement bed. This provides a means of stabilizing the setts, a seal against water, which is presumably capable of absorbing movements resulting from expansion and contraction. However, it must be emphasized that the method requires a very high degree of care and workmanship, and ensuring a clean surface may involve careful supervision. Where open joints are required it may be the best approach to adopt the same dry grouting technique for filling up the joints although the setts may be set into a wet cement bed.

Traditional granite setts are either 75 mm or 100 mm cubes, or 225 mm x 100 mm x 100 mm and may be either British or imported in origin. They are an expensive material and as such should be used only where they can be seen to the best effect and well appreciated. For this reason too, it is worth emphasizing that the methods of construction, using these materials should be designed to ensure that the qualities of the material are not in any way compromised. In recent years the principal source of granite setts in redevelopment areas in cities, particularly, has been the 19th century street surface. A great number of second-hand setts have become available, and this is indicative of the great durability of the material. In many cases the sett paving has subsequently become covered by a tarmac or bitumen surface, and cleaning setts so affected may not be regarded as worthwhile. Nevertheless, there are often a sufficient number of clean surfaces for the setts to be re-used, with the natural qualities of the stone unimpaired.

Apart from granite very few stones are sufficiently hard and durable, although whinstone is an alternative found in use in the North of England. This may be used in the rectangular or cube form, or may be in smaller random shapes sometimes known as 'chips'. The stone itself is darker, and generally very much less interesting in texture.

Brick paving. A similar textural and small scale effect to that achieved by the use of granite setts may be obtained by the use of bricks. For durability and public safety these should be engineering quality, or at least to high standards of impermeability. Although a path covered with moss and lichen may be an attractive feature in a private garden, it is unacceptably hazardous in public areas, as is a surface made uneven by frost damage crumbling the brick faces. The majority of bricks used for paving are made in sizes different from those for building and will be only 40 to 50 mm in thickness. A wide range of colours is available, dark 'blues' and brown being traditional. Stable paviors with diamond pattern surfaces or with 'chocolate bar' indented surfaces ranging in scale from two outlines on a 225 x 112 mm brick surface to sixteen on the same area are traditional. Bricks not specifically manufac-

Fig. 4.20. A random sett paving pattern.

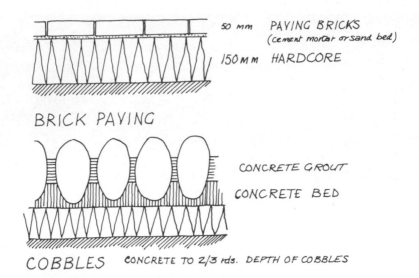

50 mm PAVING BRICKS
(cement mortar or sand bed.)

150 MM HARDCORE

BRICK PAVING

CONCRETE GROUT

CONCRETE BED

COBBLES CONCRETE TO 2/3 rds. DEPTH OF COBBLES

Fig. 4.21. Cross-sectional diagrams of paving brick and cobble construction.

Fig. 4.22. The use of recessed man-hole covers in which the paving material can be inset enables the paving pattern to be continued uninterrupted by the cover.

tured for paving purposes may be used laid flat, depending on the surface exposed, or laid on edge. The use of these depends on their frost resistent qualities, and laid on edge they may be an expensive means of paving. Because, like granite setts, the brick surface consists of small units the base upon which they are set will play a considerable part in supporting the paving, and its specification will depend on the volume and intensity of the traffic to be accommodated and the nature of the soil. For pedestrian use a bed of hard core, blinded with ashes, and 75 mm in thickness should be provided as a minimum specification. For vehicles this may be increased, depending on the ground conditions to between 150 and 300 mm of hard core. Alternatively a base of concrete may be provided which may typically consist of 75 to 100 mm of concrete with one part of cement to nine parts of aggregate, or of lean mix concrete in thicker layers. The choice of material for the base may well depend on the relationship of the area to be paved to adjoining materials, their depth of excavation and the use of base materials for them.

It will not normally be necessary to place the base course of hard core or concrete on any sub-base unless the ground conditions are particularly bad. Under concrete it is sometimes necessary to provide a satisfactory surface upon which to lay the material and this may be provided by clinker or hoggin, building paper or bitumen sprayed on. Any structures will require excavation down to solid ground and thus obviate the use of hard core.

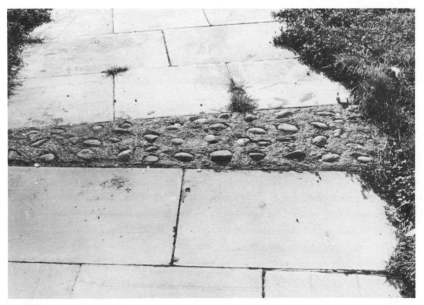

Fig. 4.23. An 'ad hoc' solution to a change in path direction which provides neither a good functional finish nor a particularly elegant one.

Fig. 4.24. Natural stone cobbles and chipping laid on the edge as a surface for a car park area in an historic town.

Bricks will usually be laid on a bed of cement mortar, although sand is not unknown. If they are laid with open joints the mortar must be brought to the surface to ensure that water is not retained to cause frost damage and this may involve dry grouting or careful trowelling to avoid dirtying the surface. An alternative of filling the interstices with soil is sometimes suggested and this is intended to encourage the growth of vegetation.

Cobbles. Where special effects are to be sought, or where, more particularly, the intention is to create a surface to deter pedestrian traffic, cobbles may be specified. For the latter purpose it is necessary to use hand selected beach cobbles which are of durable stone and will not be subject to 'knapping'. For this use stones will need to be between 50 and 75 mm (2 − 3 inch) in

diameter at their centre, and to be ovoid in shape with a maximum dimension
of between 175 and 250 mm (7 — 10 inch). They should be laid by hand
with their long sides vertical, each stone butted up close to the next and
pressed into a bed of between 50 and 75 mm of concrete. In this way the
lowest 1/3rd of the cobble stones are set into the concrete. The stones are
subsequently grouted up so that they are set into approximately 2/3rds of
their depth, and this is a sufficient proportion to make the stones stable
and not liable to be disturbed or prized up as long as they are tightly butted.
A dry mixture should preferably be used for this grouting up, and the surface
watered. Cobbles can be laid on a base of hard core 75 mm in depth, although
a stronger specification may be adopted if there is any danger of trespass by
vehicles.

It should be noted that the use of materials such as this results in some
problems of maintenance, as where litter is prevalent it is often difficult to clean
between the stones. The use of smaller hand selected stones may be adopted
and provide a surface which is less positively discouraging to pedestrian traffic.
Stones which are 50 mm in diameter may be set in cement and mortar (1:3) on
a bed of 50 mm of concrete and 75 mm of hard core. These may be set in so
that they are abutting although this means that only a small proportion of the
stones can be allowed to project from the mortar to ensure that they are held
satisfactorily in place. A more strongly textured effect can be obtained by
allowing a 10 — 15 mm gap between the stones, but even then it will be necessary to ensure that over half the depth of each stone is embedded in the mortar
to ensure adequate bedding.

Tiles etc. Because of the danger of damage by frost, few tiles being proof
against this, the use of tiles in the United Kingdom is very limited. There
are, nevertheless, a wide variety of tiles available in sizes ranging down from
230 mm square, and 30 mm in thickness. They are made with clay, and as
well as rectangular tiles, a number are made in interlocking shapes. Their
use may be justified in special circumstances, protected terraces or covered
sitting areas for example. In other climatic conditions they have a much
more widespread application. The same observations apply to the use of
mosaics which, although they may be used more freely in climates not
affected by extremes of cold and frost may be limited by reason of their cost.

Slab paving. The most common material used for paving pedestrian areas
in the 20th century is the precast concrete slab or flag. In Britain this comes
in a number of standard sizes principally 900 x 900 mm, 600 x 600 mm,
and 600 x 450 mm. The specification of these slabs is covered by a British
Standard B.S. 368:1956, and they are produced by a large number of
manufacturers. They may be 50 mm in thickness although slabs with the
additional strength afforded by increasing this to 63 mm are often specified by
engineers. The majority of these slabs are pressed hydraulically and have a
plain surface which is grey in colour depending on the nature of the aggregate

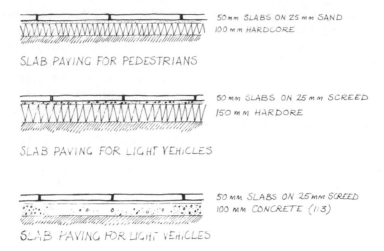

Fig. 4.25. Cross-sectional diagrams of slab paving construction for different uses.

and the cement used. However this may be varied both as to colour and texture, although economics dictate that the majority of situations, street footways etc. should be paved with standard pressed grey slabs. Variations are achieved in three basic ways as follows.

(1) *Surface pattern.* Pressed slabs can be formed in moulds which are patterned so that an impression of a pattern is left on the surface of the paving slab. The production of slabs with this effect involves virtually no increase in cost over that of plain slabs.

(2) *Surface texture.* An extremely wide range of textures achieved by the use of different aggregates which are exposed on the surface of slabs is available from manufacturers. These range from very fine textures to textures with large aggregate portions. Aggregates always need to be selected from durable stone but may consist of crushed rock or gravel and could comprise granite chippings or variably coloured brown gravel, to give only two examples.

(3) *Pigmentation.* The third way in which variation is achieved is by the use of pigmentation in the concrete. In this way self coloured slabs may be produced although it is often the case that the visual effect is not totally satisfactory. The colours of many pigments give slabs, particularly those with smooth surfaces, an appearance reminiscent of ice cream! The use of a pigment may be combined with that of aggregate exposure to produce a pleasant effect. This, in fact, is the basis of the manufacture of reconstructed stone slabs, in which the stone aggregate is crushed to a fine texture and cast with a concrete with appropriately coloured pigment.

Precast concrete slabs are laid on a base which will depend on the traffic to be supported. They will not be damaged by the weight of traffic as long as this

Fig. 4.26. A pedestrian area, which allows delivery vehicles to drive and park, calls for good base construction under paving slabs.

Fig. 4.27. This picture shows damage to the slab paving as a result of inadequate strength in the base. In the foreground additional paving can be seen. This is not only ill designed but poorly carried out.

Fig. 4.28. Specialized paving units providing access of water to tree roots, within the overall paving pattern. This is exposed aggregate Monoconcrete metric 4 square paving (photograph by Mono Concrete Ltd).

weight can be transferred to the base without creating any tension within the slabs. Where it is necessary to allow vehicles to travel over a slab surface it is most important to ensure that the base course beneath the flags will give them the fullest support all over. For pedestrian surfaces it is necessary to lay slabs over a base course of hard core of 100 mm thickness blinded with ashes and to set these on a bed of sand which will not exceed 25 mm in thickness.

The use of sand enables access to services beneath the paving, and easy replacement of slabs, but it may result in some movement. Although the sand will be largely held in place by edging materials this is not always entirely reliable and it may be washed out. The most stable way of laying slabs is to place them on a mortar bed which can consist of lime and/or cement and sand, or better, on a screed of cement and sand. A screed of cement should be 25 mm minimum depth and consist of a 1:3 mix of cement and sand. Depending on the nature of traffic anticipated and ground conditions, the screed will be laid on a base to consist for vehicle traffic of 150 mm of hard core or 100 mm of lean concrete as a minimum. It is too common to see examples of slab paving which have been cracked as a result of inadequate provision of base material. For this reason it is preferable to err on the side of providing an over-generous base, unless it can be a certainty that a lesser specification will be adequate.

Fig. 4.29. Pressed slabs with indented patterned surfaces (photographs by
S. Marshall and Co. Ltd, Halifax).

Fig. 4.30. Paving slabs with distinctive surfaces (photographs by S. Marshall and Co. Ltd, Halifax).

Natural stone. The same arguments for the provision of an adequate base which are advanced in the case of precast concrete slabs apply to natural stone, with the added point that as natural stone is an expensive item it is even more important that it should be protected from unnecessary damage. Some thin natural stones may be particularly liable to breakage, and, therefore, in need of the best support. A wide range of stones is available and selection will be on purely aesthetic grounds, not necessarily depending on the local availability of a costly material required to serve a prestige purpose. Traditionally local stone was used as the material for footways as well as buildings and in this way the individual character of particular cities and towns has been developed. Stone may be used with a sawn or a riven finish. In the case of riven finishes in particular, it is important that the method of laying allows for the variation in thickness arising from the process of riving. This will usually mean laying the slabs on a bed of mortar, or on sand on a concrete screed. The thickness of any sand bed should be the minimum which will allow for the variations in thickness so that the most stable bedding is achieved.

The methods of laying slabs on a pattern of five spots of mortar has been recommended from time to time, primarily because it provides a method of laying which gives accurate results and easy laying. It is not advisable particularly for thin slabs, or for small slabs, or for small slabs which would require a large number of dots in a comparatively limited area. In fact, it has the disadvantage that almost any slabs laid in this way will be left with voids beneath them and may thus be subject to stress from traffic, resulting in damage. This applies both to natural and precast concrete slab paving.

Grouting. A very important point in laying paving slabs of whatever kind is the method of ensuring that the interstices are properly grouted up. It is essential that the method adopted should not leave any residue on the surface of the slabs. A dry cement or lime mortar grout should be brushed over the surface of the slabs to fill up the cracks, but a wet mix should not be used under any circumstances, as it will almost inevitably result in some deposit or staining.

Other surfaces. The casual, or occasional use of some surfaces has led to a number of developments in methods of strengthening and supporting grass surfaces. This means that a green appearance can be maintained on surfaces which will be used perhaps only on a few days in the year for heavy traffic. Clearly the choice of any material to give the required reinforcement will depend on a large number of circumstances, of which the nature of the ground, the frequency and duration of the intensive use and the alternative and more regular use of the area will be the primary factors. A number of methods of providing a framework of concrete within which grass can be established has been devised, and these are marketed as proprietary products. They may consist of precast concrete slabs with a series of protuberances which will take the weight of traffic moving over the surface. The interstices are filled with soil and grass is allowed to grow. The depth of soil should not extend to the surface of the concrete to avoid compression of the soil and plant life. This method of creating a surface which is intermediate between grass and hard surface is well exemplified by the Mono Concrete Company's 'Mono BG' slabs. These are manufactured in blocks 600 mm x 400 mm x 120 mm in depth. It will be necessary usually to give additional

Fig. 4.31. Natural stone paving giving a texture and interest that is unrivalled.

support to these materials by the use of a base course of hard core, although care must be taken that, while adequate drainage of the areas of this sort is an important consideration, excessively dry conditions which militate against satisfactory plant growth, are not created.

A variation on this is laying *in situ* concrete within light polythene moulds. The use of *in situ* concrete is likely to result in a greater area being

Fig. 4.32. The use of mono-bg slabs, or monoslabs, is a valuable addition to the range of paving where a grass appearance is required and where infrequent traffic is anticipated. Monoslabs at the Tower of London (photograph by Mono Concrete Ltd).

covered by concrete, and whereas the 'Mono BG' slabs create the effect of small concrete points within the predominantly soiled area, the *in situ* concrete process gives the impression of small insets of grass, etc., in a matrix of concrete. In this case, the concrete will be laid on a base course of hard core which for

Fig. 4.33. Monoslabs provide an ideal surface for occasional traffic, extensions to car parks for use in peak periods for example, where the grass appearance is valued at other times. The car par extension at Brockhole (photograph by Mono Concrete Ltd).

most purposes will not need to be in excess of 75 mm. When the concrete is set and the plastic moulding has been removed, or if necessary burned off, the interstices can be filled with soil and seeded or may in some special situations be filled with plugs of turf. The latter is a very slow and costly process and is rarely justified.

The use of these techniques has been adopted and/or recommended for the maintenance of banks, for which purpose, it must be said, they do not really seem appropriate. From the visual point of view they are less effective seen from vertically above than in perspective, and their use in embankments presents the surface in a manner which is closer to that of the vertical view than the perspective. While these materials certainly help to hold soil in place and enable

Fig. 4.34. The use of a wet grout over the surface of paving slabs results in cement marks disfiguring the slabs.

vegetation to become established this can often be achieved more cheaply and simply with other techniques. One of the major difficulties of laying structural materials on banks is the fact that they are liable to be undermined as a result of the movement of water below the surface. Among the means adopted for combating this danger is the careful sealing of the surface so that no water percolates under it and into the bank, but entry of water into the soil is a major feature of these materials. As a structural material for the support of banks its value is very questionable. Where structural support is required other, more certain, means will need to be devised. Where a method of stabilizing the surface vegetation is required, this may be achieved in any one of a number of simpler and cheaper ways.

One of these, involving the placing over the soil surface of a mat, or net, of material has been recommended widely as being suitable to provide some support for such uses as occasional car parks, where the interaction of the mat spread over the surface with the plant root dissipates the vertical force of any traffic. The development of modern man-made fibres such as polypropylene has resulted in a product which is virtually indestructable in the soil. The strength of this method must increase as the growth of vegetation increases the density of the turf mat. It is suitable only for a very specific range of circumstances, in which it will not be used with any other form of base or support.

Edging and trims

The subject of paving cannot be discussed without reference to the ways in

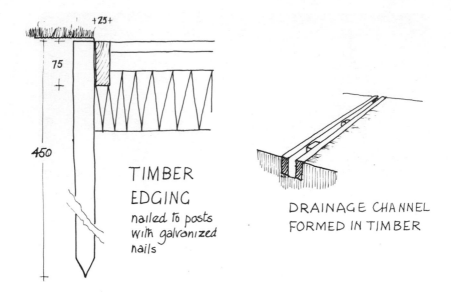

TIMBER EDGING
nailed to posts with galvanized nails

DRAINAGE CHANNEL FORMED IN TIMBER

Fig. 4.35. Edging construction.

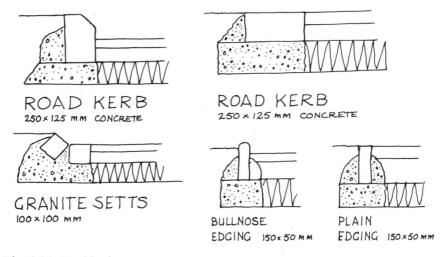

ROAD KERB
250 × 125 MM CONCRETE

ROAD KERB
250 × 125 mm CONCRETE

GRANITE SETTS
100 × 100 mm

BULLNOSE EDGING 150 × 50 mm

PLAIN EDGING 150 × 50 mm

Fig. 4.36. Road kerbs.

which paving materials and paved areas are contained and the junctions between different materials are treated. In design terms, the handling of such details assumes an importance out of all proportion to the area displayed or the cost involved. The use of edging materials relates to the use of paving materials as dictated by their individual character. Overall the uniform surfaces such as

asphalt, tarmac or hoggin are suitable on undulating ground with free flowing
horizontal and vertical curves. These materials can be bounded by similarly
free edge lines Slab paving, whether natural stone, or P.C. concrete, will be in
formal, rectangular, or in the latter case, sometimes more complex shapes and
will be most suitably edged in a formal manner. Standard methods of edging
are units of quite large individual length in wood or metal or shorter lengths of
concrete. Other unit materials of quite short individual length may be used
in certain circumstances.

Timber edging. The use of timber for edging is usually limited to hoggin or
bound surfaces which are to be used for light traffic or pedestrians. The
timber which should be elm, oak or larch will be cut in lengths of 4 − 5 m,
will be normally of 75 x 25 mm (3 x 1 inch) cross-section, and will be held
in place with pegs 500 mm x 50 mm x 50 mm) (20 inch x 2 inch x 2 inch)
approximately every 2 m (say 6 ft), depending on the alignment. The timber
cannot be bent into very tight curves but can be reasonably freely used. In
some cases it may be necessary to set the pegs into concrete. The edging
should be used with the paved surface flush to its top and preferably the
surface at the opposite side should also be flush with it.

An adaptation of this use of timber can be applied to the control of surface
water on paths when channels consisting of two pieces of timber separated
by distance pieces may be set across sloping paths at regular intervals.

Metal edging. The same or similar effects as are achieved with timber edging
may be attained by the use of metal edging. Like timber edging this is secured
in place by pegs, although these are likewise metal and have special clip

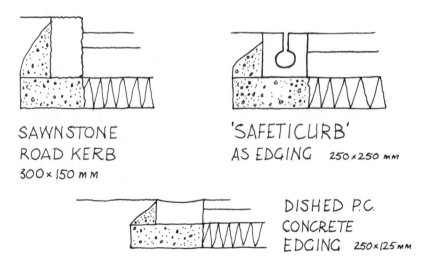

SAWNSTONE
ROAD KERB
300 × 150 mm

'SAFETICURB'
AS EDGING   250 × 250 mm

DISHED P.C.
CONCRETE
EDGING   250 × 125 mm

Fig. 4.37. Other types of road kerbs.

Fig. 4.38. A traditional arrangement of roadside edge and raised kerb in natural stone. It is not only the dimensional difference but also the textural qualities of the stone that give it a distinctive quality in comparison with precast concrete.

attachments. Metal edging is commonly available in two ranges; light and heavy duty, with the latter being suitable for reasonably heavy vehicular traffic.

For most normal purposes the edging material is used flush with the adjoining paving surfaces. One of the advantages of this material over timber, is that it can be laid out to very much tighter radii.

Concrete edging strips. Concrete edging, which is covered by British Standard B.S. 340, is traditionally available in the following dimensions: 450 x 50 x 150, or 450 x 50 x 100 mm (18 x 2 x 6 inch or 18 x 2 x 4 inch). The length of the individual units limits very severely the radius to which these can be laid without creating a very curious visual effect. This material is laid flush with the paving material it edges, and the adjoining ground surface and is usually haunched in concrete, on a concrete bed 100 x 75 mm in dimension. Where, as an alternative to flush laying it is desired to have some upstand, half round edging or bull nosed edging may be used. Maintenance problems may, however be encountered when these are used adjoining grass.

Kerbs. Where, as in the case of roads and adjoining footpath, a change in level is required this may be effected by the use of a kerb-stone. A range of standard kerb-stones is manufactured in precast concrete either as straight units, or to standard highway radii. Principal dimensions are 450 mm x 250 mm x 125 mm, 450 mm x 300 mm x 150 mm, or 450 mm x 125 mm x 150 mm (18 inch x 10 inch x 5 inch, 18 inch x 12 inch x 6 inch, or 18 inch x 5 inch x 6 inch) the last being less commonly in use than the former. The profiles and dimensions of kerbs commonly used are set down in B.S. 340. While the larger sized kerb is set on a concrete base of approximately 200 x 100 mm and haunched, the 450 mm x 125 mm x 150 mm (18 inch x 5 inch) x 6 inch) was designed to be used as an edging curb, to be actually set on to the surface of a rigid road. This method of construction is not as sound as the others, and in a good number of cases these kerbs have been found to come loose. Precast concrete kerbs may be obtained with a bull nose, with a raked top, or with one chamfered face. The use of a kerb of this nature may be to demarcate an area of formal grass or a planted space, and in these circumstances the use of a sawn stone kerb may be preferred, appropriate dimensions are found in B.S. 435.

Some stone kerbs may be employed which have been split or hewn rather than sawn and these give a finish which while attractive is less precise than standard units and may lead to problems when used with certain materials.

Other edgings Precast concrete channel sections 125 x 250 mm with a flat or dished top may be used as an edging material. These are cast, like kerbs, in lengths of 450 mm. Additionally smaller units such as bricks or granite setts may be employed for this purpose A specialist material such as the patent 'Safeticurb' may be used to form an effective and visually clear edge.

Drainage of paved surfaces

The subject of the drainage of paved surfaces has been discussed in the chapter on drainage. Table 3.4 gives a range of recommended minimum crossfalls for different paving materials dictated primarily by the considerations of surface water drainage. It is most important that water is not permitted to stand on paved areas, as this might result in damage to the surface, particularly in cold weather. It is also a nuisance to pedestrians in public areas. The minimum angle of slope for satisfactory drainage will depend on the texture and the composition of the surface, the lowest angles being attainable with monolithic paving with a smooth surface.

Summary

In this chapter the attempt has been made to enumerate the range of hard surfaces used in landscape work. The purposes for which hard surface areas are adopted are listed and in particular the relationship between the choice of materials for a special purpose, and the methods of construction for that purpose are shown to be important. The strong influence of detailed construction on overall design and the relationship between the choice of construction details and the setting, position, and character of the site on which they are to be employed is emphasized.

References

Ashworth, R. (1966). *Highway Engineering.* Heinemann: London.
Arnison, J. H. (1967). *Roadwork Technology.* (3 Vols) Illiffe Books: London.
British Standards Institutions (1967). *Glossary of Highway Engineering Terms* B.S.I.: London.
Concrete Society London (1974). *A guide to good practice for road edge details* (Report **10**).
Department of Education and Science (1966). *Playing Fields and Hard Surfaces.* Building Bulletin **28** H.M.S.O.: London.
Department of Environment (1970) (Traffic and Road Research Laboratory). *Road Note No. 29* (3rd Edn.) a guide to the structural design of pavements for new roads. H.M.S.O.: London.
Lowe, G. (1971). *Modern Flexible Road Construction.* Asphalt and Coated Macadam Association: London.
Ministry of Agriculture, *Soil Cement Roads.* Fixed equipment of the Farm Leaflet **19**. (O.P.) H.M.S.O.: London.
Ministry of Agriculture, *Farm and Estate Roads.* Fixed equipment of the Farm Leaflet **12**. H.M.S.O.: London.

Ministry of Transport (1969). *Specification for Road and Bridge Works.*
    H.M.S.O.: London..
Tandy, C. V. R. (1972). *Handbook of Urban Landscape.* Architectural Press:
    London.
Weddle, A. E. (1967). *Techniques of Landscape Architecture.* Heinemann:
    London.

5 Construction of simple structures

Landscape architects are frequently called upon to construct simple features as part of their work. These may consist of small free standing walls, retaining walls, flights of steps, plant boxes, or man-holes and silt traps for drainage work. Additionally, knowledge of types of fencing and their methods of construction are essential, as are elementary principles of timber construction. One of the first requirements for the landscape architect who is not either qualified as an architect or a civil engineer, or, still more unlikely, as a structural engineer, is for him to become able to judge the appropriate methods to be adopted in different circumstances, and according to the scale of works involved. While small scale retaining walls, for example, will be perfectly satisfactorily constructed in mass concrete, larger ones will be more efficiently designed to precise structural tolerances using reinforcement and the refined design techniques of engineering. This is work for which the landscape architect is not trained, and which he cannot be expected to undertake. It is important for the landscape architect to recognize those situations where an engineer should be consulted, either because of the intrinsic difficulty of the design problem, or because the extent of the work involved could result in savings in construction costs from the application of critical design criteria. The former may be the case with very large retaining structures, river bank supports and the like, where understanding of the critical basis of soil mechanics becomes a mathematical science. In the latter instance the decision whether to build a retaining wall in, for example, either mass concrete or precast concrete may depend on the height and length of wall to be constructed. The size will dictate the economics, with large walls being capable of effecting sufficient economies in the use of materials to justify high design costs, whereas smaller walls will be more cheaply constructed by rule of thumb methods which are not critical in design terms.

On a small free standing wall, similarly, the designer might well decide to accept a degree of over designing, whereas if this was a large wall or a situation where a design was to be extensively repeated, it would be worth investigating whether a more critical approach to design could result in a saving of costs. The same criteria might apply to timber structures or to bridges as related to size or use.

Free standing walls

DRYSTONE WALLS

It has always been said traditionally that it was necessary to ensure that a wall
had 'a good hat and good boots'. The most common form of walling in Great
Britain and probably in many other parts of the world, is the dry stone wall,
forming the boundary of upland fields, and constructed largely from the natural
stones occurring in the soil. These are usually no more than 1.5 m (4½ – 5 ft)
in height, and there must be many thousands of miles of them in England

Fig. 5.1. Traditional dry stone walls in Derbyshire.

alone. They are built on a broad base, often, where shallow soils permit, taking
advantage of solid rock at or near the surface. In other cases they may be built
on a foundation of large stones, or in some modern cases on concrete. The
base of the wall may be up to a metre across, and it is built to taper inwards,
as it rises to achieve a width of, perhaps, no more than 300 mm at its top. The wall
may be built dry, as was traditionally done, or may be built with cement within
the core, in such a way that the stones appear externally to be uncemented. The
wall is traditionally topped off with stones specially selected and laid to form a
reasonably weather proof coping. Dry stone walling depends on the way in
which the stones are selected and interlocked for its strength and durability,
and it is a particularly skilled trade. It is often the case that the techniques of
dry stone walling are adapted to the construction of low garden walls, using
flat shale stones, very commonly. In such situations the use of a more formal

Fig. 5.2. A dry stone slate wall typical of the Lake District.

coping stone may be adopted, to give a more precise finish. From the simplest type of wall construction has developed a number of variations and improvements. The use of mortar adds strength and durability to a wall, and will result in the ability to build both narrower and higher walls.

Random rubble uncoursed

The roughest form of stone wall is that described as uncoursed random rubble, consisting of stones picked at random and laid to form bonds although without any attempt to put them down actually in courses. These walls are built with a slight taper, frequently, but only from, say, 350 mm (14 inch) at the base to 300 mm (12 inch) at the top. The base will be on a foundation at least twice its width, and this in modern examples will consist of concrete 75 mm (3 inch) thick and 700 mm (28 inch) wide. Traditional practice was to use stones of this width and depth to form the foundations. A coping would be formed of hand selected stones laid with the grain at right-angles to the natural bedding line, or 'edge bedded' as it is described.

Random rubble coursed

A greater degree of strength is achieved if a wall is built approximately to courses, and this, naturally, requires greater care and attention in the selection of

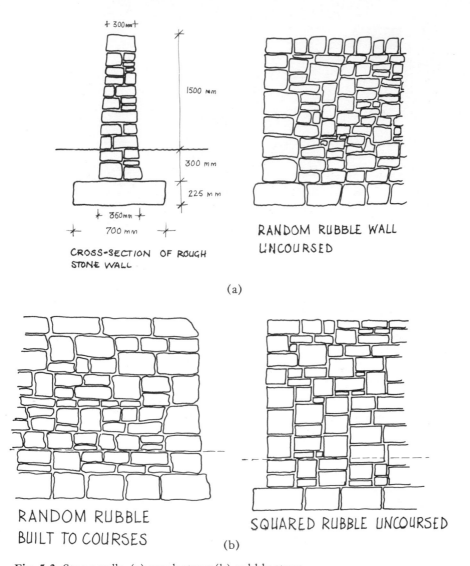

CROSS-SECTION OF ROUGH STONE WALL

RANDOM RUBBLE WALL UNCOURSED

(a)

RANDOM RUBBLE BUILT TO COURSES

SQUARED RUBBLE UNCOURSED

(b)

Fig. 5.3. Stone walls; (a) rough stone (b) rubble stone.

stones to be fitted into the wall. For this reason it is marginally more laborious, and costly. A similar taper is usually built into the walls as with uncoursed random rubble. The width might be 125 mm at the top and 150 mm at the base, with a foundation of up to 300 mm in width. The foundation would either be stepped, in the case of natural stones or not, in the case of concrete. Either way this would be set on to solid ground, usually at least 300 mm below the ground surface.

Fig. 5.4. A wall built of square rubble in courses with a rounded stone coping. The stones have, in most cases, been bush hammered to give texture. The iron straps are a late addition to carry iron posts with barbed wire and have resulted in some staining.

Squared rubble

Further refinements in walling result in the use of squared stones to form squared rubble walls. These may be stones which are split in the quarry in this way, or can be easily squared up. The material can be built up uncoursed, with what are known as riser stones, which are larger than the majority of stones in the wall, extending the height of two other stones. A number of reconstituted stone walling types produced commercially, adopt this pattern for their construction. Squared rubble may also be built to courses, although this will also often involve the use of riser or bonder stones. An alternative is that which is known as regular coursed rubble where the courses consist of stones of different thickness but the stones are all the same thickness in each individual course.

OTHER FORMS OF WALLING

Other forms of natural walling are polygonal walling, or the use of particular materials such as flint or slate. Polygonal walling is usually only used for facing and may need to rely on a backing of brickwork or other material for adequate strength. Flint walls or brick and flint are traditional in East Anglia where there is little other natural stone. Flints here are traditionally 'knapped' or split to reveal a flat shiny surface, and laid with that surface outwards. The use of slates in the Lake District with their natural flat bedded block shapes has resulted in an unique method of walling, laid 'watershot'. This means the bedding of the stones is such that on buildings the bedding is tilted so that water getting into the wall, should there be any, will always be brought out to the face of the wall.

Ashlar

'Ashlar' is the name given to the finest dressed stone, cut into rectangular blocks with sawn faces and straight edges. It is laid with very fine joints and requires very precise cutting and fitting. It is a most expensive method of walling and

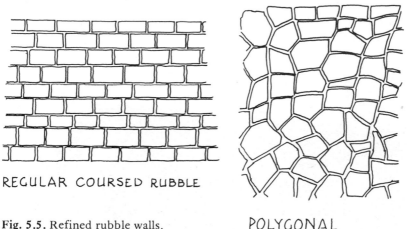

REGULAR COURSED RUBBLE

Fig. 5.5. Refined rubble walls.

POLYGONAL

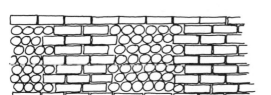

BRICK AND FLINTS

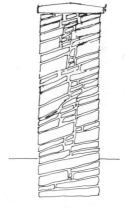

'WATERSHOT' OR
TILTED SLATE

Fig. 5.6. Other forms of walling.

only used nowadays where some attempt is being made to create a stone facade in an area where anything different might be out of place. Because of the cost, it is common practice nowadays to use the material as a facing often with no more than 25 mm thickness of stone. This will be built up upon a backing of brick or a similar material to which it is bonded with mortar and held by cramps. The structure of the wall will be entirely dependant on the bricks with the ashlar face giving only a visual effect. The same bondings as described for squared rubble are used with ashlar, with regular coursed bonding being the most suitable arrangement for the character of the stone.

The use of the stone walls and other specialist materials as described above is becoming less and less of a practical proposition with rising costs of labour and material. Nowadays the emphasis in the majority of design situations must be on devising building methods which will give satisfactory results with minimum cost. This implies using cheaply produced materials that can be quickly

Fig. 5.7. Dressed ashlar stone in its historic use at Belsay, Northumberland.

and easily built into the desired form. The most common and popular of these
is brick.

BRICK WALLS

As bricks are half as wide as they are long the method of measuring the width of
brick walls by 'bricks' and 'half bricks' is a logical approach. The usual free
standing wall is commonly a 'one brick' wall with a 215 or 219 mm length.
Standard bricks are either imperial or metric standard in Britain (see Table 5.1)
(see page 178). Half brick walls may occasionally be erected in some situations

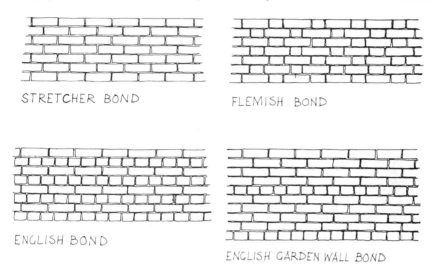

STRETCHER BOND   FLEMISH BOND

ENGLISH BOND

ENGLISH GARDEN WALL BOND

Fig. 5.8. Brick walls.

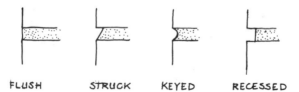

FLUSH   STRUCK   KEYED   RECESSED

Fig. 5.9. Typical brick joint treatments.

but they are limited in their application. A number of methods of bonding is
frequently described in the literature, but we must remember that the modern
bricklayer spends by far the greatest part of his working life laying bricks in
stretcher bond, as a result of cavity wall construction. This is quick and
comparatively easy to do, and may result in a disinclination on the part of
many to become involved in more complicated patterns of laying. English

Table 5.1 Brick and brickwork dimensions with dimensions of concrete blocks

	Metric dimensions (mm)	Imperial dimensions (inches)
British standard imperial brick	219 x 105 x 67	$8\frac{5}{8}$ x $4\frac{1}{8}$ x $2\frac{5}{8}$
British standard metric brick	215 x 102.5 x 65	8.46 x 0.04 x 2.56
Half brick wall	102.5	$4\frac{1}{8}$
One brick wall	215	$8\frac{5}{8}$
One and a half brick wall	327	$13\frac{1}{4}$
Vertical joint (standard)	10	$\frac{3}{8}$
Vertical joint alternatives (standard)	6 13	$\frac{1}{4}$ $\frac{1}{2}$
Four course height with metric brick and 10 mm joint	300	
Four course height with imperial brick and $\frac{3}{8}$ joint		$11\frac{3}{4}$
US Standard Brick		8 x $3\frac{3}{4}$ x $2\frac{1}{4}$

Concrete Blocks, made to a range of sizes both in the UK and the USA. These may be hollow or solid. Common dimensions are

UK	USA
$17\frac{5}{8}$ x $8\frac{5}{8}$ x $2\frac{1}{2}$ or 3, $3\frac{1}{2}$ or 4 in	
$15\frac{5}{8}$ x $7\frac{5}{8}$ x $5\frac{5}{8}$ or $7\frac{5}{8}$	$15\frac{5}{8}$ x $7\frac{5}{8}$ x $3\frac{5}{8}$ in (described as 16 x 8 x 4 in
and	to allow for joints)
$17\frac{5}{8}$ x $8\frac{5}{8}$ x $8\frac{5}{8}$ in	$17\frac{5}{8}$ x $7\frac{5}{8}$ x $7\frac{5}{8}$ in (described as 18 x 8 x 8 in to allow for joint)

garden wall bond consisting, as it does, of one course of header bond to three courses of stretcher bond may be an acceptable alternative, calling for only limited concentration. Such variations of bonding as Flemish bond, or Flemish cross bond, or monk bond, or modern face bond and others depending to some extent on the use of different tones of brick for their effect are unlikely to achieve wide general use in future. As with stone walls certain factors are critical in the design of brick walls to ensure durability and stability. These are as follows:

1. Foundations

It is important that walls are constructed upon adequate foundations. A good rule of thumb for this which has been accepted for many years is that the foundation should be twice the width of the wall at its lowest point. This should give it an adequate base, spreading the load of the wall. For the depth of the foundation itself the traditional rule is that this should be at least one and one-third times the distance by which the foundation projects on each side of the wall, assuming these to be equal. This arrangement coincided very well with the old Imperial dimensions of brickwork, and does likewise with the metric. Not only is the actual foundation built with the wall important, however, the stability of the ground upon which the wall is to be built is of vital importance and it is frequently necessary to excavate to some depth in order to ensure that the ground is solid. This is a common experience in areas of redevelopment where the ground surface may consist of disturbed land or the rubble from

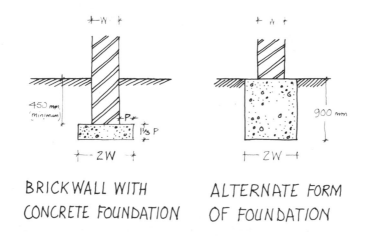

BRICKWALL WITH CONCRETE FOUNDATION

ALTERNATE FORM OF FOUNDATION

Fig. 5.10. Foundations.

previously demolished buildings, when it is necessary to dig down to a reasonably strong natural stratum. Sometimes the placing of a layer of hard core beneath the foundation is illustrated in drawings but this, in fact, solves nothing and should not be permitted.

The acceptance of a need to provide such a layer is the acceptance that the ground in question is incapable of supporting a brick wall satisfactorily. The answer to such a problem lies in a different direction; deeper excavation, or special measures designed to compensate for the weakness of the ground. Hard core may be laid to improve poor ground conditions under more broadly base structures such as roads, but cannot be expected to solve the difficulties of more concentrated loading such as occur with walls and which will by their nature be subject to lateral movement pressures. It has usually been considered necessary to excavate to a depth of at least 900 mm (3 ft) in natural soils to obtain stable conditions. This may need to be increased in the case of wet conditions and particularly in clay soils which are always subject to expansion and contraction. Gravel and other dry soils may not require excavation to such depth, but it is frequently suggested that at least 450 mm (18 inch) of cover should be provided above the foundation to ensure that it is not subject to the action of frost.

An alternative method where shallower foundations are acceptable is the concrete strip foundation. This is a comparatively recent innovation and one which is gaining support as a means of saving labour. It consists of excavating as would be done for a standard foundation, and filling the trench up to ground level instead of providing the minimum thickness of concrete. This avoids the

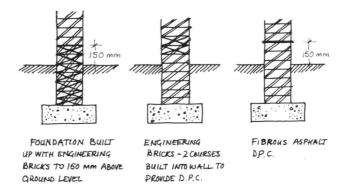

FOUNDATION BUILT
UP WITH ENGINEERING
BRICKS TO 150 mm ABOVE
GROUND LEVEL

ENGINEERING
BRICKS ~ 2 COURSES
BUILT INTO WALL TO
PROVIDE D.P.C.

FIBROUS ASPHALT
D.P.C.

Fig. 5.11. Damp proofing.

need to lay bricks below ground level, and where the wall is used, for example, in conjunction with grass surfaces, performs the function of a mowing strip. This method has been cautiously accepted for house building in some localities, but its use will naturally depend on the volume of concrete required and the resultant cost compared with traditional construction.

2. Damp proofing

It is important that walls should be protected against the effects of damp whether rising from the ground or soaking in as a result of precipitation on the upper surface. Thomas and Korff (1972) recommend the use of special quality bricks to form a damp proof course (D.P.C.) at the base of free standing walls, these to be in accordance with the standards laid down for D.P.C. bricks in B.S.:3921. The selection of bricks for such walls is something requiring considerable care and it may be necessary in many cases to choose bricks of an engineering quality, particularly those of low porosity, to ensure durability. Where design considerations call for the selection of any other brick it is important that the best protection is given. Bricks used below ground level should be engineering quality or, at least, sound well burnt bricks of low porosity, and they should be built up with cement mortar. Depending on the quality of brick used below ground and those to be used in the wall itself it may be necessary to put in a D.P.C. comprising either two courses of D.P.C. bricks to B.S.:3921 as indicated above or fibrous asphalt felt or some similar material

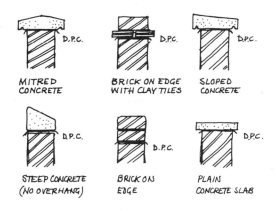

Fig. 5.12. Forms of concrete and brick copings.

forming a continuous flexible damp proof course. This material should be allowed to project from the wall on both sides to ensure that the vertical passage of water is prevented. It is, however, liable to the criticism that it creates a very marked line of weakness along the base of the wall, a fault not attributable to brick D.P.C's. The D.P.C. should not be less than 150 mm above the ground surface.

It is relatively difficult to protect the face of the wall against driving rain. Where this is anticipated to be a problem it is probably necessary to select a weather proof brick. It is possible to paint brick surfaces with clear silicone paint to give some protection and this may be the appropriate solution to some design problems but should be undertaken only with specialist advice as to its relative cost and merit.

3. Copings

The top of the wall is an area requiring particular care in detailing to ensure that the whole wall is properly protected. Ideally the wall should be provided with a coping which will shed water off so that it falls to the ground and not on to the face of the wall. This involves an overhanging coping, grooved on its lower side to prevent water running back to the face of the wall. Coupled with this will be a D.P.C. at the top, just beneath the coping to prevent water which is not shed off from penetrating into the wall. Fibrous asphalt may be used for this purpose. There are unfortunately many circumstances in which the use of such copings is doomed to failure as a result of vandalism, and alternative methods, which may well be less ideal, have to be adopted.

Overhanging copings present an ideal target for vandals on public housing areas and are usually avoided for this reason. In these circumstances the use of brick on edge may be a satisfactory answer although even here it has usually been found necessary to make special provision for the end and corner sections of such walls to ensure their protection. Bricks on edge can easily be prized off at the ends and corners and the solution of either having special end sections precast in plain or coloured concrete, or concreting a block *in situ* may be adopted. Where it is important for the design, that the brick on edge runs through the full length it may be necessary to anchor the bricks with special steel end anchors. Brick on edge should ideally be allowed to overhang when used as a coping, and it may well be that this is possible when it has not been selected purely to give a vandal proof finish. In these circumstances bricks may be used with a course of tiles beneath to provide the overhang necessary to protect the wall itself. It should be remembered though that the choice of a suitable coping for the circumstances may dictate the choice of brick in the wall itself, and limit quite significantly the possibilities open to a designer.

4. Mortar

Standard free standing brick walls are built in a mortar consisting of 1 part of cement to ½ part of lime to 4½ parts of sand. Where however, conditions of extreme exposure exist it may be necessary to increase the element of cement at the same time reducing the ratio of lime to sand. Thus a mixture of 1:¼:3, cement: lime: sand, may be used. Below ground level and for the building on of D.P.C. brick courses, cement mortar is often recommended, in which case a mixture of 1:3 cement: sand, should be adopted. Further details of the selection of mortar are set out in the BDA practical note no. 2 (1973).

5. Stability

One aspect of the design of free standing walls which, on occasion, tends to be overlooked is the need to ensure that the wall is designed to withstand the lateral forces of wind pressure. This will vary in the UK from 285 N m⁻² (6 lbf ft⁻²), which is only to be expected in Central London, to 575 N m⁻² (12 lbf ft⁻²) in relative shelter throughout the country, to pressures in excess of 1150 N m⁻² (24 lbf ft⁻²) in exposed areas. The Brick Development Association proposes the use of simple ratios of width to height of wall, according to the anticipated wind pressure of an area. In the first example quoted it would be safe to build a

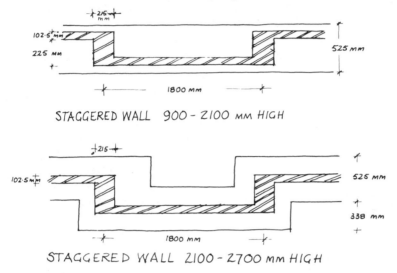

Fig. 5.13. Dimensions of staggered brick walls.

wall to a height up to ten times its width. In the worst quoted condition, the height should not exceed four times the height. From this, low walls can be seen not to pose any critical problems, a 900 mm (3 ft) wall built in 219 mm (9 inch) nominal brickwork being perfectly adequate in all circumstances. In the majority of the country away from the severely exposed locations, particularly around the coast, a 219 mm (9 inch) wall can safely be constructed to a height of 1125 mm (3½ ft approximately). Above this height, or the appropriate alternative according to wind and weather conditions, special provision must be made to give additional support against lateral wind. This could be done by increasing the wall thickness, and there will be circumstances when the selection of a 'one and a half brick' (327 mm) wall may be the desired solution. This would raise the safe height of construction of a free standing wall to 1635 mm (5¼ ft) for the major part of the country. This is not always an acceptable solution in economic terms and the use of piers where a straight face on one side of the wall is required, may be adopted. An alternative is the use of 'staggers', in which the wall is built in sections of 1800 mm (6 ft) maximum, with a set back between alternate sections which in fact form piers, although without the obvious effect of piers as traditionally built.

The Brick Development Association recommend that walls up to 900 mm
(3 ft) can be built with half bricks (102.5 mm) with piers of 215 mm (8⅝ inch)
at 1800 mm (6 ft) centres. Over 900 mm (3 ft) and up to 2100 mm (7½ ft)
walls may be built in the same half brick thickness (102.5 mm) to include
staggers at the identical 1800 mm (6 ft) centres as for piers, and the depth
between the outside faces of alternate sections should be one and a half brick
327.5 mm. The width of the overlap between the staggered sections is recommended to be one brick (215 mm). These dimensions are based upon the most
sheltered conditions as encountered in the area of Central London, compared
with a straight forward wall of one brick (215 mm) up to the height of 2100 mm
(7½ ft). Elsewhere than Central London, unless the wall is to be built in an
extremely sheltered position these dimensions need to be amended. Foundations for staggered walls of this size are built on a continuous straight line, and
do not reflect the staggers. They will be wider than the dimensions for foundation derived from twice the wall width. A wall whose depth from the outside
face of one stagger to the opposite outside face of another is one and a half
bricks (327.5 mm) would require a foundation 525 mm (1¾ ft) wide and 225
mm (9 inch) deep. For higher walls it may be desirable to lay the foundations to
the same arrangement as the wall to avoid excessively wide foundations.

Expansion and movement joints

It is most important that in any wall of over approximately 9 m (30 ft) in
length, there should be built joints to allow expansion and movement. 9 m is the
maximum length that should be erected as a single section for small walls, for
one brick (215 mm) walls the preferred distance between joints is likely to be
less and probably no more than 6 m (20 ft) although the greater length may be
allowable if unavoidable. A vertical joint is usually constructed, perhaps 12.5
mm (½ inch) in width and unlikely to be more than 25 mm (1 inch), and this
may be filled with a mastic jointing material, or alternatively left as a gap. It is
important, incidentally, to remember to extend the break in the structure
through to the coping so that this is not subject to displacement or damage as a
result of any movement.

A great deal of very helpful information on the design and construction of
brick walls is contained at the publications of the Brick Development Association, 3 − 5, Bedford Row, London WC1R 4BU. Some have been referred to in
the text, and some are listed in the bibliography.

Concrete block walls

An alternative to bricks is the use of concrete blocks for the construction of
walls. Solid blocks are normally standard sizes (Table 5.1). Because of the

different size and weight of the units, different safe dimensions of wall construction will operate. As blocks are lighter, generally, than brickwork, more stringent design criteria for the thickness:height ratio will need to be applied. There is less guidance available on the relevant sizes than is the case for brickwork. It is probably wise, however, to reduce slightly the proportions of width to height that would be used for brickwork, when working with solid concrete blocks. It is equally important with concrete blocks as with bricks that the wall should be protected, at top and bottom, from moisture. The use of damp proof courses (D.P.C.'s) will usually consist of the standard asphaltic felt, always bearing in mind the inevitable weakness that this will create. The use of D.P.C. bricks or slates might be worth consideration although this would need to be acceptable visually as a design feature. Both the colour and texture of the material would be strikingly different, and variations in dimension in the case of bricks would need to be accommodated. This might extend to building a block wall on a brick footing, in which case a feature could be made of the change of materials. This may be particularly appropriate when use is being made of the numerous ornamental screen blocks, which are made with a pattern of apertures on each block so that a patterned open screen effect is achieved with the wall construction. It is worth mentioning that the fact that such a wall does not present a solid barrier to the passage of wind will reduce the care which it is necessary to devote to the design of such walls. With these a feature can be made of a precast concrete coping, and this can similarly be done in the case of plain block walls.

Retaining walls

The design of retaining walls is a further area where the approach to design will depend on the extent of the problem. Retaining walls may be 'mass' walls, depending for their strength and durability on the mass of material of which they are built whether it be of stone, brick or concrete, or designed walls relying on concrete reinforced, usually under stress, to provide the necessary strength. Walls below a certain size, say 2 m in height (or 6 ft) and 25 m in length (or 27 yd) can be built quite easily and cheaply in mass materials. Above this size range the use of designed walls in which the reduction in the volume of materials built into the wall offsets the costs of preparing the design must be considered. It need hardly said that the latter is specialist work to be undertaken only by a fully trained structural or civil engineer. It is also difficult to be precise about dimensions for the choice.

Retaining walls need to be designed to withstand the pressure of the retained material which is exerted in such a way that it might either tend to overturn the wall or to move it laterally. Walls which are 'surcharged', i.e. walls having a steep slope, above the retained section must be designed to account for this and must be more robust than those which are supporting ground which has an horizontal surface or a slope not exceeding 1:10 for a reasonable distance back from the retaining wall. A simple rule of thumb method can be used for the design of mass walls in either brickwork or concrete. In brickwork, it may be assumed that a wall will never be less than 1 brick thick (219 or 215 mm) and that for every 600 mm (2 ft) in height the width of the brickwork will be increased by a half brick width (105 or 102.5 mm). This specification is sometimes varied to increase the width at heights of 750 mm (2½ ft). The alternative of *in situ* concrete will usually consist of walls 300 m (1 ft) in width as a minimum. This would be stepped out to increase to 450 mm (1½ ft) as the wall reached 750 mm (2½ ft) in height and would be similarly stepped out at similar intervals. It is quickly seen how the volume of material can mount with a wall of any significant height. The wall will be built upon a foundation of twice the width of the lowest section of wall.

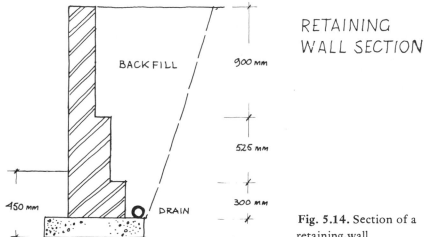

RETAINING
WALL SECTION

BACK FILL

900 mm

525 mm

300 mm

DRAIN

450 mm

Fig. 5.14. Section of a retaining wall.

In situ concrete retaining walls require the use of 'shuttering' against which to pour wall structure, and, because it can be an expensive material, this calls for careful thought to ensure that a design can be built by a reasonably economic use of shuttering material. Often for this reason or because of the height of the wall it is found necessary to pour the concrete in a number of 'lifts', usually coinciding with the steps in the wall width. When this happens it is often desirable to take special precautions to 'key' together the sections of concrete poured into the wall at different times. This may mean placing reinforcement bars projecting from the lower layer into that above, or leaving timber slats in when the concrete is setting so that when these are subsequently removed they provide a keyed surface for the next layer to fit into. In some circumstances where bricks or a similar ornamental finish is required an outer skin providing the required surface may be built before the concrete is poured and this can be used as the shuttering. The inclusion of butterfly clamps or a similar device to form a firm junction between the facing material and the mass of the structure is recommended in those circumstances. It is probably safer not to include any such 'skin' of brickwork or other material in the structural thickness of the wall if making any assumptions about the structural strength of the wall. The construction of retaining walls, of whatever material, will involve excavations into the retained material to such a slope as will provide a reasonable degree of safety for the duration of the work. This excavation must then be back-filled, and this should be done with inert fill which is reasonably free draining. Coupled with this must be arrangements for the removal of any excess moisture at the rear of the wall.

It is important that retaining walls like free standing walls have proper D.P.C.'s and protective coping and that the rear face of the wall is protected from penetration by damp. An ideal means of achieving this is the use of a 'vertical' damp proof course comprised of bitumen painted on. Suitable back-fill material leading moisture down to the base of the wall to drainage outlets may suffice to prevent this sort of damp, in the wall itself. The alternative methods of removing water from behind retaining walls are either weep holes, or a tile drain laid along behind the wall. The use of weep holes is frequently specified, and this can be a simple and relatively cheap method of dealing with the problem. In some stone walls, or indeed in brickwork weep holes may be created by leaving gaps between the stones or bricks unmortared. This is not a very satisfactory arrangement as these tend to become clogged up. In brickwork it is common practice to insert glazed drainage pipes. As these are frequently projected from the wall surface they act as a natural attraction for children, and for vandals, as they may poke things up the pipes or break off the protruding ends. The other disadvantages with weep holes is that they frequently lead to discoloration of the brick surfaces and the adjacent ground surface if these are paved or hard surface. Unless the water is carried clear of the wall surface there may be a temporary discoloration resulting from dampness as well as the more permanent effects of salts on the surface. There is also a possibility that the movement of water behind the wall will bring down fine silt and this can be deposited on the exposed surfaces resulting in disfiguration and even some nuisance. The alternative of laying a continuous pipe behind the wall at or about foundation level may result in additional cost but may be justified. It will need to be connected to a drainage system to carry away any excess water. This will involve either leading a drain-pipe around the end of the wall, or beneath the foundations, where this is necessary, or through the wall with the structure constructed to 'bridge' over the pipe in such a way that no strain will be placed on the pipe itself.

Facing of retaining walls

It is a very common practice, where retaining walls are to be given a special decorative treatment, for them to be faced with stone, or bricks when they have in fact been constructed of mass concrete or even of reinforced concrete. Even a mass brick wall might be faced with a thin outer skin of ashlar or slate. For example where brick is used as the external surface, this will be built as a 'half brick' skin with concrete, although it would be integral in the case of a wall built of mass brickwork. For such brick 'skins' constructed with mass concrete, as has been previously mentioned, the brickwork may be employed to form the shuttering or formwork of the wall, thus reducing the cost. This may also be possible with some forms of stone walling although ashlar and slate are now commonly cut to such thin sections that they could not stand by themselves unsupported, acting only as a cladding on the main structure. Any formwork or shuttering must be able to support the weight of the concrete wall both individually within the sheet and with the framework behind it. This weight will be of the order of 2400 kg cm^{-1}.

Frequently nowadays the concrete of the wall structure is left as the external surface material, in which case it is specially treated or made to rely upon the particular nature of the shuttering used. Steel sheets may be used to give a smooth and even finish. Timber, on the contrary leaves an impression of its own patterns, and the imprint of planks has been used to good effect quite widely recently. Corrugated sheets may be used to add interest, and in some cases expanded polystyrene in which a design has been cut with a hot iron might be used to give special interest. For particular design requirements shuttering with designs in moulded glass fibre might be considered. With all these techniques there is the possibility that additional variation in the effects can be achieved by treatment of the surface. This may be before the concrete is fully set, when it is green, that is to say, or it may be when the concrete is completely cured. In the former case the brushing of the surface, usually with a wire brush, may be undertaken to leave an interesting textural and colour variation depending on the aggregates used. In the latter case the use of hammers to create an interesting texture may be adopted. This technique is often used appropriately in conjunction with a form of shuttering which leaves raised patterns, which in turn can be hammered off to leave a 'rustic' finish.

Steps

The construction of most formal flights of external steps, however finished, will commonly involve the use of a concrete structure, usually reinforced with a mesh reinforcement. There will be relatively few occasions when it is necessary to construct flights to cover very large changes in level, and the majority of cases will involve construction of four or five steps. In most of the cases it will be possible to cast the concrete as a single piece. The use of reinforcement is recommended in all but the most stable of ground to guard against any danger of differential movement. It is not necessary except when temporary ground surface conditions are unsatisfactory to lay the concrete on hard core. Where ground surface conditions are poor it may be necessary to dig out excessive depths of material, and back-fill with hard core to provide a stable base on which to lay the concrete. It is also quite in order to lay the concrete on a formation layer which is on a slope. If this is done, it is advisable to shape the concrete at top and base to give flat sections which will avoid any danger of the steps slipping with the angle of the slope.

The construction of steps of this sort will involve a considerable amount of shuttering or formwork as the top surface will follow the line of the final steps, whether to be left as exposed concrete or being clad with some other material. Shuttering or formwork of some complexity will thus need to be constructed. It may be that this will be used in sections, the lowest part

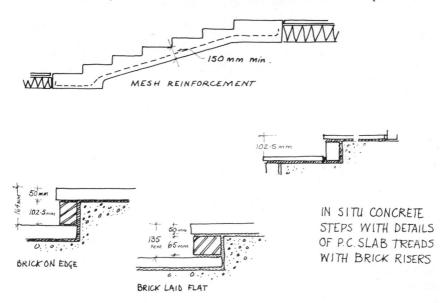

Fig. 5.15. *In situ* concrete steps with details of P.C. slab treads with brick risers.

of the steps being cast first and the same shuttering re-used up the steps until the work is completed. This is one way in which it is possible to save on the price of shuttering. At the same time the concrete can be formed into a single mass, although this may involve keying between the different castings to ensure a good joint. In some cases when flights of steps are flanked by retaining walls it may be advisable to build the steps into the walls, particularly where the ground beneath the steps has been back-filled and there is some danger of move-

Fig. 5.16. Very simple details can often be the most effective even in such grandiose designs as Versailles, where the plain steps make a fine contrast with the ornate vase.

ment. Obviously this bridge effect will place additional strain on the walls and their foundations, and this must be allowed for in the design. It does, on the other hand, avoid the danger of differential settlement which might take place were the steps and the walls not linked in this way. Beasley (1960) gives very comprehensive advice on the scale and proportion of steps which it is desirable to use for external purposes, and helpfully includes the dimensions of a number of famous and admired examples. It can be noted in general terms that the use of dimensions which are quite acceptable internally for outside use, results in a mean and unsatisfactory appearance. The 'going' or horizontal surface of each individual step must be adequate for comfort. For internal steps this has led to the recommendation of a minimum width of 280 mm (11 inch). For external purposes 450 mm (1½ ft) is probably nearer an acceptable minimum. The 'riser' or the height of each step can be almost equally unsatisfactory if it is too low as if it is too high. Very high steps create actual physical difficulty and this is likely to be felt when the riser is more than 165 mm (6½ inch). Very shallow steps confound people in a different way particularly as they descend them. Steps shallower than about a 120 mm (4½ inch) riser tend to be uncomfortable, as one is generally used to something deeper and when one arrives at each step slightly before one anticipates one may be quite badly jarred. This effect may be somewhat mitigated by the use of a design with a very long 'going', say 1 m (3 ft) and a very shallow step giving more the effect of a stepped ramp or where there are only two or three steps.

Fig. 5.17. A grand staircase designed as much for effect in relation to the column at the top of the steps.

It is quite common for the materials chosen for the facing material to dictate, within the broad overall limits, the precise size of going or riser to be used. The selection of materials also will dictate whether the steps can be built with a projecting nosing. This can be done, for example, with concrete slab treads and brick risers although not, obviously, with steps constructed entirely of brick. It is important, in the choice of construction, to ensure that the surfaces of the steps fall in such a way that all surface water is easily and quickly shed away and removed. It is also worth considering the ease with which any design proposed can be kept clean, both of sweet wrappers, chewing gum, and the like, and of soil which might be trapped in corners. When steps are constructed up planted or grass banks, it is important to give thought to the design of the edging of the steps so as to provide a junction which is easily cleaned, as well as simply maintained as far as the vegetation is concerned.

Fences

An alternative means of creating an enclosure structurally is by the use of fences. The choice of whether to use a fence or a wall will depend to a considerable extent on the nature of the enclosure required. This is also true of the exact sort

Fig. 5.18. Simple construction using natural materials gives the right feeling in many rural settings.

of fence chosen. In these days of universally available materials thought must be given to the character of the neighbourhood or area where the fence is to be erected, particularly as this is influenced by existing walls and fences. The traditional selection of materials for enclosure has depended on the local availability of materials, and ground conditions, as well as upon the nature of the enclosure required. Stone walling developed from the removal to the edges of fields of excess stones in the area of cultivation. This was often in areas where timber was in any case not very easily obtained, with the development of timber fences in areas where, conversely, stone was a comparatively rare commodity. The nature of both stone and wood available, the way it cleaves or grows, further influences

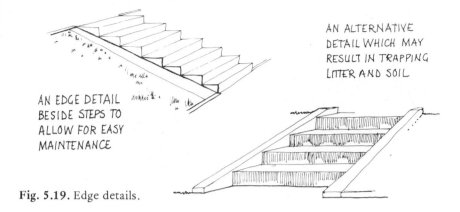

AN ALTERNATIVE DETAIL WHICH MAY RESULT IN TRAPPING LITTER AND SOIL

AN EDGE DETAIL BESIDE STEPS TO ALLOW FOR EASY MAINTENANCE

Fig. 5.19. Edge details.

the design of such means of construction. In this way regional characteristics have developed both in walling and fencing.

The traditional use of fencing material of different character in relation to different forms of land use and occupation has become familiar and for many visitors to the countryside provide quite strong symbolic indicators of the landscape. In Britain this is particularly so in the use of traditional continuous metal bar fencing associated with the parks of great country houses, and to a lesser extent the use of horizontal timber fencing associated with equestrian establishments and activities, to name only two examples. Other forms of fencing have a strong local character associated with availability of material; Cleft Chestnut paling in Kent, or woven wattle hurdles in Somerset, although the

Fig. 5.20. Chestnut pale fencing on horizontal post and rail fencing.

Fig. 5.21. Typical post and rail fence.

regional concentration of these is now less strongly exhibited than in former times. More modern and more urban forms of fencing also have their associations and areas of appropriateness. Fencing consisting of round metal bars topped with ornamental arrow heads would be associated with a building of some consequence, a palace or public edifice or an important metropolitan park. At the opposite extreme, woven wooden fencing is perhaps most at home in the stock-brokers' Tudor leafy suburbia. Other railings are typical of or associated with, other situations, and more modern activities and developments give rise to the need for particular types of fence, for example, motorways and other roads, and sports activities. In many cases it has to be borne in mind that the need for fencing arises as a result of the density we need to achieve in the layout of land uses and activities when different sports need to be placed 'cheek by jowl' and some form of physical separation which takes up practically no space is necessary to contain individual uses.

Fencing has a very wide range of applications and vast numbers of patterns and designs are available to meet the requirements. It seems likely that the range is likely to continue to extend as the pressure on land becomes even more acute and new activities and uses become developed. The visual significance of what is erected can be very great indeed, and this must be borne in mind. It is worth repeating that besides the appropriateness for the function which is essential to the choice of fence, materials should be chosen with an eye for the contribution that any such feature will make to the existing character of an area. Cost is a factor which it will be impossible to overlook, and durability will need to be considered at the same time, and equally.

A most useful review of methods of enclosure was prepared a number of years ago by the Central Electricity Generating Board (1966) under the title

Design Memorandum on the Use of Fences. This compared and contrasted walls, fences, bollards and other forms of enclosure and provides very useful detailed information on the design and construction of different forms of fence, as well as of the other methods.

The methods of construction of a number of commonly used fences have been specified by the British Standards Institution who have provided in each case a number of alternative specifications for the design and construction and the use of materials to meet particulat situations. The different forms of fencing listed below are covered in British Standard number 1722, which is divided into eleven parts as follows:

(1)   Chain link fences   (1972)
(2)   Woven wire fences   (1973)
(3)   Strained wire fences   (1973)
(4)   Cleft chestnut pale fences   (1972)
(5)   Close board fences   (1972)
(6)   Wooden palisade fences   (1972)
(7)   Wooden post and rail fences   (1972) .
(8)   Mild steel or wrought iron bar fences   (1966)
(9)   Mild steel or wrought iron unclimable
        fences with round or square verticals
        and flat studs and horizontals   (1963)
(10) Anti-intruder chain line fences   (1972)
(11) Woven wood fences   (1972).

The British Standard 3854:1965 dealing with Farm Stock Fences has been withdrawn, and another useful publication of the Ministry of Agriculture (1969) in the Fixed Equipment of the Farm Series (no. 6) entitled *Farm Fences* is also out of print.

Fences are of two types, those of metal, usually either mild steel or wrought iron, and those of timber chosen from a wide range of timber. Traditionally timber would be home grown, but increasingly, imported softwoods are employed for a wide range of uses, including fencing, and provide the major part of our needs.

TIMBER FENCES

Wood used for fences consist of hardwoods and softwoods, and include those which can be used, and are durable, without any treatment, those which can be dipped into a preservative to be made so, and those which need to be treated with preservative under pressure to ensure their proper protection and long life.

Timbers that are commonly used without any treatment include oak, larch, sweet chestnut and western red cedar. Those that can be easily treated include alder, hornbeam, sycamore, lime and horse chestnut. Those by contrast which really require pressure treatment for the best results include ash, elm, Scots

Table 5.2 Classification of timber for natural durability (commonly used exterior timbers)

	Very durable (over 25 years)	Durable (15 – 25 years)	Moderately durable (10 – 15 years)	Non-durable (5 – 10 years)	Perishable (less than 5 years)
Hardwoods	Teak Iroko Afrormosia	Oak		Elm Poplar	Alder Ash Beech Horse chestnut Sycamore
Softwoods		'Western red cedar' Yew	Larch	Fir Pine Spruce	

Table based on that of the Forest Products Research Laboratory, Princes Risborough. Durability is based on untreated timber, kept damp and in contact with the ground. A number of African hardwoods are very durable and these are used for practically all external furniture. Three of the most popular are listed.

Fig. 5.22. Horizontal timber fence.

pine, spruce, and Douglas fir. Other timbers may also be suitable but these
are the principal timbers used. It is very important to the success of any work
of this nature that the timber should be in the proper condition for the job.
For this reason it is important for the landscape architect to have some understanding of the methods of treatment required for different timbers. In addition
to treatment, the condition of the timber to be used on a job needs careful
control. The most sensitive parts of any fence are clearly the posts, which
are subjected to the effects of ground moisture and soil borne organisms.

For this reason it may, under some circumstances, be acceptable to treat the
base of fence posts up to at least 300 mm (1½ ft) above ground level only.
Methods of treatment may also need to be adapted to meet certain circumstances. On site, application of preservative may only extend to brushing on,
which is a short term measure of limited value.

Other timbers, however, also need to conform to a standard, and need to be
sawn smooth, with square edges, without any large or dead knots, and without
the bark remaining. Only timber of this standard and without 'shakes', cracks,
occurring usually as a result of the wood having been dried out too quickly, can
be certain of remaining sound for a reasonable time. Any timber which has
surface indentations, of any sort, is liable to decay as a result of the retention
of water, and the growth of organisms which may follow this. It is particularly
important that the top surfaces of timber should be sound, and true, as these
are most prone to the effects of weather. It is for this reason that the measure

of capping the tops of posts, where the grain is exposed 'end on' to the elements
has sometimes been adopted. At one time this was common procedure with
ornamental garden fence uprights where small cut timber squares would be
nailed on. This was intended to serve a practical as well as an ornamental
purpose, although the precise value of the additional protection it affords would
be difficult to quantify. On the other hand farmers often go to the trouble of
capping farm gate and fence posts with sheet metal, and one may assume that
with practical men the value of such protection is real, and proven.

  Sizes of timber. The sizes of timber to be used in the construction of various
  types of wooden fence specified in the relevant British Standards are given
  within those standards. In many cases the specification will cover a range of
  alternative sizes. It is important to remember that timber, certainly both in
  Great Britain and the United States is specified to nominal sizes, to which
  it is originally cut but that as a result of shrinkage it is rarely, if ever, found
  to be the nominal size. Because fences are such commonplace everyday objects
  it is easy to take them for granted and forget that the dimensions of the members and the setting out of the fence uprights and rails follow traditional
  patterns because these have been arrived at by trial and error. This is because
  they represent the best alternatives taking into account the lengths of timber,
  and the natural properties of wood resulting in the need to have a reasonable
  relationship between the cross-section and length.

  It is important not to require rails to span excessive distances otherwise this
will result in them being too weak and liable to fracture, or alternatively they
will require an unduly large cross-section. In the selection of timber sizes the
most economical use of timber must of course be taken into account.

  The methods of fencing are described in detail in the B.S. 1722 as previously
stated. Nevertheless it may be useful to set down here some of the principal
features of construction of each. These are set down in the order of numbering
of the relevant parts of the British Standard.

Cleft chestnut pale fencing (B.S. 1722, part 4)

Cleft chestnut pales each with one end pointed are secured at top and bottom
with wire twisted between the pales to provide a gap when erected of 75 mm
(3 inch) between the pales. The wire usually consists of four twisted strands
of 14 s.w.g. wire. Pale lengths are variable between about 600 mm (2 ft) and
1500 mm (5 ft). In the case of longer pales over 1 m (or 3 ft), a third, central,
wire needs to be added to give additional support. Individual pales are difficult
to size because of the uneven results of cleaving but will be of the order of
between 25 and 40 mm (1 — 1½ inch). This sort of fencing is used frequently
as a temporary fence which can be erected for short time protection of, say,
shrubs or grass, and subsequently retrieved and used again. In these circumstances it can be used with vertical posts to support it at centres of 2 — 3 m.

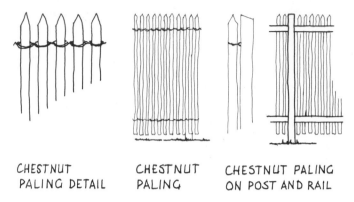

CHESTNUT   CHESTNUT   CHESTNUT PALING
PALING DETAIL   PALING   ON POST AND RAIL

Fig. 5.23. Timber fencing.

Depending on the height of the palings the dimensions of the posts will vary from 50 x 50 mm (2 inch²) up to 100 x 75 mm (4 x 3 inch). Unless the pro-tection is for a very temporary period it is usual practice to strain the fencing to straining posts set at distances of not more than 70 m (75 yd). These posts need to be set into the ground for about one-third of their total height and to be supported by struts at 45° from the horizontal in the line of the strain. In this way considerable tension can be developed. It is quite common for this type of fencing to make use of straining posts and intermediate posts of 'unwrot' timber, i.e. round sections as grown, and not sawn rectangular sections. This, of course, is cheaper although the bark should be removed before use. Straining is usually with galvanized eye bolt strainers and ring nuts.

Where a more permanent version of the same effect is required the practice of combining this material with a horizontal bar fence may be used. This provides a very satisfactory and comparatively impenetrable fence which may well be cheaper than alternative methods of construction. It is necessary to staple the chestnut paling to the horizontal rails at frequent intervals with strong wire staples. It is usually suggested that stapling should be carried out after every third staple at top and bottom. It will be necessary, of course, for the post and rail fence to be constructed so that the horizontal rails coincide with the wires of the chestnut paling.

Close board fencing (B.S. 1722 part 5:1972)

In contrast with cleft chestnut paling fencing, close board fencing is constructed to form a rigid framework, the strength of which is principally dependent on the way in which the members are bracketed together. Cleft chestnut fencing is dependent on the straining effect of the wire with which the timbers are woven, opposed by the solidity of the straining posts and struts. The tension of the wires provides the basic rigidity, and in this respect this sort of fence is more properly classed with post and wire type fences than with solid post and rail close board or paling fences. Close board fencing is usually erected between 1.2 m (4 ft) and 2 m in height with rectangular vertical posts between

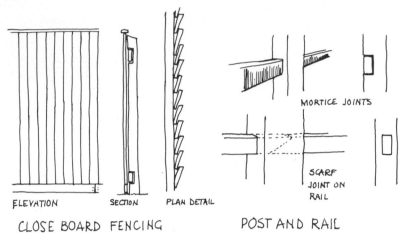

ELEVATION   SECTION   PLAN DETAIL

CLOSE BOARD FENCING   POST AND RAIL

MORTICE JOINTS

SCARF JOINT ON RAIL

Fig. 5.24. Timber fencing and joints.

100 x 100 mm (4 inch²) and 150 x 100 (6 x 4 inch) in section according to height. These will be inserted into the ground for one-third of their length.

Post holes should, as in the case of all fence posts be dug as small as possible in relation to the size of the post to ensure a good solid and firm bedding in of the post, although not too small to allow for ramming the material back to steady the post. In most cases it is considered desirable to set the posts into concrete for at least half their depth in the ground and this should in any case be for a depth of 450 mm (1½ inch). Where this is done holes will be larger to allow an adequate volume of concrete.

Horizontal rails will be attached to the vertical posts by means of screws and may be rectangular (from 75 x 50 to 100 x 75 mm) (3 x 2 to 4 x 3 inch) or arris rails, which are triangular rails formed by cutting rectangular rails diagonally. Rails may be jointed with butt joints or morticed set into the posts, provided that the cutting out of the mortice space in the post does not result in its being weakened. A recessed joint may be used in preference to a true morticed joint where the post is not to stand out from the line of close boarding. On higher fences there will need to be three rails to give adequate support and the maximum distance apart of the posts will be 2.75 m (9 ft). It should be borne in mind that the same criteria that affect the design of brick walls govern close board fencing, although apart from solid concrete fencing it does not govern other types. For this reason it is important to ensure that the fence will be strong enough to meet the wind pressures of any particular locality. The close boards which give the fence its name are nailed to the rails slightly overlapping with two galvanized nails to hold each board or pale to each rail, and are sawn 100 mm wide (4 inch) and to a thickness varying from 20 to 7 mm (¾ to ¼ inch). The best form of this fence consists of oak pales which may be sawn or more traditionally cleft. These are 90 mm (3½ inch) in width and 12.5 mm to 7 mm (½ to ¼ inch) in thickness when sawn and approximately 10 mm (⅜ inch) when cleft. The advantage of using cleft timber is that this runs with the grain and this results in the timbers being less liable to entry of moisture and consequently injury.

In order to improve the life expectancy of close board fences it is common practice to protect both top and bottom in the same way that damp proof courses and copings are used on walls. Fence posts are usually cut on a slant at the top or 'weathered' as it is described. A thin top rail with a mitred top is frequently nailed along the top of the boarding or pales to protect the boards which are with the grain 'end on' to the worst weather effects. At the base of the fence a gap is left between the base of the boards and the ground and this is filled in by what is described as a 'gravel board'. This is a board laid horizontally between each upright. When this begins to rot, as the area near the ground of such a fence always does before any other, the gravel board can be removed and replaced, without affecting the remainder of the fence which thus remains sound and durable for much longer.

In common with other forms of fencing involving rails, close board fence rails are placed to follow the lines of the ground and the vertical boards similarly will take up this line. Fencing of this sort should not be stepped, as would be the case with a brick wall where it is necessary to have the foundations on a horizontal base.

Wooden palisade fencing (B.S. 1722 part 6:1972)

Oak pales do not require any treatment with preservative but posts, rails and boards in other timber should be treated prior to erection. It is also desirable to paint these after erection every few years with creosote or proprietary preservatives. This form of fencing is structurally very similar to close board fencing. In use however it is different, providing only partial screening and not the total enclosure of close board fences. For this reason it is frequently used to define formal enclosures such as front gardens. The heights are usually between 1 m (say 3 ft) and about 1.5 m (say 4½ ft). Taller fences up to 2 m (6 ft approximately) may occasionally be used where a high partial screen is needed. The tops of the palisades are usually either cut to a point, described as twice weathered, or are rounded, and the posts are cut to match. Post and rectangular or arris rails are the same sizes as used for close board fencing while the palisades are normally 60 mm (say 2½ inch) wide and 20 mm (¾ inch) thick. These are nailed to each rail with two galvanized nails from each palisade to each rail. The palisades are set their own width apart.

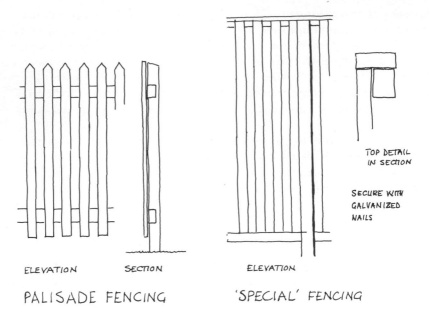

ELEVATION　　SECTION　　　ELEVATION

PALISADE FENCING　　'SPECIAL' FENCING

TOP DETAIL
IN SECTION

SECURE WITH
GALVANIZED
NAILS

Fig. 5.25. Other sections of timber fencing.

For very tall palisades it may be desirable for design reasons to leave the top line flat or even cap the fence with a continuous capping. Where special circumstances call for ornamental fences as features, board or palisade fences, where the boards are attached on alternate sides of the rails to provide a three-dimensional screen, may be designed. These provide slightly changing views and a varying sense of enclosure according to the angle from which the fence is viewed. The design of such features usually involves a longer board and raising the top rails to the very top of the fence and bringing the lower rail almost to the level of the ground. For these reasons it may be necessary to use a larger dimension of timber. It is probably unwise, however, to increase the width of boards much beyond 150 mm (6 inch) as there is an increasing tendency to warp with wider boards. This sort of feature will normally be painted rather than treated with wood preservative and it should be borne in mind that this will increase the maintenance liability. Some manufacturers now supply artificial materials which take the place of painted boards for use as either vertical painted boards or for horizontal 'ranch style' fences, as they are called. Rigid hollow section P.V.C. boards provide a pleasant, maintenance free, alternative to white painted boards. These will usually be required to be bolted or screwed to the posts with galvanized bolts or screws that will not result in any staining of the P.V.C. and the manufacturer's advice should be sought if any doubt arises.

Post and rail fences (B.S. 1722 part 7:1972)

A traditional stock fence consisting of vertical posts and three or four horizontal rails, the post and rail fence may be either of the morticed type or nailed construction. In the morticed type the vertical posts are cut, or morticed, to take the horizontal nails. These, in turn, will be jointed with 'scarfed' joints, with the end of each rail cut at an angle to fit into the same angle cut on the next rail. Morticed fences are laid out with a maximum of 3 m (9½ ft) between posts. Rails are cut to this length so that the scarf joints can coincide with the mortices. Intermediate posts known as 'prick' posts are set between the fence posts, one, or occasionally two, to each length of rail, and these may be set on alternative sides of the fence. The height of this fence to the top rail is usually 1.3 m (4¼ ft) and the main posts are 150 mm x 75 x 2.25 m (6 inch x 3 inch x 7 ft). Prick posts are the same dimensions as the rails which are 100 x 37.5 mm (4 x 1½ inch), and are driven 450 mm (1½ inch) into the ground and nailed with galvanized nails. Nailed post and rail fences will be constructed of the same basic dimensions of post and rail. In this case the posts will be set at intervals of 2 m (6 ft) and there will be no prick posts. The rails which will be cut in 4 m (12 ft) lengths will be butt jointed at every alternative post and nailed to the posts with galvanized nails. Half round timbers may be used as an alternative to rectangular sections in this method of construction.

Woven wood fences (B.S. 1722 part 11:1972) and wattle hurdles

An alternative to the use of close boarded fencing may be the selection of panels of woven wood anything from 0.6 m (2 ft) to 1.8 m (6 ft) in height. These are often selected to give 'character' to a private garden, or may be useful to provide a more temporary enclosure such as at flower, or agricultural shows. Because of the size of the individual panel units this sort of fence needs to be used on ground which does not have any significant changes in level, when an ugly stepped effect would result. Panels made by a number of manufacturers can be supplied as 'interlace' or 'overlap' where the slats of the panels are interwoven horizontally between vertical slats. In the former case the slats, usually 100 x 5 mm (4 x ³⁄₁₆ inch), are butted up to each other, whereas in the latter case these are overlapped by 12.5 mm (½ inch). In both cases the panels are framed and braced with wrought timber. Panels 1.8 m (6 ft) in length are set between vertical posts 150 x 75 mm (6 x 3 inch) or less for the lower heights, and are held in place by beading, nailed to the posts on either side. This avoids damage to the framework of the panels from nails. Panels should be treated with timber preservative prior to erection and may be dipped by the manufacturer. They will need periodic painting with creosote or some proprietary preservative and for protection from most serious effects of weathering, the panels should be held off the ground.

A more traditional panelled fence is the wattle hurdle, consisting of hazel twigs or wands interwoven to form a panel similar to that of interwoven fencing in construction. The character and appearance is, of course, quite different. Wattle hurdles have been used for centuries in rural areas particularly associated with sheep, where these types of fencing may be adapted either for permanent enclosure or for temporary use. At Priddy on the Mendips, in Somerset the use of wattle hurdles for temporary pens at the time of the sheep fair is hundreds of years old and these hurdles were kept in a carefully stacked pile which was thatched over to protect them and so stored from one year to the next. For temporary use the wattle hurdles may have spiked verticals that can be driven into the ground. More permanent erection will call for vertical posts, usually in round timber 75 − 100 mm (3 − 4 inch) in diameter. The hurdles will be held in place as is done for interwoven fencing, and should be held free of the ground for maximum durability. Hurdles are made in lengths of 1.8 mm (6 ft) and from 1 m (3 ft) to 1.8 mm (6 ft) in height. In some areas there was at one time a tradition of weaving fences of wattle *in situ* which has some advantage on undulating ground.

An alternative to wattle fencing is the use of wands of willow, or 'withy' to form a similar interwoven fence of an equally rural character. The dimensions and construction are similar to wattle fencing for this.

METAL FENCING

Like timber fencing a number of forms of metal fencing are covered in the specifications of the British Standards Institution. Mention has already been made of the traditional use of continuous metal bar fencing associated with landscape parks in Great Britain. This is perhaps an appropriate introduction to metal fencing because of its traditional nature and because like wattle this sort of fencing can be obtained in long lengths erected *in situ,* and in 'hurdles' 1.8 m (6 ft) long.

Continuous bar fencing (B.S. 1722 part 8:1972)

For continuous fencing the uprights with slots for the horizontal bars, of which there are commonly five, are set at intervals of 450 mm (3 ft). The horizontal bars are 4.5 m (15 ft) long and at this interval joiner posts are used to accommodate the junction between the bars. Standard posts have either a thrust plate at the base or alternatively two pronged feet. Horizontal bars are either circular or flat metal. The top rail is usually bigger in diameter or section than the others to give additional strength to the fence. Metal fences are usually dipped in boiled linseed oil or varnished, by the manufacturer and then require to be painted with red oxide primer and two coats of oil paint, or in the case of varnished fences painted with two coats of bituminous paint.

In some ways akin to this form of fencing is the vertical bar or 'unclimbable' fence.

Mild steel or wrought iron unclimable fences with round or square verticals and flat studs and horizontals (B.S. 1722 part 9:1963)

This is another very traditional method of fencing which has a clean and simple design and is therefore satisfactory in a wide range of uses in basically urban conditions. This type of fencing is manufactured in panels as either solid units or as self adjusting, at slightly increased cost. This means that the fence material

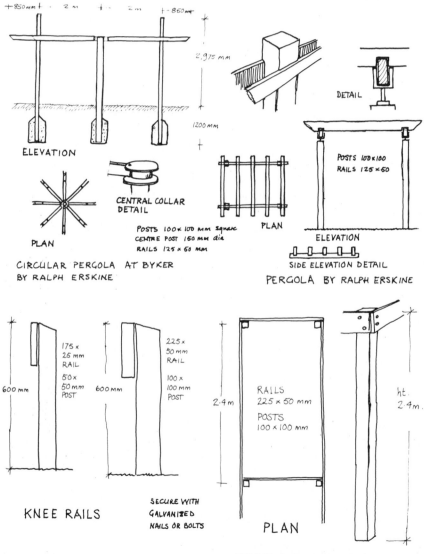

Fig. 5.26. Other fences.

can be adjusted to run up or down slopes of up to 1:9 while the posts remain
vertical. The fence, which must be very familiar to all, consists of panels of
vertical bars set in horizontal rails, usually strap shaped. The verticals are usually
finished either with pointed ends or hooped ends and may, in the former case,
carry quite elaborate ornamental 'spear heads' in more sophisticated examples.
It is most important that a really firm method of fixing is adopted to avoid
any danger of removal of the verticals which could be dangerous weapons in the
wrong hands.

Heights of the fencing range from 1 m (3½ ft) to 2 m (7 ft). Panels are
usually 2.75 m (9 ft) in length and these are bolted to mild steel upright posts
38 x 10 mm, to 58 x 10 mm (1½ x ⅜ inch to 2¼ x ⅜ inch) in cross-section.
These should be set for at least one-third of their length into the ground and
may be set in concrete not weaker than 1:10 concrete aggregate. The uprights
should be fitted with stay plates at their bases, although this may not always
be necessary when the posts are set into good concrete foundations. It is most
important that adequate treatment is given after erection. Sections and posts
may be delivered either dipped in boiled linseed oil or varnished and must be
thoroughly protected on site, either by lead oxide primer and two coats of gloss
paint, or two coats of bitumen paint over varnish. At alternate posts it is recommended that there should be side stays to support the fence laterally; these are
set at an angle of 60°, should be at least at two-thirds of the fence height, and
should have plates at their bases. These may or may not be set into concrete.

Woven wire fences (B.S. 1722 part 2)

The use of woven wire fencing is associated principally with stock rearing,
and consists of wire woven vertically and horizontally to give an open textured
net with rectangular apertures anything from 300 x 75 mm (12 x 3 inch) to
300 x 225 mm (12 x 9 inch) in size. British Standards allow for posts in timber,
concrete or 'iron' (usually mild steel). Timber is probably the most common,
and the appropriate material in the majority of cases, as this is likely to be
cheaper than and almost equally as durable as either concrete or iron. The height
of woven wire fencing ranges from 750 mm (2½ ft) to 1125 mm (3¾ ft) based
on the width of rolls of wire available. The wire is fixed to posts which are
set at intervals not exceeding 3.5 m (say 12 ft) with straining posts at intervals
of not less than 150 m (165 yd) and at any change in direction. The straining
posts are supplemented with stays in line with the fence line. Straining posts
for the 750 mm (2½ ft) should be 1.6 m (5¼ ft) long, 100 mm (4 inch) square
with stays 1.35 (4½ ft) long and 75 x 50 mm (3 x 2 inch) across. For the 1125
mm (3¾ ft) height the equivalent posts would be 2m (6½ ft) by 125 mm
(5 inch) square, and the stays 1.725 mm (5¾ ft) by 100 x 75 mm (4 x 3 inch).

Strained wire fencing (B.S. 1722 part 3)

This, like the previous fence discussed, is used primarily in agriculture but may be adapted for other uses. It has been widely used in the division of garden spaces in local authority housing, although this use is open to some question as it fails to provide any privacy, which many occupiers find essential to the full and proper use of such areas. Again British Standards allow for timber, concrete, or 'iron' posts with galvanized wire. Like woven wire fencing this is a non-traditional type and so it might be argued that the choice of material for the posts is not critical. In rural conditions, however, timber is almost certainly most appropriate, and in terms of maintenance and durability compares very favourably with the other two materials. In terms of cost it is the favourite. Special circumstances may call for mild steel or concrete posts.

The height of this fence is very similar to the previous one and ranges from 825 to 1350 mm (2¾ to 4½ ft). At the latter height the fence would be supported by posts 2.150 m (6¾ ft) by 100 mm (4 inch) square set at least 600 m (2 ft) into the ground. These would be placed at intervals not greater than 3 m (10 ft) apart. At every 150 m (165 yd), and at changes in direction it would be necessary to place straining posts 2.2 m (7¼ ft) and 125 mm (5 inch) square, set 750 mm (2½ ft) into the ground and supported with stays 2 m (6½ ft) long and 200 mm (4 inch) in section. The stays are placed in line with the fence at an angle of 45° to the vertical. Both straining posts and stays are commonly set in concrete, although this is often considered to be unnecessary in the case of wooden posts when the ground material can be well consolidated. Wires are strained by the use of winding brackets or eye bolts at straining posts. In some cases top and bottom wires may be of barbed wire.

Chain link fences (B.S. 1722 part 1:1973)

Chain link fences provide a good protection between sporting activities and the like. They range in height from 900 mm (3 ft) to 2.135 m (7 ft) and the higher fences are probably more commonly used. For tennis courts the height will increase to 3.6 m (12 ft). Posts may be in mild steel, concrete or timber, and it is perhaps the first of these that is the most appropriate for the majority of situations in which chain link fencing is used. They intrude less into the overall pattern of fence and posts consist usually of angle irons, so that the horizontal wires to which the chain link is affixed can be threaded easily through holes in them.

Posts will be 38 to 50 mm (1¾ to 2 inch) angle iron up to 6 mm (¼ inch) thick with straining posts 50 to 62 mm (2 to 2½ inch) and 6 mm (¼ inch) thick. The latter will be supported with angled stays and set into the ground 600 mm (2 ft) for the lowest height of fence and 750 mm (2½ ft) for the highest. Straining posts and stays are either set in concrete (1:10) in which case they are spragged, i.e. the ends are splayed open to give a greater contact with the concrete mass, or are fitted with special plates which helps to stabilize the posts when soil is rammed around them. Intermediate posts are also either fitted with plates or set in concrete. These should not be more than 3 m (10 ft) apart with straining posts 70 m (75 yd apart) and at ends or corners where stays will follow the lines of the fences.

The chain link material must be galvanized and comply with stringent requirements as to the diameters of wire. This is true also of plastic covered wire when both the gauge of the wire and the thickness of the plastic covering it, should be taken into consideration. From the design point of view the colour of material must be given careful thought particularly as it is often forgotten that seen from oblique angles chain link presents an almost solid impression. Some colours, and paradoxically green is one of them, present a very obtrusive effect in many circumstances. It is important that posts are properly treated either before or on erection. They may be galvanized or metal coated, or coated with an annealed plastic coating before delivery, or they may be painted on erection, arriving on site only primed.

Anti-intruder chain link fencing (B.S. 1722 part 10)

These are basically chain link fences of the highest range extended with cranked extension arms to carry three lines of barbed wire. They are used, as the name implies, for industrial and commercial security. As such it is the aim of designers that they should be as unobtrusive as is compatible with their deterrent effect. If the use of such fences can be limited to the rear and sides of vulnerable premises this is very desirable from the aesthetic point of view. Posts are usually concrete or steel and conform to the same dimensions as for normal chain link.

Other fences: specialist manufactured types

There is a wide range of fences available commercially for particular purposes, among these are a number that have been developed largely as a result of traffic hazards, and these are manufactured by specialist engineering manufacturers. Names such as pedestrian guard-rails, parapet railing, and safety fencing are used to describe variations of vertical bar fencing in which welded panels with rectangular hollow tube top rails typically 50 mm square (2 inch) and 13 mm (½ inch) square uprights are set between standards at 1.8 m (6 ft) centres and jointed to them with sleeved joints, giving a smooth finish. Safety barriers for traffic may consist of very substantial horizontal rails, set on strong verticals. There are also a wide variety of large scale industrial versions of vertical bar fencing using big section corrugated, or pressed metal poles, and these are tradi-tionally employed on industrial sites. Major manufacturers of these types of fencing have specialist design expertise, and it is reasonable to rely on this for detailed design and consultation for major specialized fences.

Selection of standard manufactured items and standard details. All of these need to be used with some caution to ensure that the material selected is really appropriate both visually and functionally for the job required of it, and in the case of some of the more visually difficult designs, that something which will give a better appearance cannot really achieve the required functional objectives equally well. The problem of universality in the field of materials is that those which are supposed to be fitted to a range of purposes in reality do not completely fulfil the requirements of any individual application. This applies not only to fences but to the whole range of manufactured products available in the field of landscape construction and the same 'caveat' may also be applied to standard details and designs which are often recommended and used in offices. It is very easy to arrive at a compromise standard detail which can be tolerated in a number of different situations but which is in fact less than the best of any of them. This is a procedure that no designer should be prepared to tolerate.

Other fences: low fences, knee rails etc.

There are many situations when the demarcation of areas or property requires little more than a low rail. Knee rails may be constructed in timber or metal. A typical timber rail might consist of short posts 75 x 50 mm (3 x 2 inch) with pointed base and weathered top, 525 mm (21 inch) long with 300 mm (12 inch) above ground to which is nailed or bolted a horizontal rail 90 x 19 mm (3½ x ¾ inch). The posts should be set at intervals of about 1.8 m (6 ft). Metal rails will consist, commonly, of galvanized tube 38 mm outside diameter welded to a series of 13 mm (½ inch) solid mild steel rods at 1.8 m (6 ft) intervals. Alternatively solid mild steel rods between 13 and 22 mm (½ and ⅞ inch) may be used for the rails with verticals consisting of flat straps, which could be up to 44 x 10 mm (1¾ x ⅜ inch). In this case the standards would be perforated near the top and the solid rail threaded through in the same way as is done for continuous bar fencing.

These forms of rail would usually be manufactured off site in predetermined lengths, in keeping with both site requirements and the process. They are often required for limited and repeated runs, demarcation of front gardens, for example. Care should be taken to ensure that lengths required can be satisfactorily transported. A number of manufacturers produce ornamental light hurdles ranging in height from 300 mm (1 ft) up to about 750 mm (2½ ft) with hooped tops similar to those of unclimable fencing and these can be used for the same purpose. Because they are individual hurdles they can be used for temporary protection of grass areas or flower-beds, although only from casual trespass. They are designed on spiked feet and stays. They can also be bolted together to form a more permanent fence. In this case it may be considered desirable to set the feet into concrete.

MAINTENANCE OF FENCING
While the life span of timber fencing, of the close board and paling type is

extended by the application of creosote or preservatives or painting, this treatment is not usually undertaken in the case of timber posts for post and wire or woven wire fences. Concrete fencing posts require no maintenance, but do not appear to have an appreciably longer life than well prepared timber of the proper dimensions for the job. Metal fencing of the horizontal bar or unclimable vertical bar type can be expected to have a long life particularly when it has been well prepared at the time of erection. This can be extended, too, if painting is undertaken at regular, if quite infrequent, intervals. Strained and woven wire fences are limited by the durability of the wires, and it is not unusual for the posts to be restrung. The same limitations affect the life of chain link fencing, whether galvanized or plastic coated and in both cases, if the metal posts have been well prepared and well cared for, these may be retained for use with a new chain link. Treatment of timber which has been discussed earlier in this chapter is covered by British Standard Specifications, and it is advisable that this should form the basis of my specification for fence construction.

A detail which is frequently overlooked where fences are erected in association with grass is the maintenance of grass up to, and around posts and indeed along the immediate face of any solid fence. This also applies to walls. Unless such a grass area is to be grazed by animals a mowing strip or some arrangement to take the fence outside the area of grass should be included in the design. Bollards and posts in the grass create the same difficulties.

Other means of demarcation: bollards and posts

Bollards may be made of timber, metal, and concrete. Like fencing there is a considerable range of manufactured products available with some metal bollards offering such sophistication as lights in the top, or hinged bases for easy removal. Other examples can be set into the ground in slots to enable their removal. Concrete bollards can be purpose made and a number of manufacturers will be prepared to undertake casting of bollards with plain or textured exposed aggregate finishes to individual designs. These features need, in general, to be set into concrete to almost the same depth as their final height above ground and all but the smallest will require some form of rod reinforcement. The choice of bollard will vary very greatly according to the function and the situation. Timber bollards may be appropriate to many less formal situations, where cars are to be kept off rural grass verges for example. In cases like this, quite short stocky timbers can be used extending perhaps no more than 300 − 375 mm (12 − 15 inch) above ground level and set at sufficiently close intervals to prevent the passage of cars. The height of bollards is of course related to the clearance beneath the vehicles. For this purpose a bollard 600 − 675 mm (2 − 2¼ ft) in length and with a cross-section of 125 x 125 mm (5 inch²) or 150 x 150 mm (6 inch²) would give a good design proportion and provide a chunky and deterrent design. The proportion of such features is very important to the final design achievement.

Fig. 5.27. Precast concrete stepping stones provide an effective and simple design detail.

Fig. 5.28. A traditional 'kissing gate' in a rural setting.

Gates

Traditional timber gates are the most appropriate features in association with woven wire, or strained wire or post and rail fencing. Posts of different dimensions will be used depending on the aperture to be spanned. It is important to note that the introduction in recent years of new forms of agricultural machinery has resulted in quite considerable changes in the countryside, not least in the dimensions of gates. These are now often much wider than before and in some cases two gates close a field aperture, swinging together, where there was one before. Traditional forms of pedestrian gates in timber are as familiar as the standard stock gates. The same can be said of traditional metal gates which go with horizontal bar rails.

The important thing about the construction of any gate is, first, that the gate post and the fittings upon which the gate itself swings is able to support the weight of the gate, and that it will continue to do so. Secondly the construction of the framework of the gate must be sound, regardless of what ornamental or stock proof details it carries. The framework of the gate consists of the vertical swinging post sometimes called the heel, the horizontal top bar and the angled brace or strut which holds the first two pieces of the structure in a constant relationship. These three form a right-angled triangle and all the other parts of the gate are hung from them. Some of these parts obviously add to the rigidity of the structure, in other designs the additional sections simply act as an additional weight dragging the gate down. Obviously the larger span of the gate the greater the strength required of the three main members.

Street furniture

Some items of street furniture present very considerable problems of design, litter bins are a prime example, and it is fair to suggest that the perfect litter bin has yet to be designed, if this is possible. Designs need to be vandalproof, easily emptied, to avoid displaying their contents, and to fit into the surroundings in which they are set. Other features have less stringent design and construction criteria but the details of all street furniture and similar items need to be considered as vital to the success of design schemes. There is nothing easier than for a grand design to be completely undermined by the presence of details that are poorly thought out and shoddily constructed. This extends to the positioning and style of notice boards, street signs, bus stops, telephone kiosks, letter boxes and other 'minor' details. It is essential to the work of the landscape architect to ensure that these are coherently designed, well constructed and add to, rather than detract from, the total design effect.

Timber structures

The majority of structures constructed by the landscape architect are generally relatively light and not load bearing, and in many cases the timbers employed will be greatly in excess of anything dictated by structural requirements. It is important however to select sound timber and to ensure that designs are undertaken in such a way as to avoid the retention of water or situations in which timber can quickly rot. For this reason metal footings are sometimes specified for posts, to overcome the dangers of posts' rotting at the most vulnerable point of ground level. This is an expensive detail but one which may be considered desirable on certain construction jobs. As a protection against the action of weather, and also to avoid vandalism, the methods of fixing timber should be

Fig. 5.29. Very simple construction details can often be the most effective and delightful. A jetty at Bolam Lake Country Park, Northumberland.

concealed, on the underside where possible. Metal fittings must be rust proof and not liable to stain the timber.

Techniques for preservation of timber have already been discussed, and where these are necessary the most stringent care must be taken to see that they have been properly carried out. For simple pedestrian bridges the simplest and most straightforward method of construction will consist of a basic structure of planks and beams. Depending on the width of the bridge the beams will be set on girders at either bank, on a solid concrete or brick wall or foundation or on individual bases. The beams are set to span the feature to be bridged and the planks nailed on to them with galvanized nails. The standard loading acceptable for normal floors is usually taken as suitable for this purpose and this is 250 kg m⁻² (50 lb ft⁻²). Beams will usually be placed at fairly close intervals, remembering that joists in flooring are commonly spaced at 375 mm (15 inch) and never greater than 800 mm (2⅔ ft) apart. Table 5.3 gives the approximate · clear spans that can be achieved for different beam sizes.

Table 5.3 Clear span and appropriate beam sizes: Distance between beams 375 m.

Clear span, m (ft)	Beam sizes, m (ft)
1.8 (6)	113 x 50 (4½ x 2)
3.65 (12)	226 x 50 (9 x 2)
5.5 (18)	275 x 75 (11 x 3)

Planks will be nailed to the beams at right-angles and these in most external examples will be square edged planks which will be set with a fine gap between planks to allow for easy drainage. Tongue and groove boards and rebated or ship lap boards such as are used commonly in interior construction will not be used other than in exceptional circumstances and when there are special provisions to dispose of any surface water on the boarding. Narrow planks or boards are preferable to wider ones as these will not shrink or swell so much individually, nor will they tend to warp so much. Planks will vary from 100 mm (4 inch) in width to 275 mm (11 inch) with thicknesses from 25 – 38 m (1 – 1½ inch). The design of bridges to take more than pedestrians will depend on an increased strength of beam, involving perhaps mild steel or reinforced concrete, together with a more substantial surface material. Planks and boards will be more than the standard 38 mm (1½ inch) maximum and might well be laid without gaps and with a wearing course of asphalt to protect the surface of the wood and provide a smooth surface which would allow the run-off of water. On wider bridges the construction may be augmented by the use of joists laid across the main beams or girders which provide the span. In that case the planks or boards will be laid parallel to the beams. Rigidity in the construction is improved if the planks are laid so that the ends of alternate boards are in different lines. This achieves the same effect as the bonding of brick work.

Summary

This section has attempted to put down some of the principles governing the construction of various elements in the landscape. A number of standard solutions has been quoted and it is hoped that this provides illustrations which enable the student designer, in particular, to understand the problems of these designs and solve them in new and original ways.

References

Beasley, E. (1960). *The Design and Detail of Space Between Buildings.* Architectural Press: London.

The Brick Development Association (1973). *Mortars for Brickwork.* B.D.A. Technical Note 2, Brick Development Association: London.

British Standards Institution (Various Dates). *Fences,* 1972 (in 11 parts).

British Standards Institution (1974). *Clay Bricks and Blocks,* **3921.**

Central Electricity Generating Board (1966). *Design Memorandum on the Use of Fences.* C.E.G.B.: London.

Thomas, K. and Korff, J. O. A. (1972). *The Design of Free-Standing Brick Walls.* B.D.A. Technical Note, Brick Development Association: London.

6 Water features

The need for water for human and animal use has led to the development of techniques for collecting and reatining water being developed from the most primitive times. In Britain a large proportion of the landscape consists of clay, impervious to water, and the simple act of digging a hole may be all that is necessary to create a pool of water. Loss of water through evaporation, however, means that such a pool must be topped up either by precipitation running into the pool direct or via streams or drains, or as a result of the movement of ground water. In warmer climates the greater problems of evaporation will demand a higher level of replenishment for a pool of the same surface area. Alternatively the availability of water supply will dictate the extent of water feature that can be constructed whether for ornamental or functional purposes.

When dealing with impounding water for domestic and industrial purposes it has often been assumed that losses as a result of evaporation can largely be discounted. In fact current investigations into the loss of water from lakes and pools as a result of evaporation from the surface suggest that a loss equivalent to 450 mm (18 inch) depth of water would be likely in an average year in British conditions. In the equatorial region this loss is likely to be nearer 1.8 m (6 ft) per annum and this clearly is a significant amount particularly in the case of water bodies which have a large surface area but are relatively shallow. However, it is reasonable to assume that in historic times and in places where the water supply is less plentiful than is normally the case in the British Isles, the use of such a precious commodity would have been subject to tremendous constraints, both physical and psychological, prior to the development of modern technology. This is well illustrated in the Moorish gardens in Spain, where the use of water in the creation of sensual delights is in a sense prodigal but where one finds that the designer has achieved an incredible economy in the way that much is made of water, a great effect being achieved by a small volume; the same water often being led through the different levels of the garden to be used again and again in different features. The historical concept of the idealized garden, which had little expression in reality both far and wide and for long periods, had always for its centre piece some water feature.

In Great Britain the development of means of providing water for humans and beasts in hill-top settlements in dry areas was achieved in very early times, possibly in the Neolithic age of husbandry. This comprised the ingenious inven-

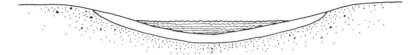

Fig. 6.1. Typical form of dewpond with 'puddled' chalk or clay lining.

tion of the 'dew pond', which must have appeared to have 'magical' properties to our suggestible forebears, and which it must be admitted, still does not seem to have been fully explained in a scientific manner.

Dew ponds consist of saucer shaped depressions usually formed in the chalk landscape and without any source of supply of ground water. The bases of these ponds are formed from puddled chalk either in a single layer or in several layers which may be alternated with straw. This forms an impervious base which will retain any water that gets into the pond. In some cases the use of chalk may be exchanged for clay, if any is readily available. Despite their name it appears that dew ponds depend largely on rain water but that the presence of vegetation around the rim of the pond may be a significant factor in the replenishment of the water supply. Water vapour from mists and fogs appears to condense more readily in the presence of vegetation, which itself may contribute to the water vapour content of the atmosphere by the exhalation of water through stems and leaves. Whatever the precise cause, it is the case that dew ponds can provide a supply of water which is replenished even in times of drought. It appears that an important part of the functioning of the dew pond depends on the form of the apron around the water itself, the area of collection of water from rain or from dew is much greater than the area of water. The shape of the pond and its apron, forming an inverted shallow cone is such that the less the water area the smaller the area for evaporation, and the larger that for rainfall and condensation. This supply however seems to rely on the pond being filled with water in the first place.

In recent times some attempts have been made to create dew ponds with concrete lining with the aim of providing a cleaner water supply. Results of such experiments have shown that they can sometimes be successful and sometimes disastrously otherwise, although it is not always clear why this should be so. The form and, as yet not completely understood, principles of replenishment that govern the design and construction of dew ponds might be very valuable to a landscape architect working in the design and construction of water features where a ground water supply was not available. When dew ponds need to be repuddled, as does happen from time to time this can be done by driving cattle through them repeatedly.

Another form of impounding water which was practised in the earliest times and which implies a greater understanding of the movement and presence of water beneath the ground than frequently displayed by modern man, is the 'spring' pond. This form of pond was frequently dug in dry valleys and often in chalk country. In this way an underground stream would be interrupted and the water impounded, for the use of man and his animals.

Both of the examples quoted show the ability of primitive man to find sources of water in rather unpromising conditions, and this leads to the point that one of the most important aspects of the design of water features must be to ensure that adequate supplies can be made available to fill and to replenish the feature constructed. This can be quite a major problem when the creation of large lakes or pools resulting from voids left, for example, by open-cast, or strip mining, are required to be filled by natural streams. Some of the larger holes of this kind might take years rather than months to fill up if dependent on natural supplies. The use of supplies of treated water from the Water Company mains cannot be countenanced on the grounds of cost and of the relative inadequacy of supplies for more socially legitimate purposes such as domestic and industrial consumption.

The construction of water bodies may be considered as falling into three main types.
(1) Those that rely largely on natural soil conditions for their water holding capacity — naturally based lakes.
(2) Those that employ some means of reinforcing the natural conditions to form an ostensibly informal or natural water body — constructed lakes with natural appearance.
(3) Those that rely on construction methods which result in a formal water body — formal water bodies.

Naturally based lakes

The construction of major reservoirs and large lakes relies on the natural soil and geological conditions of the ground on which they are placed. Unless there is a substantial layer of material which forms, or can be made to form, an impermeable layer the task of forming an extensive reservoir becomes impossible and the structural requirements to ensure retention of adequate water supplies for a large population would probably preclude some of the simpler alternatives which might be adopted in less critical circumstances. The design of a reservoir will involve, in simple terms, the selection of a suitable valley which when dammed will retain an adequate volume of water due to its topography and basic geology. The selection of the position of the dam and its form of construction will likewise depend on the topography and geology. On the larger scale the choice will be between reinforced concrete and earth dams, stone or brick construction only being appropriate at the very smallest scale of water impound-

ing structures, if at all. This area of design and construction is a good example
of the relationship between the structural constraints on designs and materials
and the visual suitability. Reinforced concrete dams are found in areas where
the strength and solidity of the underlying rock is expressed in the rugged
topography. Whereas less dramatic and more gently rolling terrain is frequently
more appropriately complemented both structurally and visually by an earth
dam of an entirely different form from that employed for a concrete dam.

All large artificial water bodies should be constructed only under the advice
of a competent civil engineer. For water bodies in excess of 5 000 000 gallons
capacity this is in fact a legal requirement under The Reservoirs (Safety Provisions) Act 1930. The design drawings must be checked and certified by a
qualified professional civil engineer, who must issue a series of three certificates,
firstly relating to the design proposals, secondly to the way in which the works
have been carried out, and finally, to certify that the construction of the entire
reservoir is sound and that it may safely be filled to a level which must be
specified. This requirement incidentally does not apply to filling up excavations,
for example, from open-cast mining operations, which might otherwise be dry,
because the act specifically refers to holding water above the natural level of
any part of the natural ground adjoining the reservoir. Even so it is worth
introducing a cautionary note in relation to the development of such features
which it is advisable to undertake only with the benefit of specialist advice,
whether from a civil engineer or an hydrologist.

The construction of precast concrete dams involving reinforcing material
and prestressing is very clearly a field of activity calling for precision engineering
skills of a very high order. This is also the case, perhaps more surprisingly with
large earth dams. This is well illustrated by the dam at the Derwent Reservoir
which was constructed to a standard pattern but for which the control had
to be very closely maintained throughout the construction process, because
principally, of the moisture contained in water bearing strata of ground beneath.
A standard earth dam shape with a wide base and low slope angles was adopted
with a comparatively narrow vertical clay core and with a clay blanket at the
base, to ensure a seal of impervious material. This method of forming an earth
dam illustrated in Fig. 6.2 may be used for dams at a wide range of scales,

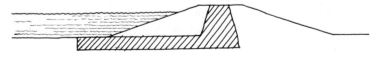

Fig. 6.2. Typical cross-section of earth dam with clay core and apron.

although the smallest water bodies are likely to be supported by dams built
entirely of clay.

The particular feature of the Derwent Dam was the drilling of vertical sand
drains used to effect the strengthening and dewatering of the substrata. As the

weight of the dam loaded these substrata they were compressed and the water in them was forced out into the vertical sand drains and out of the structure. It was most important that there should be no uneven displacement of the strata or distortion of those layers and for this reason an extensive system of monitoring was introduced so that the effects of loading could be measured accurately throughout the entire process of the work. This involved the use of piezometers and settlement gauges to measure the moisture in the material and the rate of settlement. In all a total of 193 different instruments were placed in the various strata. The new construction and these were connected to gauge houses especially built to allow constant monitoring, to continue after construction.

The extreme care necessary to ensure that a stable structure is established and maintained in these conditions tends to act against achieving a satisfactory visual effect. The lines of dams are often unsympathetic in relation to the surrounding topography and it may not be possible to devise any means of softening them. Tree planting, for example, will meet with the most vociferous objection from the engineers as likely to affect the stability of the dam by root action except at the furthest extremities of any construction. The use of more informal outlines may also be considered undesirable as adding undue or uneven loading at certain points. Some thought should be given in relation to the visual effect of such designs to the creation of shadows because it is sometimes possible to find that designs which, in all other respects fit into the surrounding landscape, become strongly intrusive when the sun's angle results in the creation of strong and geometric shadows. It may be that a landscape architect will have the opportunity to give advice which improves the visual aspects of the design of major dams.

Other aspects of the construction of large water bodies with which the landscape architect will be confronted are the margins. The results of variation in water level and the effects of wave action on large water bodies, either due to the weather or the movement of water craft can lead to problems with both the appearance of the banks and their stability. Problems associated with appearance and stability vary in significance in relation to the shallowness or steepness of the bank concerned, and are almost exactly in inverse proportion one to another. Thus a long shallow margin will have relatively minor problems of stability, whereas the smallest reduction in level will result in extensive exposure of mud. A steep margin will not create such a marked visual effect at times of low water, but may result in greater problems of erosion from wave action or from other causes.

TREATMENT OF BANKS

The solution of the treatment of water margins may be principally dependent on either constructional or vegetative means. The latter are really beyond the scope of this book but the former are not, and should be discussed in relation to big water bodies and to smaller ponds and lakes and even streams where some measures for structural protection are needed. The choice of method for the protection of banks will depend to a very large extent on the appropriate visual treatment. Many structural means of bank reinforcement and protection are

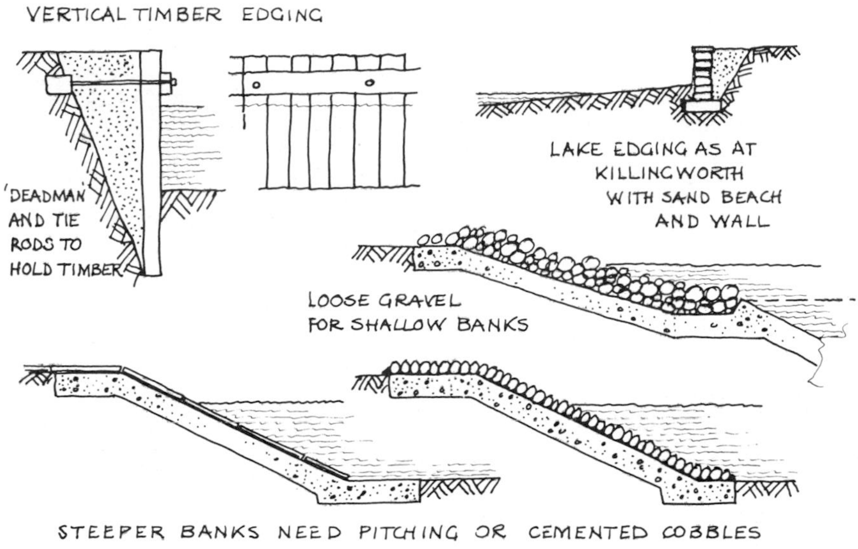

VERTICAL TIMBER EDGING

'DEADMAN' AND TIE RODS TO HOLD TIMBER

LAKE EDGING AS AT KILLINGWORTH WITH SAND BEACH AND WALL

LOOSE GRAVEL FOR SHALLOW BANKS

STEEPER BANKS NEED PITCHING OR CEMENTED COBBLES

Fig. 6.3. Treatments of banks.

quite unsuitable in naturalistic situations and planting methods which are commonly seen as the most appropriate way of solving the problem in the wild may in some circumstances be both visually and functionally inappropriate. In many situations the use of planting is undesirable because it will prevent or reduce interaccessibility of land and water.

Another circumstance is when the designer takes the view that, on purely aesthetic grounds, there is a need to retain a clean and uncluttered line between land and water, and the presence of planting along this junction interferes with the visual clarity of the design. In relation to large water bodies, techniques for the treatment of edges need to be simple and cheap unless they are limited to specific short stretches of the margin. Areas which are particularly vulnerable are the dam area which must clearly be protected from any erosion which could weaken the structure in any way. Additionally shores which face the prevailing wind and could, for this reason, be subject to wave action, may particularly require treatment. Dam surfaces will often be protected by 'pitching', the covering of the surface with paving materials cemented together and laid on a firm base of concrete, and this sort of treatment ensures total protection as long as it is adequately done, although it may be regarded as an inappropriate design in a large number of cases. Alternatively the area may be protected by boulders, or 'rip-rap'. This comprises a layer of stones, which are sufficiently large individually to be proof against the effects of the moving water and thick enough to be able to dissipate the forces it exerts on the shore without disturbing the soil beneath. In many instances natural lakes are bordered by shingle or sandy beaches and this can be simulated on the shores of created water bodies where gravel or sand occurs naturally at the appropriate level,

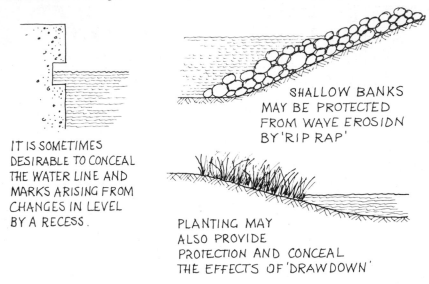

IT IS SOMETIMES DESIRABLE TO CONCEAL THE WATER LINE AND MARKS ARISING FROM CHANGES IN LEVEL BY A RECESS.

SHALLOW BANKS MAY BE PROTECTED FROM WAVE EROSION BY 'RIP RAP'

PLANTING MAY ALSO PROVIDE PROTECTION AND CONCEAL THE EFFECTS OF 'DRAWDOWN'

Fig. 6.4. Other treatments of banks.

or where it can be simply and cheaply obtained. A number of other methods of bank treatment relying on a larger amount of constructional work may be adopted for limited lengths of the margin on a large water body. These are referred to later in the text.

Constructed lakes with a natural appearance

Only very exceptional circumstances would justify the use of special techniques to construct a waterproof water body in a situation where the substrata were permeable, in the case of large water bodies. There might, of course, be examples where in a predominantly impervious substratum there was a need for reinforcement in specific areas, although this might, in practice be an extremely difficult structural problem to resolve. By and large the design and location of large water bodies must rely on the natural impermeability, and the formation, of the natural geology. In the case of smaller water bodies, however, a number of methods for constructing an impermeable base are commonly available. It is not possible to be precise about size limits for some methods, as so often the financial constraints and stringencies governing the use of a particular method

will be seen in a different light by different clients depending on their
enthusiasm, and also on local conditions. Thus the use of puddled clay as a base
for a pool where such material was not the natural substratum might be very
expensive and one which it was thought only appropriate for a very small
feature in terms of area. Where clay was present on the site but fissured, for
example and therefore needing to be puddled before it would be impermeable
it would probably be more worth-while developing a larger area of pool.
Impounding of considerable volumes of water does call, however, for a high
degree of certainty as to the durability of the method of retaining water. For
this reason the use of puddled clay on extensive bodies of water may not be a
very wise choice.

In many parts of the country where the level of ground water, the 'water
table', is near the surface the excavation of minerals may result in the formation
of water features without any need for special measures to retain the water.
There will, of course, be occasions when it is possible to take advantage of this
to provide a water body by excavation although there may be no immediate
advantage to be gained from the material excavated. It is likely that except
where there is some economic reason for the excavation of materials the extent
of any feature of this sort will be comparatively limited. The disposal of such
material will in any case raise problems of removal and deposition.

The employment of explosives experts to excavate pools by blasting is an
option which should not be ignored. Clearly a job for the expert, it is something
which can only be undertaken in very open conditions. It does nevertheless have
the advantage of dealing with the disposal of the excavated material, although
obviously the size of feature that can be treated in this way is comparatively
limited.

There are two alternative systems of lining naturally shaped water bodies,
the use of puddled clay as previously mentioned, and the alternative of putting
down impermeable sheets of material.

CLAY PUDDLING

The main disadvantage of this process in economic terms is that it is one which
is very intensive in terms of labour. It is important that the clay to be used
is in the right condition, which means that it must be reasonably damp and in
a malleable condition. The work is all hand work and consists of spreading the
clay with a shovel and consolidating it in thin layers either with hand tampers
or with Wellington boots. It is necessary to build up an adequate thickness of
this impermeable material to achieve a satisfactory waterproof pond in the light
of any expected uses. Thus, while some authorities will suggest a thickness of
150 mm (6 inch) as the minimum for a clay lining, such a very thin lining will
only be suitable when conditions of use can be closely controlled and there is
no danger either of cattle entering the water or the pool drying up. In both
circumstances very thin layers of clay would be liable to suffer from the slightest
damage.

It is probably more advisable to regard the minimum desirable thickness as 300 mm (1 ft) with 1 m thickness (3 ft) not being uncommon. Ponds with linings of that thickness can be constructed without much fear of damage by cattle, and indeed the traditional method of the repair of leaks in puddled clay is to drive cattle through the pond to improve the puddling. Clay linings are liable to crack when they dry out, if the pond water level falls to a very great extent through evaporation or some other cause. It is reasonable to suggest that serious cracking will more easily occur in clay layers of limited thickness than in the thicker layers. When this happens it is necessary to repuddle the areas where the cracking has taken place. One way in which leaks can be discovered is by the use of a chemical powder 'flourescein'. This turns a 'fluorescent' green in water and when the water in the pool flows through any crack it remains on the soil along the crack so that the position of the leak or leaks can be identified from the deposition of the green substance. By careful digging it is possible to trace the leak right through the clay lining and effect a complete repair. The same technique may be adopted with polythene linings. It is often possible, of course, to localize the likely area of damage to the lining if, for example, there has been any draw down and drying out of part of the pond wall, or if there has been any disturbance by machines, humans, or animals. Such indicators frequently lead one to the locality of the leak.

A special type of clay formed from aluminium silicate and known as 'Bentonite' can be used for lining pools, canals and reservoirs. It is very costly and has the disadvantage that it is much more easily damaged than ordinary clay. It may be used on large schemes where mechanical operations can be involved, and where adequate protection can be given to margins and other areas of weakness or likely damage. The Bentonite is usually spread at rates of between 5 and 10 kg m^{-2} (1 − 2 lb ft^{-2}) and mixed with soil to form a 75 − 100 mm (3 − 4 inch) layer. For protection a layer of soil of at least equivalent thickness should be placed over this. This material is all placed dry and the water introduced subsequently. It should be noted that Bentonite cannot be used on any but the gentlest slopes, because it will be easily displaced.

FLEXIBLE LININGS

There are three principal materials used for the formation of flexible pond linings. These are polythene, P.V.C., and butyl. For small ponds it will be possible to obtain a single sheet of material, specially made or jointed if necessary to cover the whole pond surface. For larger water bodies this is not so easy, and to have large sheets leads to problems of handling. It is often simpler to use standard sheets and deal with the problem of jointing on site. Polythene of a suitable thickness, 1500 gauge, is sold in standard sheets 7.5 x 20 m (24½ x 65½ ft). It is the least long lasting of the materials used, and may be useless after as little as two years if exposed to sunlight.

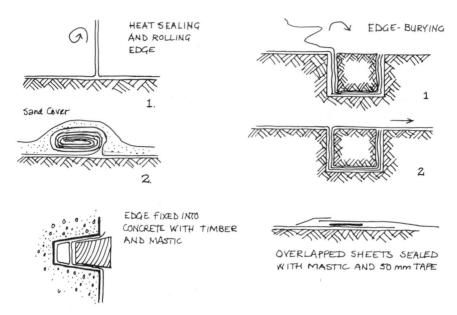

Fig. 6.5. Joints in pool lining sheets.

P.V.C. sheeting is more durable than polythene and can be expected to last up to 10 years when exposed to the action of sunlight. P.V.C. sheeting reinforced with terylene may be used for greater strength, and this material comes in a variety of sizes. It can be prefabricated to suit a particular pond design, although an area in excess of half an acre is difficult to manage with a single sheet. The material can be joined on site in one of the ways described below for large pools.

Butyl rubber is the most expensive, and most durable, material in use for this purpose. In the case of large water bodies it may be considered to be too expensive to use, and P.V.C. preferred. For small pools a single prefabricated sheet will be used while for large projects the sheets can be laid to allow joints on site.

Jointing may be undertaken by welding, by making a sandwich joint using the appropriate adhesive or by a technique known as 'edge burying' which involves folding the sheets and may, for this reason, not be suitable with butyl. Illustrations of these methods are shown in Fig. 6.5.

Whatever method of lining is used it is important to obey certain simple rules in laying the sheets to avoid damage to the material, either in the process of laying or subsequently. It is most important that the surface upon which the sheeting is to be laid is even and well compacted. Undue settlement could result in strain being placed upon the sheeting by the weight of water, and the presence of stones could also strain, and might even rupture, the material. It may sometimes be necessary to spread suitable material over some substrata of sharp rocks. When the sheeting is laid it should be allowed to be placed sufficiently loosely that it will take up the natural shape of the ground without strain. For protection it is advisable to cover it with a reasonable depth of suitable soil, without large or pointed stones. An absolute minimum of 200 m (8 inch) soil cover round the edges of pools may be reduced for the centre to 100 mm (4 inch). Where any traffic of any sort is anticipated in the shallows a depth of at least 300 mm (1 ft) should be provided. It is essential to ensure that a detail is used which enables the liner to be brought up to near the ground level around the pool. This is to ensure an adequate water level is maintained in relation to the surrounding land. When a natural appearance is sought this will usually involve the design of a shallow sloping bank and the construction must ensure that the soil placed over the sheeting is not liable to slippage. The sheeting obviously provides a smooth surface with relatively little frictional hold and slumping of material placed on it on slopes can occur all too easily. Although P.V.C. and polythene sheeting can be pleated or folded this cannot be allowed in the case of butyl rubber.

An alternative method of sealing a pool, which may be appropriate when there has been a leak in the sealing material is the use of a water borne sealer. 'SS13' is a product of Environmental Chemicals Ltd of Arundel, Sussex. It consists of fine particles of material which settle out of the liquid added to the pool water and fill up the interstices of the soil causing it to seal. Its use is limited to fine soils, and it is an expensive method. It should only be used with the greatest care as its properties are fatal to fish for obvious reasons, and this is likely to extend to other pond life. The material is supposedly safe after it has settled, but the dangers of it being stirred up by subsequent disturbance are not clear. The seal achieved is, in any case, not complete and so the use of this material as the sole sealant for the creation of a pool is likely to have only very limited application.

CONCRETE CONSTRUCTION

Where there is a very strong need to ensure the best water retentive qualities in a pool it may be advisable to design this with a concrete lining. This does not preclude the achievement of an informal finish as the edges can be concealed and the base of the pool can easily be covered by gravel or soil. The pool should be flushed with water a couple of times before this is done so that the salts contained in the concrete, which might be harmful to aquatic life can be washed out. It is probably wise to allow a period of about a month for seasoning but the pool should also be filled with water early, and at any time after 24 h from the placing of concrete, because the 'set' is harder underwater than in the air. Small ponds can be made quite informally with a single 'pour' of the concrete if their dimensions are not much greater than 8 x 5 m (25 x 15 ft) and no great depth is involved, less than 1 m say. In such cases, provided there is a good solid base, a thickness of 150 mm (6 inch) of concrete may be specified, without any reinforcement. On very small ponds this can, in favourable circumstances, be reduced to 100 mm (4 inch). In many cases the use of mixes of concrete which are standard and do not include any special additive are recommended. The sorts of mix which are recommended will be very dependent on the circumstances, the smallest structures being least demanding in terms of strength.

Thus the suggestion is sometimes made that for very small informal water features in private gardens it is acceptable to use a 1:3 cement: sand mixture. In contrast with this, larger pools, although not those requiring reinforcement, will often be constructed in a mix of 1:3:6 (1 part of cement, to 3 parts of fine aggregate or sand, to 6 parts of coarse aggregate or gravel). For the design of reinforced concrete pools the use of a mix of 1:2:4 is recommended, a particularly rich mix being desirable to protect the reinforcement mesh from the action of water. In the case of works of this kind involving sea water the use of an even richer mix is usually recommended namely 1:1½:3. It is important that the proportion of water in the mix of concrete is carefully controlled to ensure a mix which is relatively impermeable to water. The best mixes will have only enough water to combine with the cement and make the mixture workable. All the surplus water in the mix which dries out, results in the creation of pore spaces which can be filled up again by the water of the pool. Besides weakening the concrete, this permits the passage of water into, and possibly through the concrete, and could result in the progressive development of leaks. Some designers will prefer to include an additive to act as a waterproofing agent. This is mixed in as a powder with the dry mix of concrete and is added as a proportion of the cement by weight, usually in quite small quantities, say of the order of 2% by weight. The powders which are available under various trade names are based on metallic stearates which make the finished mix of concrete more water repellant. It is probably more important than ever that when one of these admixtures is used there should be really good mixing and compaction of the concrete.

In larger pools it is necessary to consider both the need to provide reinforcement and to lay the concrete in a series of slabs. Reinforcement is usually used in the form of wire mesh and the actual choice for a particular purpose is likely to be governed by the British Standard Code of Practice 2007 'Design and Construction of Reinforced and Prestressed Concrete Structures for the Storage of Water and other Aqueous Liquids. It should be noted that vessels for storage of quantities of water may have different dimensions and structural properties from the designs at present under discussion in which the visual or ecological aspects are paramount and in which the volume of the capacity is not usually important. The mesh is specified according to the spacing of the wires in the mesh and the gauge of the wire itself and may vary, as in the United States from 4 to 10 gauge wire, and from 100 m^2 spacing between wires, up to 200 m^2. In

Great Britain the practice is to specify the mesh according to its weight in kg m⁻² (formerly lb ft⁻²).

When the concrete is laid in separate sections it is necessary to make some provision not only for the prevention of water seeping through cracks between different sections of concrete which have been separately laid, but also for the

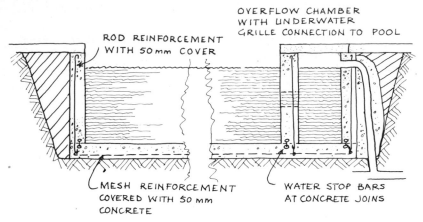

Fig. 6.6. Diagram to show outline construction of concrete pool with concealed overflow chamber.

expansion of the concrete at certain times. This is a more significant influence than perhaps the joints which must also be provided to allow for contraction. Expansion joints may be formed in pools using asphalt although rubber joints are not unknown. Joints such as these can be used equally well to take account of the results of contraction as well as expansion and may eliminate cracking of the material. Where any form of jointing between concrete slabs laid at different times is involved it is important that a satisfactory method of ensuring a seal against seepage is used. This commonly takes the form of what is known as a water-stop bar or a water bar and consists of a rubber or similar flat sectioned strap which has an indented section. This is set into the concrete so that one-half is embedded in the slab just laid and then the new concrete poured around the projecting half of the strap. In this way the best possible seal is achieved, as the concrete wraps around the protruding indentations of each half of the strap and this minimizes the likelihood of water seeping around the joint. Where these junctions occur there is likely to be some danger of weakness and in particular the likelihood of vertical movement. Where reinforcement is needed it might result in damage or distortion to the structure if this was to be placed as a rigid mesh right over joints. Accordingly this is likely to be placed in panels to coincide with the pouring of the panels themselves, but reinforcement to span the different pours may be included and may traverse the joints, in order to counteract the possibility of vertical movements which

were differential as between adjoining slabs or panels. An alternative to this
method might be to set down strips of concrete to form pads beneath the
joints so that each panel was supported by the pad and in this way the danger
of differential movement would be minimized.

In informal pools the use of concrete will be completely concealed and there
will be no vertical sides or strongly formed shapes. What shapes are formed
in the concrete will conform generally to natural ground shapes, and in fact
concrete is unlikely to be used in these circumstances except in particular
cases. It may be used in formally engineered areas, such as the dam face in
reservoirs when its appearance will not be concealed, but when the object
is to create a lake with a natural appearance, concrete will not be appropriate,
and it will be concealed under a surface layer of sand or boulders or some
similar natural finish. The same is true of the means of regulating water flow
and retention. While it is difficult to design such features to belie their
engineering nature and function, they are frequently placed in such a way as
to be most inconspicuous. This is true of almost all the lakes in landscape
parts of the 18th and 19th century which are found to have penstocks or similar
gates to control the flow and level of water discreetly placed out of the eye
of the casual visitor.

Formal water bodies

It is possible to go to elaborate lengths with materials like concrete to conceal
the construction of the pool and create the illusion of a natural feature. More
usually, the sort of pool involving extensive structural work of this nature
is not treated as a natutalistic feature but accepted as a formal, although not
necessarily geometrical element in any design. Pools such as this may be associated with buildings, or they may be designed according to functional requirements which call for vertical sides or the achievement of particular depths.
The structural use of concrete for such formal pools is exactly as has already
been described. Pools of any size will obviously be constructed with reinforced
concrete to the best specification of concrete (1:1½:3) with or without
additives. The construction of vertical walls will call for the use of mild steel
rods also placed vertically, to reinforce the walls. These need to be overlapped
over the mesh reinforcement on the floor of the pool, probably by about 150 —
200 mm (6 — 8 inch). For small pools rods of mild steel 7 mm (¼ inch) diameter
will be used, at intervals of 150 mm (6 inch) apart. For larger pools with walls in
excess of about 1 m, the specification and dimensions should be worked out
by a structural engineer. The rods, besides being overlapped with the floor at the
lower ends should be bent over at the top to come within 75 mm (3 inch) of
the top of the wall. In order to ensure that the rods remain in a vertical position
and fulfil their purpose adequately in the wall, it is often necessary to use a
series of horizontal rods to tie the verticals together. These will be placed at

intervals of about 225 mm (9 inch) apart. The minimum thickness of the walls will be about 150 mm (6 inch), although it is often considered desirable to increase this to 300 mm. The thickness of the concrete is less critical in the case of concrete which is reinforced.

Very small pools and shallow walls may be built with brick or blocks although this method will result in a need to render the wall with a waterproof element to ensure that the walls are waterproof. This is perhaps less sound structurally than building in solid concrete from the point of view of water retention, because thin renderings of cement, which are sometimes also recommended for the final treatment of concrete walls are liable to be easily damaged or to crack and thus become unserviceable. The brick walls will be built on the floor of the pool laid in concrete which will be extended to form a foundation for the walls. An alternative to putting on an internal cement rendering is to use an asphalt 'tanking' to achieve a waterproofing effect, and this may overcome the difficulties of sealing the joint between the floor and walls which can be a serious problem when brick walls are used. It is important that the bricks used are of engineering quality and that the concrete of the pool floor is roughened so that a really well keyed junction between the concrete and the mortar base of the wall is achieved.

Although concrete is the ideal material from which to make the pool structurally it is not always regarded as being the best finish from a visual point of view. For this reason it is often the practice to face the walls of pools with the desired finishing material. Thus a thin skin of ashlar, or a half inch brick wall or a wall of stones with a random finish might be constructed as a facing to a concrete wall. In all these cases it is desirable that the stones or bricks should be impervious to water and should consequently not be liable to break down as a result of being wetted and perhaps occasionally dried. In a number of examples thin polished marbles or sawn slate have been used successfully for this sort of facing to good effect. Where this sort of facing is used it is most important to ensure that the facing material is tied into the solid wall in such a way that there is no danger of it breaking off. This involves the use of butterfly cramps in the case of brick and stone walls and small cramps made of tin or copper in the case of thinner section facings. Where plant growth and an ecologically balanced aquatic community is intended to be developed in a pool, the floor may be covered with a depth of soil to stimulate a nature soil pond floor, or alternatively gravel sand or cobbles may be laid on the concrete. In some circumstances the concrete floor may be so constructed as to allow individual pockets of soil, for the growth of particular aquatic plants, or plants may be limited to moveable plastic plant containers set on the floor of the pool. The exact method of design adopted will depend to a very great extent on the nature and situation of the pool, the circulation of water, and the requirements for emptying and cleaning the pool. These details are considered in a subsequent section.

FORMS OF NATURAL STONE FACING ON CONCRETE

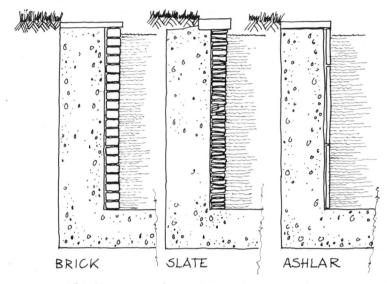

BRICK   SLATE   ASHLAR

Fig. 6.7. Forms of natural stone facing on concrete pool.

In addition to pools with a formal finish based on concrete walls, or
apparently in stonework, some pools are occasionally encountered whose walls
are constructed in timber, oak being a timber which is particularly durable
under water with elm also being a suitable alternative. However it does not
need to be pointed out that this does not provide the waterproofing necessary to a pool. In some cases the use of the timber is merely to provide a vertical
side to the pool in a chosen finish, alternatively it may be used to act as a
retainer for a material such as clay which may provide the waterproof walls.
A third possibility is that this sort of pool may be constructed in conditions
in which the water body is dependent on the levels of ground water in the
soil, in which case no actual water retention by impermeable walls is necessary.
The use of timber to provide the vertical walls of pools calls usually for a very
complex system to retain these in an upright position, and held together, one
against the next. A number of examples of this sort of feature have been illustrated in recent years, showing what are sometimes described as 'deadmen',
heavy beams or blocks of concrete buried in the ground at some distance back
from the pool wall and to which the vertical timbers are fixed by bands or
straps across their faces and linked by metal bars. In this way the timbers are
kept in position. This, it should be repeated, is a rather costly and complicated
way of creating what is only generally a visual effect. The alternative to this
approach is to drive the timbers into the substrata to a sufficient depth to
ensure that they will be properly retained. This will usually require that at least

one-third of the total length of the timbers are buried in solid ground. At the same time this method should be assisted by the use of metal straps placed horizontally along the face of the timbers in such a way that they help to hold one another in place.

An alternative to the use of timber in these circumstances is that of steel sheet piling which may be used in this way to provide a virtually waterproof wall. This sort of finish is particularly applicable in the case of moving water features where a vertical side which is proof against erosion is required: this might apply to canals or rivers navigated by boats of various sizes. Another method of ensuring a boundary to walls, whether a pool, river, canal or even the edge of the sea is the use of walls of gabions which can be used to provide vertical or near vertical sides, although this material, comprising wire boxes packed with stones, provides no actual waterproofing in itself. It is invaluable where it is necessary to protect such banks from erosion by moving water in rivers or the effects of waves, whether created by the sea or the movement of watercraft. All the methods of creating or supporting banks just described may be used in connection with large water bodies where on specific sections there are particular problems of erosion or the creation of particular conditions for the landing or mooring of boats call for vertical banks.

Formal pools have perhaps the most stringent requirements for the maintenance and control of water quality and conditions, on visual grounds alone, but a certain number of requirements which can be stated for them apply as well to other forms of pool. It is important in the design and construction of pools to allow for:

(1) Control of level of water, with means of disposing of surplus volumes, and replenishment of losses.
(2) Means of emptying and cleansing of water body.
(3) Method of circulating water, where this is not kept moving by natural flows.

CONTROL OF WATER LEVEL

The control of water level in pools depends on a number of factors related to the size, situation and nature of the water body under discussion. Very precise regulation and careful maintenance of water at a constant level may only be necessary from a visual standpoint and then only perhaps in formal waters, or small pools. Although the visual consequences of extensive draw down on reservoirs can be unpleasant, they are something which are acceptable having become so as a result of the relative inability of human organization to overcome the difficulties they present. Some levels of pools with vertical sides can be allowed to fluctuate without giving rise to serious visual problems, although more than a certain depth of dry wall between the water surface and ground level can be disturbing. Some pools, of course, will be designed in such a manner as to allow for the control of storm water, by the simple device of

holding up the product of a heavy precipitation. This is, thus, contained in a
water body which has the capacity to hold a considerable volume of water
until it can be released slowly into the drainage system, whether natural or

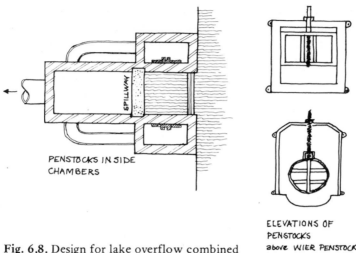

PENSTOCKS INSIDE
CHAMBERS

ELEVATIONS OF
PENSTOCKS

Fig. 6.8. Design for lake overflow combined   above WIER PENSTOCK
with penstocks for drainage.   below CIRCULAR PENSTOCK

artificial. In this way the design of a drainage system on a much smaller scale
than might otherwise be needed can be undertaken, or existing facilities may be
made use of in very different circumstances from those in which they were
originally constructed.

A good example of this was the development of the Killingworth Lake,
which was a major feature of the New Town in Northumberland. This was
devised to allow the storm water resulting from the development of the area
to be collected and held until such time as it could be carried away at the
capacity of the existing sewers. The drainage aspects of this have already been
discussed in Chapter 3. The design of this water feature relied first of all on
the construction of a water level control device or 'penstock'. This can be
raised at times of heavy precipitation to retain the main volume of water in
the lake. Subsequently it would be lowered progressively until the normal lake
level was once more reached. The visual problems of changes in level are overcome by the provision of a sandy shingle beach and a low wall, actually built
of granite setts. Small changes in water level are accommodated in the shingle
beach itself, whereas greater increases above the normal level are contained
within the vertical wall which although no more than about 750 mm (2½ ft)
in height provides for a considerable increase in volume of water over the entire
area of the lake surface. This has created a lake with a functional purpose as

well as visual quality, not to mention its value as a recreational resource. The visual aspect is not in any way diminished by the functional requirements and the entire scheme is most successful. It is clear however that such treatment is only appropriate in the right setting with an appropriate scale of water body.

In contrast the control of water bodies to precise levels calls for control of the supply and the disposal of surplus water. The supply of water in small pools where the level needs to be maintained constantly is often dependent on mains water. The alternative to this is the use of another source of impounded water which can be brought into use to 'top up' a pool at will. Natural supplies of clean water may not be sufficiently reliable; certainly this is true as far as surface water run off is concerned and may be the case with small streams. In both of these cases the times when the need for topping up arises, often in quite small quantities, may well be the times when water is unavailable from these sources. The use of mains water for the purposes of supplying orna-mental pools is something that should be envisaged after consultation with the water authority concerned. This source of water may well not be available in periods of drought and in any case the use of large volumes of mains water is hardly likely to be viewed favourably by any water authority. On the other hand, topping up is likely only to involve small volumes of water. On small pools the use of a ball valve similat to that used in the supply to cisterns, and most commonly associated with water closets may be adopted. This will involve the construction and siting of a suitable chamber in which such a valve can be discreetly housed. Depending on the relationships of the water surface to ground level, this may or may not need to be above ground. The incorporation of features such as this into designs for pools and their surrounds which do not obtrude into the design is often a task calling for extreme ingenuity. This sort of system does, however, provide an automatic means of topping up the water level. An alternative which is probably structurally simpler is to provide a con-cealed tap. Even this may be subject to some complications because there is frequently a requirement to ensure that there is an adequate vertical separation between the outlet of company mains water supplies and any body of water which could possible contain any form of impurity.

Thus some water authorities will require that there should be a vertical gap between any tap and the highest possible level of any pool of at least 225 mm (9 inch). Such a requirement could lead to the need to construct a raised chamber to provide for the supply. Control of the supply must be accessible to those who have to use it but should be concealed from the public, and of course does not need to be at the point of supply itself. Where it is possible, the most satisfactory arrangement is to have the pool fed by a natural source so that fresh water is constantly flowing through and oxygenating the pool. This can usually be achieved without difficulty in the case of naturalistic pools in 'open settings' where either there are small streams or open water courses running naturally or where the system of subsoil drainage can be designed to feed into the pool. In more formal example this is not so easy and although drainage water from roofs and hard surface areas may be plentiful it is important to ensure that any such supply diverted to feeding pools is only used when it is quite certain that this can be done without any fear of pollution from oil, or salt or any chemicals either in the materials of construction, or likely to be used in the vicinity. It is not necessary to emphasize the need to relate the levels of any underground drains which might feed the pool to the level of the water in the pool. It is sometimes difficult to ensure that these drains are above the pool level and do not result in the water 'backing up' in the drains, particularly if the pool level is allowed to rise, with resultant waterlogging and damage to the ground and drainage system.

The method of disposal of excess volumes of water from a pool will depend to some extent on whether this is to be into an open water course with a naturalistic effect or whether the excess has to be carried away into the sewers or some undergroud drain. In the case of the former some quite simple penstock arrangement may be all that is required. It will be desirable for this to be adjust-

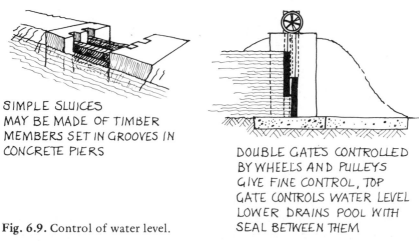

SIMPLE SLUICES
MAY BE MADE OF TIMBER
MEMBERS SET IN GROOVES IN
CONCRETE PIERS

DOUBLE GATES CONTROLLED
BY WHEELS AND PULLEYS
GIVE FINE CONTROL, TOP
GATE CONTROLS WATER LEVEL
LOWER DRAINS POOL WITH
SEAL BETWEEN THEM

Fig. 6.9. Control of water level.

able for two reasons, firstly so that the water can be drawn down even on naturally formed lakes to allow for periodic cleaning, cutting of reed growth and digging out of silt, and also because there may be very good reasons for wanting to maintain some flow, if not continuously then intermittently along the stream below the water body. This might be necessary to replenish smaller pools along the stream, for example.

In the case of overflows into a drainage system of underground pipes there will be a need to provide a system which will not be liable to be damaged by vandals or become easily clogged by floating matter. The need to be able to obtain easy access to such a feature for cleaning purposes is in opposition

to the need to make access difficult for the general public. For this reason
it may be that the development, in public places, of a locked chamber adjoining
a pool with a connection below water level, possibly with a fine meshed grille to
exclude any fish from the chamber, should be devised. In this way access to
the actual overflow, through a simple pipe in the wall of the chamber as it
might be, would be obtained only through a man-hole cover which could be
locked. Having the connection between the pool and the chamber below surface
level would prevent the likelihood of the overflow becoming choked with
floating debris, even without the grille (Fig. 6.6).

Another alternative would the use of a bellmouth pipe placed away from the
pool edge but in a position where it was not too clearly visible to the casual
observer. This is constructed so that the top of the pipe is at the desired water

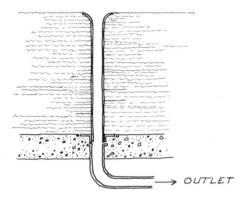

Fig. 6.10. A 'bell mouth' overflow.

level when the pipe is in position, either screwed or sleeved into a socket in the
bottom of the lake and connected into an overflow pipe. When the water in the
lake rises above the desired level the excess lips over the edge of the bellmouth,
down the pipe and away through the outflow. This sort of design is liable to
severe damage if vandals are able to discover the way it works and for this
reason its use must be very carefully considered. It does, however, provide a
simple and straightforward method of maintaining the requisite water level and
it has the advantage of also providing a means of emptying in the same simple
design.

MEANS OF CLEANING POOLS
The requirements for emptying the pool will dictate the position of the overflow pipe as it will usually be desirable that this should be in the deepest part
of the pool. In many cases it is desirable to be able to control the rate of

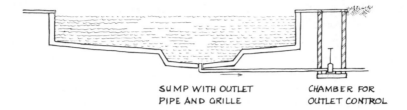

SUMP WITH OUTLET
PIPE AND GRILLE

CHAMBER FOR
OUTLET CONTROL

Fig. 6.11. Sketch section of pool to show sump for collecting fish but no over-flow.

emptying of a pool so that stocks of fish, for example, can be trapped and transferred elsewhere during cleansing operations. This may mean the provision of a stopcock on the pipe taking the overflow away which can be controlled with ease. This will usually be concealed in a chamber below ground level and with a man-hole cover for protection against anyone tampering with the system. It is often convenient to design the pool in such a way that a particular limited area of greater depth is constructed around the outfall pipe so that when the water is drawn down a small area of water remains in which the fish will be brought together and can be easily trapped. The size of such a 'sump' can be no more than 1 or 2 m across and, say, ½ m in depth. Pools with a hard bottom or with gravel or stones at the bottom can be designed with this shape without introducing any complication, but other pools with soil or mud bottoms may become choked up if this design is adopted without any special provision being made to retain the soil against erosion into the sump. It may be necessary to protect the drainage sump against silt by enclosing it in walls which may be designed to allow the passage of water but hold back solid material.

RECIRCULATION OF WATER

Where there is no natural flow of water with a regular supply it may be necessary to provide a method of recirculation of the water. This is often considered desirable for purely visual reasons when the sight and sound of moving water are regarded as a desirable addition to the qualities of an otherwise static design. Even where the quality of still waters providing a reflective surface is the primary aim, the use of some device to circulate the water may be incorporated so that the water does not become stagnant and thus unattractive. In such a case the reintroduction of the circulated water will be devised so as to disturb the actual surface as little as possible.

It is probably sensible to seek specialist advice when approaching the problem of designing a means of recirculating water. There is a considerable range of pumps available according to the nature of the work that is to be required in any particular situation. It is convenient to think of them as being of two types, those that are actually placed in the pool and are simply used to drive a fountain at the surface or which can alternatively pump the water to a small waterfall at or near the edge of the pool. These pumps, known as submersible pumps have a comparatively limited capacity and are usually used in small private garden pools. They are quite frequently used in ornamental pools inside buildings where water features are introduced. They are driven by electricity and are supplied with insulated cables which are sealed by the manufacturer. They are very quiet in operation. Some industrial versions however are capable of delivering up to 90 l (20 gal) min⁻¹ and are very compact in design. This volume is much more than is necessary for small fountains which may not need more than about 9 l (2 gal) min⁻¹ flow.

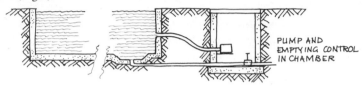

PUMP AND
EMPTYING CONTROL
IN CHAMBER

Fig. 6.12. When a pump chamber is installed it is probably wise for it to be separated from the pool to minimize danger of flooding, the pump should also be raised from the floor.

Larger volumes of water however call for a more powerful form of pump, and one which cannot be submerged. Water pumps need to be 'primed' in order to work satisfactorily, i.e., they need to be filled with water in order to draw up water from the source from which they are to pump. It is possible to obtain self-priming pumps in which a special arrangement of chambers allows the retention of water in the pump. The majority of pumps however, are not self-priming and need to be either sited so as to be primed by gravity or have some primimg arrangement especially made for them. It is also true that to suck up water from any depth requires very considerable force. For both of these reasons it is desirable to place a pump, which is to be used in recirculation of water from a pool, in such a position that it can be primed by gravity from the water in the pool so that no suction pressure is required. It is the case that the pump needs to work very much less hard to pump water up above itself than it does to draw the water up to its own level from below. Thus the position of the pump in relation to the pool will not only affect the need to make special provision for primimg but will also have a bearing on the power of the pump selected. When for some reason the pump has to be placed in a position where it cannot be primed by the gravity of the pool, it may be necessary to provide a small priming tank which can be kept full of water to prime the pump.

The output of pumps is dependent upon the head or the resistance that the pump has to overcome to raise the water, either to the top of a jet in a fountain, or to the outfall point where a less exuberant form of display is intended. This is measured in height vertically in mm. Clearly where the 'head' is not excessive the power of the motor can be reduced considerably in relation to a situation where with the same required throughput the head is much greater. Standard pumps operate at a fairly high speed of revolution (about 2 900 rev min⁻¹) and are consequently more noisy than submersible pumps. A reduction in the level of noise can be obtained by specifying slower running motors which run at about 1 450 rev min⁻¹. These motors are driven by electricity and can be placed in specially constructed motor chambers which should be reasonably well isolated from the water body because it is important that the pumps should not get wet. When these are placed in an enclosed chamber this will further reduce the effect of noise and in an urban situation a low level of noise from a pump may well be easily submerged beneath the general level of noise. If a completely noiseless system is necessary a submersible pump may be the only answer, although this may result in a reduction of the output that it is possible to achieve. It is important that filters are fitted to the input pipe so that any particles which could damage the pump cannot be allowed to enter the system.

It is worth mentioning that several well known and impressive water effects have been achieved without any mechanical devices, pumping engines being, in relation to the history of garden and park design, a comparatively recent innovation. The great fountains of Versailles were supplied by natural

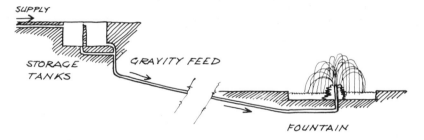

Fig. 6.13. Diagram of gravity fed fountain as at Versailles.

gravity-fed streams, the water from which was stored in vast covered containers. The great fountains of Appollo's basin are entirely dependent on the effects of gravity for their display. The supply of water to these storage tanks was augmented by the pumping efforts of the legendary machine of Marley, but this only added to the natural supply which failed to provide an adequate volume for the fountains to be played as frequently as was required. Another example of fountains dependent on natural conditions were those in Trafalgar Square, London. These were at one time operated by the Artesian pressure of the water held in the chalk basin beneath the London clay. This depended on the water level within the chalk being maintained at a high level so that when the London clay beds were penetrated, the water in the chalk in the centre of the basin which was under pressure rose to the level of the water in the surrounding higher levels of chalk. Where the opportunity arises to adopt this method for the feeding of fountains there are clearly advantages in doing so. It means for instance that there are very few maintenance costs and the motive power is supplied free.

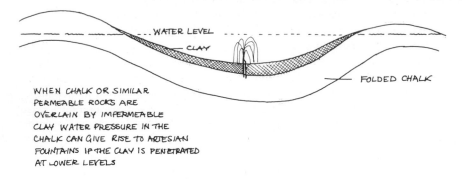

WATER LEVEL

CLAY

FOLDED CHALK

WHEN CHALK OR SIMILAR
PERMEABLE ROCKS ARE
OVERLAIN BY IMPERMEABLE
CLAY WATER PRESSURE IN THE
CHALK CAN GIVE RISE TO ARTESIAN
FOUNTAINS IF THE CLAY IS PENETRATED
AT LOWER LEVELS

Fig. 6.14. Diagram of Artesian fountain.

Another alternative which may be adopted in certain circumstances when there is an adequate supply of water is the use of an 'hydraulic ram'. This is a pump which depends on the flow of water past the 'ram' to pump up water to a head. A great deal more water flows past the ram than is pumped up and the system is probably most successfully used where the water can be stored in a tank for occasional use. Nevertheless it has the advantage of providing a method of pumping which does not depend on an expensive source of power and which because of the simplicity of the machinery involved requires only small maintenance outlay.

Irrigation

It is perhaps desirable to append a brief note on the use of methods of irrigation which may be met in landscape construction work. On many golf courses and similar areas of recreational grass, it is necessary to provide means of watering in conditions of drought. Nowadays the emphasis is on the use of methods which do not call for a great deal of labour involvement. For this reason the use of lines of water-pipes set beneath the ground and connected with sprinklers which 'pop up' when water pressure is turned on has been devised. These sprinklers when not in use remain at soil level and so do not interfere with and are not damaged by mowers. The appropriate design and arrangement, with spacings needs to be the subject of special enquiries for each individual case.

Two other areas of landscape design particularly may give rise to the need for controlled watering: these are trees in hard surfaces, and plants in containers. The former may be irrigated by drainage from hard surface areas provided no deleterious materials are introduced to the roots. In this case only drainage measures to ensure the removal of excessive soil water will be necessary. In the case of plant containers it may well be necessary to make some provision for the

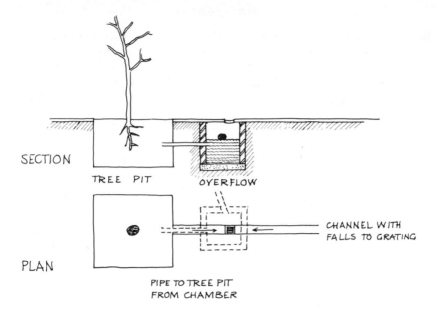

SECTION

TREE PIT   OVERFLOW

CHANNEL WITH
FALLS TO GRATING

PLAN

PIPE TO TREE PIT
FROM CHAMBER

Fig. 6.15. Diagram of a watering system for trees in a hard surface.

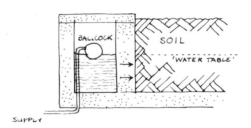

Fig. 6.16. Raised planters may need some artificial watering: a chamber with ballcock and perforations in the wall.

supply of water to provide an artificial water table. This can be done by creating a cistern chamber which is accessible to the soil and in which the water is kept at a constant level by a ball valve. In this way the dangers of excessively dry conditions, often a problem in plant boxes can be avoided. The plants remain in good condition without any need for hand watering.

˙References

British Standards Institution (1970:2007) Parts 1 and 2. *Design and Construction of Reinforced and prestressed concrete structure for the storage of water and other aqueous liquids.* London.

Brooks, A. (1976). *Waterways and Wetlands.* British Trust for Conservation Volunteers Ltd: London.

Index

Acorn Bank Northumberland, 49
Agricultural Land Classification Maps, 8
Air survey, 8, 39
    black and white, 9
    coverage, 8, 10
    false colour, 10
    true colour, 9
Angle of repose, 61
Artefacts, 27, 28, 29
Asphalt, 127
    cold asphalt (B.S. 1690), 131
    hot rolled (B.S. 594), 131
    mastic, 131

Base plans, 5
Basildon New Town, 36
Bean sizes, 214
Bell mines, 29
Bilhams formula, 85
Bitumen cover for grass seed, 67
Blade dozers, 69, 71
Block paving, interlocking, 142–4, 146
Bollards, 212
Brick paving, 145, 150–2
Brick walls, 177–8, 230
    bonding, 177
    English garden wall, 177
    Flemish, 177
    Flemish cross, 178
    modern face bond, 178
    monk bond, 178
    stretcher, 177
Brickwork dimensions, 178
Bulking, 59
Bunds for rainfall, 85

Buttress drains, 61, 101
Butyl rubber pool liners, 225

California bearing ratio, 19, 122
Castle Howard, 1
Channels, drainage, 89, 90, 109
    gradients, 109
Check dams, 91, 93
Cistern, ball valve, 240
Clam shell, 69, 70
Clay, Bentonite, 224
Climate, 2, 15, 18, 183
Coated macadam, 128
    bitumen macadam (B.S. 1621), 128
    tar macadam (B.S. 802), 131
Cobbles, 150, 152
Compaction, 59, 60
Computer, 48, 49, 53, 54
Consolidation, 59, 60
Concrete blocks, 184
    ornamental screen, 185
Contours, 46, 57
Copings, 181, 187
Country parks, 4, 213
Cross-sections of levels, 51

Damp proofing, 180, 187
Dams, earth, 219
    concrete, 219
Dense tar, 131
Derwent dam, 219
Dew pond, 217
Ditches, 65, 93
Dolomite, 137
Drag lines, 69, 70
Drainage, 81

bowling greens, 105
chambers, 112, 114
channels, 89, 90, 109
ditches, 65, 91
grid-iron, 97
gulleys, 109
herringbone, 97
parallel, 97
paved areas, 107, 108, 168
playing fields, 105
reclaimed land, 104
retaining walls, 187
sewers, foul, 112, 113
    surface water, 112
Drain pipe sizes, 87, 88, 112
Drains, 88 et seq.
French, 100, 101
forestry, 102, 103, 104
maintenance, 111
mole, 99
plastic, PVC, 96
tiles, clay, 96

Earthmoving machinery, 69 et seq.
Earthworks calculations, 42–60
Ecology, 1
Edging, concrete, 164, 165, 167
for steps, 193
metal, 165
stone, 165
timber, 165
Erosion, 90, 91, 121
Evaporation, 216
Excavators, 69, 71
Expansion joints, 184, 228
Explosives, 223

Face shovels, 69
Facing to walls, 188, 231
Fascines, 66
Fence maintenance, 209
Fences, 191–210
Fences, anti-intruder, 195, 208
chain link, 195, 207–8
metal, 204–10
mild steel, etc. bar, 195, 204
specialist, 208–9

strained wire, 195
unclimable, 195
woven wire, 206–7
Fences, cleft chestnut, 193, 198–9
close board, 198–9
timber, 195–204
wooden palisade, 201
wooden post and rail, 194, 203
woven wattle, 193, 203
Field drainage, 92
Field survey, 38
Flexible roads, 123, 125
Flourescein, 224
Forestry drainage, 102–4
Foundations, 171, 179
concrete, 171, 179
stone, 171
French drains, 100, 101

Gabions, 93, 232
Gates, 212
Geological maps, 8
Geology, 2, 14
Graders, 71
Gravel, 135
scaled, 136
Grid, levels, 44
Grouting, 159, 163
Gully, drainage, 109

Hackett, B., 1
Highway Optimization Programme
    System (HOPS), 52
Hoggin, 133
Hydraulics Research Station, 87
Hydro seeding, 67

Inspection chambers, 117
Instructions to contractors, 76
Interlocking Paving Association, 143
Impermeability, 84
Irrigation, 240
    'pop-up', 240

Joints expansion, 184, 228

Killingworth lake, 86, 233

Knee rails, 205, 209
Kutters formula, 89

Lake lining, 222-6
  puddled clay, 223-4
  sheets of material, 224-6
Land from design criteria, 41
Land Use Capability Classification, 10, 21, 22
Land Utilization Survey of Great Britain, 8
Legal restraints, 32, 33
Levels, 43 et seq.
  grids, 43, 44, 45
Litter bins, 212

Macadam, J., 128
MacAlpine, Robert (Sir) and Sons Ltd; computer programme, 52
Mac math formula, 85
Man-holes, 114
  back drop, 115
  brick, 114
  concrete, 114
  interceptor, 116
Ministry of Health rainfall formula, 85
Mole drains, 99
Mono BG slabs, 159
Moorish gardens, 216
Mortar, 182

Newcastle-upon-Tyne, Town Moor, 36
Norris formula, 85

Ordnance survey, 8

Paved area drainage, 92 et seq.
Paving, blocks, 141, 142-4
  bricks, 145, 148, 150-2
  concrete slab, 141, 153-7
  in situ concrete, 160
  stone, 158
  tiles, 153
Pedestrian bridges, 214
Pergolas, 205
Piezometers, 220
Piling, steel sheet, 232

Pipes, 87, 187
  flow in, 87
Pitching, 64, 145
Planimeter, 57
Polypropylene netting, 67
Polythene pool liners, 224, 225
Polyvinyl acetate, 67
Pool construction concrete, 226-9
Pool finishes, 221 et seq.
  Ashlar, 230
  brick, 230
  concrete, 221
  marble, 230
  slate, 230
  stone, 221
Pools cleaning, 232, 236
Priddy on the Mendips, Somerset, 204
Prismoidal formula, 50
Puddling, 219, 223
PVC pool linings, 225

Rainfall, 81 et seq.
  frequency, 81, 82
  intensity, 81
Rational formula for rainfall run off calculation, 85
Reinforcement, concrete, 138, 140, 227-8
Reservoirs, 219
Reservoir (Safety Provisions) Act 1930, 219
Retaining walls, 185-8
Rigid roads, 123, 138
Rip rap, 222
Road, base, 127
  formation or sub-grade, 126
  pavement, 126
  sub-base, 126
  surfacing, 127
Road surfacing, base course, 127
  wearing course, 127
Rotational slip, 61, 101, 121

'Safeticurb', 109, 110, 111, 165
Scobey charts, 89
Scrapers, 69, 73
  box, 73

design limitations, 75
elevator, 73
operating gradients, 74
operating distances, 75
Services, 30, 31, 32
overhead, 30
underground, 30
Settlement gauges, 220
Setts, granite, 144, 146, 147, 233
whinstone, 144
Sewers, outfalls, 113
surface water, 112
foul, 112, 113
Shrubs, 27
Shuttering, 186
Silt traps, 116
pits, 117
Simpson's rule, 50
Slab paving, 153–9
Slope, angles, 16, 60, 61, 63, 89
Slope, critical angles, 16, 17, 60
Soakaways, 117
Soil cement stabilization, 136
Soil storage, 23, 24
Soils, 2, 18, 19, 20, 90
engineering, 19, 25
vegetable, 125
Soils, cohesive, 61
non-cohesive, 61
Spot levels, 43, 47
Spring pond, 218
SS13 water borne pool sealer, 226
Steep banks, 61, 101
Steep slopes research project, University
of Newcastle-upon-Tyne, 63, 67
Steps, 188–91, 193
in situ concrete, 189
Stone walls, 171–6, 231
Ashlar, 175
random rubble, 172
squared rubble, 173
Street furniture, 212
Structure plans, 2, 3
action area, 3
local, 3
Subsidence, 120
Surface slip, 61, 120

Surface water runoff, 83, 85, 110
calculation, 85
Surfacing, 120, 127 et seq.
bound, 127
grass/concrete, 121
of banks, 120
proprietory, 137
unbound, 127, 133
Survey table, 11
Survey grids, 39
Survey methods, 37

Tartan track, 106
Theodolite, 47
Tiles, paving, 153
Timber, 196, 197, 231
quality for fences, 197
sizes, 198, 200
Timber structures, 212–15
Topography, 14, 15
Trafalgar Square fountains, London,
239
Transport and Road research labora-
tory, 49, 52, 81
Trapesoidal formula, 50
Trees, 24, 25, 26, 27
Turf pegging, 65

Vanburgh, Sir John, 1
Vegetation, 24
survey, 24–27
Vergil, 1
Versailles, 190, 239
Marley machine, 239
Volume; variations, 59
Volumes earthworks, 42

Walls, 170–88
brick, 177–8
concrete block, 184
dry stone, 171
facing, 188
free standing, 171, 182
in situ concrete, 186
retaining, 185
stability, 183–4
stone, 171–6

Water bodies, 218
control, 232–6
Water level, 232–6
Water margins, 220
planting, 220, 222
structural treatments, 221, 222
Water proofing, 223, 232

Water pumps, 237–9
submersible, 237–8
Water supply, 234
mains, 234
natural, 234
Water table, 95, 96, 223
Weep holes, 187
Wind, 183, 221